Human Rights and Development

Human Rights and Development

Peter Uvin

Kumarian
Press, Inc.

Human Rights and Development
Published 2004 in the United States of America by Kumarian Press, Inc.,
1294 Blue Hills Avenue, Bloomfield, CT 06002 USA.

Index by Robert Swanson.
Proofread by Jody El-Assadi.

The text of this book is set in 10/13 Sabon.

Production and design by Joan Weber Laflamme, jml ediset.

Printed in The United States of America by Thomson Shore, Inc. Text printed with
vegetable oil-based ink.

∞ The paper used in this publication meets the minimum requirements of the
American National Standard for Information Sciences—Permanence of Paper
for printed Library Materials, ANSI Z39.48–1984.

Library of Congress Cataloging-in-Publication Data

Uvin, Peter, 1962–
    Human rights and development / Peter Uvin.
        p. cm.
    Includes bibliographical references.
        ISBN 1–56549–185–8 (pbk. : alk. paper) — ISBN 1–56549–186–6 (cloth : alk.
paper)
    1. Human rights. 2. Economic development. 3. Human rights—Developing
countries. I. Title.
JC571.U95 2004
323'.09172'4—dc22

                                        2004001529

---

13 12 11 10 09 08 07   10 9 8 7 6 5 4 3   First Printing 2004

Contents

Boxes and Tables

Acknowledgments

This book grew out of a presentation I gave at a ceremony for the establishment of the Henry J. Leir Chair in International Humanitarian Studies at the Fletcher School of Law and Diplomacy, Tufts University. I am greatly indebted to Mr. Leir and the people who manage his estate for creating a position devoted to exploring the sort of interdisciplinary linkages I deal with here. More generally, I cannot think of a better home for this enterprise than the Fletcher School, with its presence of stimulating, engaged, and experienced colleagues and students. An early discussion of the ideas contained in this book received excellent feedback from Ellen Lutz, Ian Johnstone, and Ellen Messer, for example—it is impossible not to do well with colleagues like those! And there are others, whose names I cannot put down here and who will consequently and rightfully reproach me for years for their non-inclusion. And then there are the students. I could wax lyrically about Fletcher students for hours, but let me synthesize that by stating that there is no doubt that their consistent engagement, their experience, and their openness all created an atmosphere of great intellectual stimulation for me. Many of the ideas in this book were discussed in a seminar I twice taught, and I can only hope they learned half as much from me as I learned from them. One student must be singled out, for he worked closely with me and provided me with amazing amounts of insight and critical feedback: Craig Cohen. At an age when I was still more concerned with acne, Craig already shows great wisdom and kindness.

I received early and encouraging comments on this project from André Frankovits, Sue Unsworth, Guy Bentham, and Alex de Waal. I thank them very much for their kindness and intelligence. Later on, I received detailed comments from Norah Niland—a person I thanked in my previous book as well. Like a Latin American country in relation to the World Bank, no matter what I do to repay her, my debt to her only continues growing over the years.

Talking about money reminds me of my wife, Susan Cu-Uvin. She runs a clinic for women and men with HIV/AIDS in Providence, Rhode Island. In many ways, without ever talking about any of the stuff I deal with in this book, without ever using the words *human rights* or *development* or even *paradigm*, she and her colleagues do exactly what much of this book is all about. They are absolutely committed to respecting the dignity of their patients, many of whom are at the fringes of American society. They treat them with consistent respect and without judgment, and they stick with them for the very long haul; they work with them in a way that is holistic, understanding that one cannot separate health problems from inadequate housing, unemployment, abuse, drugs, depression, and so on; they seek to influence legislation and assist grassroots and self-help efforts to create social guarantees for more dignified lives. Susan and her colleagues exemplify much of what I believe a rights-based approach to development is all about. And, of course, they are great people, one of whom I am married to (and to whom I owe much more than merely a great professional example). I hence dedicate this book foremost to Susan Cu-Uvin, my wife, but also to her two great mentors and colleagues in the same clinic, Charles J. Carpenter and Timothy Flanigan.

Abbreviations and Acronyms

ACP countries	African, Caribbean, and Pacific countries
ANC	African National Congress
AREU	Afghanistan Research and Evaluation Unit
CBO	Community-based organization
CDF	Comprehensive development framework
CIDA	Canadian International Development Agency
CP rights	Civil and political rights
CSO	Civil society organization
DAC	Development Assistance Committee (of the OECD)
DFID	Department for International Development
EBRD	European Bank for Reconstruction and Development
EC	European Council
ECDPM	European Center for Development Policy Management
ESC rights	Economic, social, and cultural rights
EU	European Union
FIAN	Food First Information and Action Network
GATT	General Agreement on Tariffs and Trade
GRO	Grassroots organization
HIPC	Heavily indebted poor countries
HRCA	Human Rights Council of Australia
ICISS	International Commission on Intervention and State Sovereignty
IDA	International Development Association
IDS	Institute for Development Studies

IMF	International Monetary Fund (often referred to as "the Fund")
KDP	Kecamatan Development Programme (Indonesia)
MSF	Médecins Sans Frontières
NIEO	New International Economic Order
NOVIB	Netherlands Organization for International Development Co-operation
ODI	Overseas Development Institute
OECD	Organisation for Economic Co-operation and Development
OHCHR	Office of the United Nations High Commissioner for Human Rights
OPEC	Organization of Petroleum Exporting Countries
OSCE	Organization for the Security and Cooperation in Europe
PRSPs	Poverty Reduction Strategy Papers
RBA	Rights-based approach
Sida	Swedish International Development Agency
UNCTAD	UN Conference on Trade and Development
UNDP	United Nations Development Programme
UNHCHR	United Nations High Commissioner for Human Rights
UNRISD	UN Research Institute for Social Development
USAID	US Agency for International Development

Introduction

Until recently, the development enterprise lived in splendid isolation from the human rights world. Individual development practitioners may well have been card-carrying members of, say, Amnesty International; they may have discussed worrying human rights trends in the countries they worked in with colleagues during the evening, with a beer on the veranda, but they did *not* think that any of this was *their* job. Doing something about human rights was the job of human rights organizations, or possibly the foreign policy establishment, but not of development workers; they vaccinated, built schools, disseminated new agricultural techniques, advised ministries. Human rights were important, surely, but clearly somebody else's job. The same attitude prevailed (and still prevails) the other way around as well; human rights practitioners have remained largely agnostic toward matters of development and social equity (Welch 1995, 265).

Katarina Tomasevski, one of the foremost experts on the matter, described the prevailing vision well: "Development and human rights work constitute two distinct areas, where development is devoted to the promotion of economic growth and the satisfaction of basic needs, while human rights work exposes abuses of power" (Tomasevski 1989, 113–14; Sano 2000, 742; Nelson and Dorsey, 2003). Let me be clear: I am *not* saying that development practitioners lacked personal interest in human rights. All I am saying is that development practitioners did (and often still do) not consider human rights issues as part of their professional domain; they historically neither considered the implications of their own work on human rights outcomes nor sought explicitly to affect human rights outcomes through their work. This tendency continued until well into the 1990s, allowing the organizers of a prestigious 1999 conference on nutrition and human rights to state that "the human rights approach to nutrition is not even on the radar screen" (Haddad 1999, 14) and that "interaction between the [UN human rights machinery] and the UN development agencies has been essentially non-existent" (Jonsson 1999, 47; see also Forsythe 1997, 334; Marks 1999, 339).[1]

1

This is slowly changing now. This book discusses the implications of the development community conferring a more central role to human rights in its work. When we work in the development enterprise, and we wish to give human rights a more prominent space in that work, how do we reconceptualize our work? What do you do differently as a result? What does this mean in practice? What can we learn from the past in this respect? Are there any insights from scholarship that can guide us? These are the sort of questions this books sets out to answer.

A few words on the personal trajectory that brought me to write this book may be in order here. Apart from being pushed by an academic incentive structure encouraging constant and massive writing, there is an intellectual logic to this venture. A few years ago I wrote a book about the relation between development aid and the genocide in Rwanda. That book was inspired by the fact that Rwanda was considered, until close to the 1994 genocide, a model developing country, doing well on the variables we cared about: decent macroeconomic growth, the presence of a great number of NGOs and peasants' associations, high vaccination rates, and the like. In the fall of 1993, a few months before the genocide, I was still able to write a project-identification report built on this vision of Rwanda as a model of development. Yet, within a few months, it would fall apart in a spasm of violence and destruction, the consequences of which it struggles with until today. If our model pupils turn out to be serial killers (to draw on US television imagery), I wondered, what does it say about our understanding of what we are doing in the development world? Why are we so blind to local dynamics of power, politics, violence, and exclusion? From there, a second question emerged: what are the interactions between our presence—the resources, discourses, and practices of the development enterprise—and the dynamics that led to genocide?

The book that came out of this reflection, *Aiding Violence*, found a wide audience. It came, I understand now, at a time when many development practitioners, in Rwanda and elsewhere, were asking similar questions. I simply wrote what many of them were thinking or feeling but had no time or inclination to put to paper. The book talked a lot about the prevalence of *structural violence*—defined as a combination of high inequality, social exclusion, and humiliation—and the way it creates a fertile breeding ground for ethnic rhetoric and communal violence; it demonstrated in detail how most development aid, unintentionally and often unknowingly, strengthens the dynamics of structural violence rather than weakening them. The book also discussed the dynamics of social polarization, rising human rights violations, and militarization of society that preceded the genocide, and criticized the way the development community's "voluntary blindness" to these factors allowed it to continue "business as usual" almost up to the last day.

That book's main limitation was that it diagnosed a set of problems, but, like so many scholarly studies, it did not offer any solutions. After its publication, though, I was increasingly asked by various agencies to evaluate their practices, to propose alternatives, to think strategically with them. This took place mostly in Rwanda, where people desperately sought answers and where I had some credibility, but also on a more general level, for example, through my work with the OECD's Development Assistance Committee. In all these ventures, I was working with people who sought to create development strategies that reduced conflict rather than promoted it, and that improved human rights outcomes rather than simply neglecting them. In other words, we all felt a need to better understand and work on the intersections between development, on the one hand, and human rights and conflict resolution dynamics, on the other. This was necessary not only in the many cases of so-called post-conflict work, but also in order to achieve the more ambitious goal of conflict prevention (Uvin 2002b).

At around the same time, I found a great new professional home, the Fletcher School of Law and Diplomacy, where other colleagues were interested in the same sort of overlaps—between human rights and conflict resolution, for example.[2] A number of us from all over the world, it seemed, were willing to leave the purity of our previous "normal professionalism" (as Robert Chambers called it years ago) and to engage in difficult explorations of intersections, overlaps, synergies, and contradictions with other fields of social change. This book reflects what I learned about one of these overlaps, namely, that between development and human rights (see also Uvin 2002b).[3] It draws on masses of reading as well as years of professional practice. I believe the subject is important, not because adding some human rights rhetoric to the practice of development will suddenly solve all the deep problems that plague the latter, but because it forces development practitioners to face up to the tough questions of their work: matters of power and politics, exclusion and discrimination, structure and policy. Indeed, ten years after the genocide, I still believe that past development practice, with its blindness to matters of human rights, politics, and conflict, was doomed to fail; the case of Rwanda was perhaps the most extreme but sadly not the only example of where blind development aid leads us. Change was, and still is, necessary. These are tough issues, but if they are not addressed, the development enterprise is doomed to fail over and over. This book is the reflection of my thinking, as well as my practice, about these matters.

For whom is this book written? It is intended foremost for people interested in development, both practitioners and students—basically anyone who wishes to reflect on the practice of development. I wrote the book to be of interest to both practitioners and scholars. I know that it is not easy to make these two worlds read the same book: different time constraints, aims, and professional habits all oppose it. Development practitioners do not often read what scholars write, considering it all too often overly lengthy, opaque, heavily footnoted, and unconcerned with operational implications. To appeal to practitioners, I tried to write this book in a language that is accessible and with aims that are practical. On the other hand, this is definitely *not* a consultancy report or a strategy paper but rather an attempt to apply serious scholarship to questions of operational relevance, so I do have to be rather wordy, referential to scholarly literature, and conceptual. Scholars, on the other hand, read little that is written by practitioners and even less that is written for practitioners. This work, to them, is too superficial, scientifically deficient, often substituting wishful thinking for dispassionate analysis. While many scholars are interested in knowing what is going on in the field, they tend to have a rather superficial and outdated knowledge of where practitioners stand. This book seeks to avoid those pitfalls and to provide scholars with good insight into development practice at the cutting edge, while at the same time being scientifically solid. On the other hand, there will be sections where the book becomes rather "how to" in tone, for my primary aim here is operational; throughout the book, the question *what does it mean in practice?* will be my main guide.

Finally, I also hope that the book is of interest to human rights scholars and practitioners. They may be stimulated by the way an outsider, like me, wearing the lens of a development practitioner, synthesizes their debates and concerns. In addition, throughout this book I regularly discuss the extent to which the development community can offer its human rights colleagues new insights for their work. The book may thus appeal to human rights practitioners too; even if they do not have a strong direct interest in development, they could learn from the parallels, the experiences, and the lessons learned by another community of principled social change.

When I began writing this book, I intended to begin with a brief reminder of the human rights regime. After all, I thought, most of this is widely known and in no need of further explanation. However, as I moved along, I kept encountering a set of conceptual issues that I could not avoid addressing explicitly, all the more so because I found them to mirror debates within the development community. Are human rights universal or relative, and how do we know? How do we choose priorities and make trade-offs among rights? What is the value of the so-called right to devel-opment? As I felt compelled to answer these questions, the first part of this book ended up being longer and more theoretical than I had originally intended. It is to be hoped that this will not constitute an insurmountable obstacle for the more operationally minded reader; this section *is* relevant to practitioners, and I *did* try to draw out the links with development practice throughout. On the other hand, for the person with significant time constraints or a serious allergy to theory, it is possible to skip the first section of this book and begin reading at Chapter 3.

Part I

Some Debates of Relevance to the Development Practitioner

1

Background

The Big Picture

By the late 1940s, the richest and most developed countries of the world had just managed to fight another world war, once again destroying their economies and killing tens of millions of people—including the deliberate slaughter of six million Jews—as well as demonstrating, in retrospect, that economic development does not automatically bring about peace and respect for human rights. The 1948 Universal Declaration on Human Rights was a reaction to this barbarism. Pushed strongly by Eleanor Roosevelt (Glendon 2002), the then US first lady, as well as a coalition of North American NGOs, it spells out a list of specific, inalienable rights all human beings possess by virtue of being human. This document was a milestone in world politics, seeking to place explicit limits on the way states could treat their own citizens, challenging as never before the "the natural right of each sovereign to be monstrous to his or her subjects" (Farer and Gaer 1993, 240).

The intellectual origin of human rights lies in the concept of natural rights, which provided some of the theoretical foundations for the French and American revolutions of the late eighteenth century. The idea of natural rights developed in seventeenth- and eighteenth-century Western Europe as a tool to protect individuals from the arbitrariness of the absolutist state. The central claim of this body of thought was that every individual possesses certain natural rights simply by the nature of being an individual. These rights are inalienable and must be respected by the state (Steiner and Alston 2000, 361ff.). The origin of natural rights is, therefore, integral to the struggle against political absolutism in the West.

Though human rights possess essentially the same raison d'être and vision as natural rights of the eighteenth century, the current notion of

9

human rights differs in many ways from natural rights and indeed does not refer to them or use their terminology. The major breakthrough in the 1948 declaration was that these rights were understood to be universal, that is, applicable to all human beings by virtue of their humanity. It was a dramatic affirmation of the equality of all individuals, wherever they live, regardless of their race, color, sex, language, religion, origin, birth, and beliefs. Indeed, natural rights had been historically conceived of as only applying to men, or propertied men, or white men (the US Constitution, a major milestone in the human rights history, was not considered by any of the founding fathers to apply to their slaves, for example; also children have not historically been considered to be rights-bearing entities). It took until after World War II for all people to become "human."

Immediately after the declaration was adopted by the UN General Assembly,[1] attempts were undertaken to solidify its legal basis; a declaration is, after all, only a statement of intent by which no one is bound. These negotiations proved to be very difficult because of the advent of the Cold War, pitting the US and its allies against the USSR and its sphere of influence. Like all wars, the Cold War was fought with weapons, money, and words, and the emerging human rights legal edifice became a hostage to that. All sides sought to use the parts of the declaration that they felt supported their ideological vision of the world and to ignore the rest. The United States sought to limit the concept of human rights to civil and political ones, typically largely present in liberal market economies, while the USSR and its allies counter-argued that economic and social rights, in which communist countries claimed they were far ahead, were the very core of human rights. As a result, it took eighteen years, until 1966, for not one but two covenants to be adopted: one on civil and political rights (CP rights), which as of late 2000 had been ratified by 147 countries,[2] and one on economic, social, and cultural rights (ESC rights), to date ratified by 141 countries, not including the United States. Both of these covenants came into legal force by 1976 (Craven 1995, 20ff.). Also lost in the process was another part of the original design, namely, a legal document containing methods of implementation (complaints and enforcement procedures) (Craven 1995, 19ff.).

In the meantime, another seismic shift had occurred on the world scene, namely, the sudden and unexpected coming to independence of scores of colonies. In less than a decade almost the entire overseas territories of France, England, and Belgium were dismantled; only fascist Portugal and racist South Africa held to their colonies, which would be freed years later after long and violent wars of independence. The empires, until

---
Box 1

The Major Rights Recognized in the Two Covenants

The UN Covenant on Civil and Political Rights recognizes the following rights:
- the right to life;
- freedom from torture or cruel, inhuman or degrading treatment or punishment;
- freedom from slavery;
- freedom from arbitrary arrest and detention; the right to humane and respectful treatment of persons lawfully deprived of their liberty;
- freedom of movement and liberty to choose one's place of residence for everyone lawfully within the territory of a state;
- freedom to leave any country, and to enter one's own country;
- equality before the courts and tribunals;
- equal protection of the law;
- the right to be recognized as a person before the law;
- freedom from arbitrary and unlawful interference into one's privacy, family, home, or correspondence, or unlawful attacks on one's honor and reputation;
- freedom of thought, conscience, and religion;
- the right to hold opinions without interference;
- freedom of expression, including the freedom to seek, receive, and impart information;
- the right of peaceful assembly, freedom of association, including the right to form and join trade unions;
- the right to marry and found a family with free and full consent of the intending spouses;
- the right to take part in the conduct of public affairs, directly or through freely chosen representatives;
- the right of minorities to enjoy their own culture, profess and practice their own religion, or to use their own language

The UN Covenant on Economic, Social and Cultural Rights recognizes, among others, the following rights:
- the right to work;
- the right to the enjoyment of just and favorable conditions of work;
- the right to form and join trade unions;
- the right to social security, including social insurance;
- the right to the protection of the family;
- the right to an adequate standard of living;
- the right to the enjoyment of the highest attainable standard of physical and mental health;
- the right of everyone to education;
- the right to take part in cultural life

recently so dominant, had fallen for lack of willingness and money to maintain themselves in the face of mounting opposition (Ferguson 2003). UN membership rose rapidly, from 48 in 1948 to 100 in 1962 and 112 in 1966. In sub-Saharan Africa alone, twenty-three new countries were born between 1960 and 1962.

It is at this time that the development enterprise emerged. With Keynesian economics dominating Western thinking and dozens of overseas territories becoming independent, the notion was born that it was possible and necessary to organize and accelerate economic and social change—and that it was the duty of the world to make that happen. Thus scholars began thinking about how to "modernize" so-called backward economies, while bureaucrats began spending money on development projects and infrastructure programs.

The intellectual history of development is much shorter than the history of human rights. Until the middle of the twentieth century, third-world development as a mobilizing ideology, an aim that could be planned for, or a professional field of endeavor did not really exist. Some countries were rich, and some were poor; that was a simple fact of life. For many, this difference translated major differentials in terms of genetic and intellectual ability: the scientific racism of the day classified peoples by their innate, typically racial, capabilities, with whites/Europeans at the top and all other races in a rapidly descending order. For others, less inclined to racial theories, differential levels of income were simply a matter of differences in resource endowments, trade opportunities, and class development—but these, too, were not really matters of urgent (or even possible) intervention. All considered it natural that change would take a lot of time and would involve lengthy processes of exposure to Western values and practices. Certainly, there was nothing very urgent about this, nor did the colonizer, the state, or the world at large have any responsibility here. This dominant view began to change only in the last years before decolonization. Colonial authorities created different systems of service provision in the fields of health and education and began investing in infrastructures and local industry with the aim of promoting economic growth. These projects all remained small, however, until the 1960s, when the development enterprise came into full bloom.

The development enterprise, then, is of more recent origin than the human rights one, both in terms of its intellectual roots and its current manifestation. It has, however, rapidly surpassed the human rights world in resources and attention, the main reason being that "development" became a widely shared goal, technical in nature and expensive in financial resources for the entire international community, including the UN system, while human rights, given their deeply political nature, remained contested and marginalized for much of the time. Thus, by the mid 1990s, development had become a $50 billion a year business, whereas the entire human rights community lived on much less than 1 percent of that amount.

By the late 1970s the development and the human rights communities looked by and large the way they do today. They had both come to involve multilateral organizations, bilateral agencies, and, increasingly, NGOs, mostly located in the West. Complicated funding patterns prevailed among these agencies, and the Cold War ideology permeated all of them. Some countries received much more aid than others because they were strategically important to the two superpower blocs; similarly, some countries were subject to much less human rights scrutiny than others, for the same reason. Within these constraints, though, practitioners did learn and innovate. In development, new schools of thought emerged: from infrastructure (1960s) to basic needs (1970s), and from structural adjustment (1980s) to human resource development (1990s). The human rights community learned as well, fine tuning its methodology of naming and shaming.

The end of the Cold War saw a major surge forward in both communities, as if their accumulated but hitherto frustrated potential was finally allowed to release itself. Major new human rights instruments were adopted, including the Convention on the Rights of the Child (1989), which was ratified by 191 countries—every country except Somalia and the United States—and the Vienna Declaration and Program of Action (1993), which was adopted by 172 countries. Development-related international conferences abounded as well, including major events on the environment (Rio, 1992), population (Cairo, 1994), women (Beijing, 1995), social development (Copenhagen, 1995), and nutrition (Rome, 1996). By the end of the 1990s, both communities were still going strong, although much of the immediate post–Cold War enthusiasm had died down. At present, both employ thousands of professionals, working for well-respected and large-budget NGOs and international organizations worldwide, engaging in lively intellectual debates, and taking part in multiple conferences.

The Human Rights Debates

Since 1948, the human rights edifice has undergone significant advancement, bringing in new rights, new claimants (those who demand rights), and new duty-holders (those obligated to fulfill rights claims). Not surprisingly, each of these extensions has caused contestation. The 1966 separation of economic, social, and cultural rights from civil and political rights, combined with the West's almost exclusive focus on the latter, has created a sense that there are two levels (often called *generations*) of human rights. The so-called first generation—which includes freedom from torture, degrading treatment, and arbitrary detention; freedom of speech, association, and religion—is by and large enshrined in the UN Covenant on Civil and Political Rights. These are often described as "negative" rights, in that they oblige states to abstain from certain actions that violate human dignity. The second generation of rights consists of ESC rights, such as the right to education, the right to an adequate standard of living, and the right to the highest obtainable standards of health. Rather than simply refraining from abuse, then, the state is charged with acting "positively" to promote and realize progressively certain social outcomes. International law is clear in saying that *all* human rights, both CP and ESC rights, are indivisible and mutually reinforcing, and many scholars are deeply convinced of that as well. At the same time, the practice of most international human rights organizations has focused almost exclusively on CP rights, and many governments similarly have professed attachment to one category at the expense of the other (schematically, rich countries focus on CP rights and poor ones on ESC rights). Finally, some Western scholars and activists still believe that ESC rights are indeed different from "real" human rights; they are at best laudable aspirations, but they are not enforceable rights (for example, see Ignatieff 2000; Neier 2003). We will come back to this later.

More recently, so-called third-generation (or *collective*, or *solidarity*) rights, such as the right to self-determination or the right to development, have been added to the rights panoply. This addition implies a profound shift in human rights thinking, which had previously been focused on *individual* rights exclusively. The collective rights notion, however, seeks to spell out the rights of groups; their relation to the rights of individuals (those who make up the group) remains unclear. In addition, in traditional human rights thinking, the state is the legal entity from whom individuals claim their rights; there is strong adversarial relation to the state built into the human rights notion (at the same time, though, states are also the main/only guarantors of individuals' rights). Collective rights, however, are often conceived of as rights held *by* states, and this, as well, poses a significant challenge to much traditional rights thinking.

The most recent addition to the human rights edifice consists of an extension not of claimants or rights but of duty-holders; it seeks to bind non-state actors such as individuals, NGOs, international organizations, and especially (multinational) corporations. In traditional international law—the context within which the human rights edifice was constructed— only states are subjects of the law. Only states create international law, and only they are bound by it. To the extent that human rights law was concerned with the behavior of non-state actors, it was the state that was responsible for ensuring the correct outcome. It was up to states to prevent, investigate, and punish human rights violations committed by non-state actors within their territory. Individuals or corporations or NGOs could be objects of international law—their behavior could be proscribed by it, or they could be granted rights—but this always happened through the intermediary of states, who were the only subjects of international law.

Increasingly, however, scholars and activists argue that human rights obligations ought to be, and can be, *directly* applicable to non-state actors, especially corporations. Part of their justification for this change is the argument that in the current globalized world states are simply not the only relevant actors anymore. As globalization, economic integration, and global corporate mobility proceed at a fast pace, and as corporations are granted increasingly strong international legal protection for their rights to trade, invest, and produce freely, should they not be subject to duties as well? And if weak, failing, or predatory states do not enforce human rights standards, should not domestic actors be *directly* bound by human rights standards? These are difficult and fundamental debates, not only in human rights law but in all of international law.

This brief outline of the history of human rights reveals some of the key debates in the human rights community. First, there is the presumed Western origin of human rights. This, it is often argued, makes them less applicable to non-Western societies. And so, for reasons of culture, history, values, or simply poverty, non-Western societies ought not to be bound by human rights standards—and a fortiori ought not to be the subject of external pressure. Second, as we move through the so-called generations, the debate about the meaning and even existence of rights increases. Are the later generations truly rights or simply aspirations? Can one really talk about generations, with all this implies in terms of fundamental differences in style and strength, or are all these rights truly instances of the same vision, equal and indivisible? Third, the issue of the direct application of human rights standards to non-state actors—foremost, to corporations—became very important in the 1990s; in some ways, much of the wrongly named anti-globalization movement has been, and continues to be, about this question.

Each of these debates is highly relevant for development practitioners. The charge that the development ideology is Eurocentric and interventionist has been leveled at the development community for decades; adding human rights to the development agenda may make that worse. Similarly, many development scholars and activists have long questioned the role of non-state actors (foremost, corporations) in sustainable development. How can we ensure that their actions promote development? And finally, the answer one gives to the debate over the validity of the various types of rights will, of course, deeply influence the discussion of what a deeper integration of development and human rights implies.

The rest of Part I discusses some of the conceptual questions the human rights community has had to deal with over the last decades. First, I discuss the ways human rights scholars and activists have dealt with the charge of Eurocentrism. Then I move on to a discussion of the status of second- and third-generation rights: what is really the nature of the obligations entailed by ESC rights? Third, I analyze in detail the value of the third-generation human right that is most relevant for this book: the right to development.

The answers to these questions are relevant to development practitioners in two ways. First, people in the human rights community have had debates that are very similar to the current debates in the development community; analyzing how the former tried to solve these challenges may thus be useful to the latter. Second, as the development community seeks to integrate human rights concerns into its own work, it will be confronted with these challenges as well. Development specialists often assume that human rights are a straightforward and uncontested "package" that can be adopted simply and directly into development work. This is wrong. There are multiple debates and divisions within the human rights community, and it is necessary to be aware of them. Human rights specialists finally may be curious to see how a development person, like me, looks at their world. Maybe the outside lens brought to bear on their work will provide a basis for some new insights.

2

The Legal Challenges

The Charge of Eurocentrism

From its very inception the human rights community (like the development one, for that matter) has been under attack on one of its very key premises, namely, the universality of human rights. Many scholars, activists, and government officials, especially but not exclusively from third-world countries, have argued that human rights emanate from Western political, cultural, or religious values and are therefore not universally valid.[1] To no small extent, such debate functions simply as a political ploy, a device in the rhetorical wars of opposing camps in the international community. This was particularly true during the Cold War, when the United States argued exclusively in favor of CP rights, while communist countries including the USSR and China argued equally exclusively and vehemently for ESC rights. A more recent but similar debate, involving both senior politicians and intellectuals, revolves around so-called Asian values. The notion put forward is that in (East) Asia, a different set of (non-Western) values hold sway; for example, that there is much greater value placed on community and the common good (as opposed to individualism), respect for authority (as opposed to freedom), hard work and savings (as opposed to consumption), and that these values are superior to those found in the West, producing societies that are characterized by high economic growth, strong families, little violence, and no drug use. Such claims are widely seen as an attempt by a number of Asian governments, including such odd bedfellows as China, Myanmar, and Singapore, to deflect criticisms on their human rights records. It is both an offensive move, allowing these newly assertive leaders to undermine Western intellectual hegemony by explicitly positioning their own values as superior, and a defensive move

17

against a Western discourse of morality that is perceived as undermining the centrality of the state. Indeed, those espousing this approach are leaders of strong states, which they consider necessary for development and stability (Ghai 2001, 13). As Ghai observes:

> There is little evidence that Asian economic success (such as it is) is due to family or community structures or to any other aspect of Asian values. Instead it is the resources and structures of the state (and their misappropriation) that have played a decisive role in private accumulation and production. Those of us who live in the more economically successful parts of Asia are not struck by the cohesion of the community, or by the care that the community or family provides, or by benevolent governments, or by a public disdain for democracy. Instead we notice the displacement of the community by the pretensions and practices of the state. Far from promoting reconciliation and consensus, the state punishes its critics, suppresses the freedom of expression—without which dialogue is not possible—and relies on armed forces rather than persuasion (and some leaders are rather "un-Confucianistly" litigious!). The doctrine of Asian values thrives on the perception of those who are perched on the higher reaches of the state and the market.

That said, behind the political posturing, there *is* a real debate, and one that is relevant and not easily solved; it is also a fundamental challenge to the human rights enterprise, denying its validity for the non-Western world, exactly the part of the world where the overwhelming majority of work performed by the major human rights organizations is done. It is a debate, finally, that is relevant for the development community as well, because its main ideological thrust, too, has often been reproached for inappropriately universalizing Western values, aims, and methods.

By now, even the least philosophically inclined development specialists occasionally worry about the degree of interventionism and the imposition of external values inherent in their work. This may not be due to the philosophical or legal concerns that have occupied many scholars but simply arises out of the fear that social change will not succeed or be durable unless it is carried and owned internally. For two decades now, every development project, program, or policy has professed a desire to build local ownership and has claimed to strengthen local capacities, to build on the expressed needs and internal dynamics of the community, and to support national policy—all ways to ensure that aid is not considered external and "Western-centric." A wide variety of practices has been adopted to achieve these aims: techniques to promote community participation, modalities of program funding and partnership, participatory assessments and programming, and the like. In short, development practitioners, in order to ensure that their work reflects local needs and strengthens internal dynamics, have developed a multitude of practical approaches and strategies. Many of these are somewhat lacking in theory, and many also do not work as well as their rhetoric promises, but at least attempts to this effect are now mainstream in the practice of development.

Human rights scholars, much more than development specialists, have done sophisticated intellectual work to think through the issues of culture and universality, intervention and ownership, yet, they have done very little in practice. At the risk of oversimplifying, one may detect a recurrent pattern here: the human rights community tends to think more deeply through the complicated and abstract philosophical questions related to its mandate but does rather little with these insights "on the ground." The development community, on the other hand, tends to develop multitudes of tools and practices for facing up to constantly changing operational challenges but typically gives these matters little theoretically informed or conceptually grounded thought, and therefore things remain at the level of ad hoc practice. This difference is partly due to the dominant professional profiles in these communities: legal scholars, political theorists, and philosophers, on the one hand, and technicians of all kinds, on the other. It may also result from the fact that human rights practitioners believe that they have a winning approach—a well-understood methodology of collecting information about human rights violations and the mobilization of shame through publicity, advocacy, and grassroots campaigns—that does not need much questioning. Why change from a winning horse? Development practitioners, on the other hand, live with much more self-doubt about the best way to do things and fear that their money buys little but token compliance, and thus they constantly seek operational innovations to overcome these fears.

In the next pages I distinguish six paths human rights scholars have developed to address the charge of "Western-centrism." The first three have been most widely adopted by the human rights community; indeed, human rights discourse and practice are permeated by these three approaches. The other three responses are advocated primarily by a small number of reputed scholars but rarely implemented. They may inform the personal understanding of some human rights actors, but they do not significantly inform mainstream practice. At the end of this section, I draw parallels with the development enterprise. We will see that it basically functions in the opposite way: it has much more operational experience with the latter three than with the former. It seems to me that this, then, is a field where human rights practitioners could learn from the experience of the development community in order to strengthen their own practice.

One small aside before I move into the subject: my argument in this section is based on the premise that one actually needs to *convince* doubters of the universality of human rights in order to change their behavior in the direction of greater conformity with such rights. In the real world, this is not necessarily a realistic assumption. First, many violations of human rights worldwide do not result from doubts about the universality of human rights. Expressing such doubts may allow the perpetrators to cover up violations committed for reasons of power or cruelty or simple indifference, but there may be no causal relation between intellectual doubt and action. Second, it is hardly necessary to convince others in order to change their behavior: the simple use of force, or bribes, often achieves the same result. Most human rights scholars would feel uncomfortable with that strategy, for they fear that what is being advanced then is not a human rights regime but a practice of power, even if couched in ethical terms (Ignatieff 1999). Practitioners are often in a bind about this. On the one hand, they typically are less preoccupied with philosophical debates and more concerned simply to stop the actual occurrence of a human rights violation. At the same time, they may feel ill at ease, and justifiably so, fearing that the type of behavioral change that flows from the simple application of power politics may well be rather unsustainable; that is, people and states will seek to reverse it once they feel that the power balance tilts in their favor (and, of course, some powerful actors will never be bothered by such power politics—think China or the United States here, or multinational corporations). In addition, while power politics may "work" in the sense of achieving the desired aim in the short term, it may in the longer run undermine the very universality that provides the moral ground for the human rights edifice. Hence, while intellectually convincing doubters of the universality of human rights is by no means a necessary or sufficient condition for the protection and promotion of human rights, a discussion of the intellectual basis of the human rights edifice does remain relevant for both practical and ethical reasons.

The Legal Solution

The first answer to the charge of "Western-centrism" is purely formal and legal: human rights are universal and bind all states because they have voluntarily ratified the relevant legal instruments—end of discussion (de Feyter 2001, 247). This is the formalist, positive law approach (Nyamu-

Musembi 2002, 3). Even if one could argue that the 1948 Universal Declaration on Human Rights was a fait accompli for the majority of the
world's states,[2] by now, the argument goes, human rights are clearly established as binding expressions of universal aims (Yasuaki 1999, 122).
More than 140 countries have ratified both 1966 covenants, while other
human rights treaties have been ratified even more widely: the 1993 Vienna
Declaration and Program of Action, for example, was adopted by consensus by 172 states after having involved most of them in years of negotiation. And this very same declaration adopted an anti-relativist position in
words that could not be more emphatic: "The universal nature of these
rights and freedoms is beyond question. . . . Human rights and fundamental freedoms are the birthright of all people" (art. I.1). Human rights instruments, this position argues, have been negotiated, affirmed, and ratified so often and by so many countries that they truly constitute the
expression of a universal agreement. As a matter of fact, according to
international law scholars, human rights may well constitute customary
law if not *jus cogens* (mandatory international law)—in both cases implying that they are applicable even to those states that have not ratified them
(Schachter 1985; Meron 1998; Steiner and Alston 2000, 367).

In short, from a positive legal perspective, there is ample ground to
argue that human rights obligations constitute universal obligations. Jerome
Shestack states it clearly: "Even as theorists have continued to quarrel
with each other, fundamental human rights principles have become universal by virtue of their entry into international law as *jus cogens*, customary law, or by convention. In other words, the relativist argument has been
overtaken by the fact that human rights have become hegemonic and therefore universal by fiat" (Shestack 2000, 60; see Tharoor 1999, 5).

This method of solving the relativity conundrum is very popular and
widely adopted in legal circles. It has three weaknesses. First, it only works
if one already accepts positive international law methodologies for arriving at conclusions about this matter. Opponents would argue that, yes,
many declarations exist, and international courts and scholars have declared some of these mandatory or customary, but all this happened in a
world of Western intellectual and political hegemony. Clearly, these opponents have a point. Imagine the frightening scenario if Hitler's Third Reich
had won the Second World War. The face of international law, and human
rights law a fortiori, would be very different. And what if we lived in a
China-dominated world? The nature of law is without doubt linked to the
dictates of power (although it cannot be reduced to these). In short, stating that all countries are bound by human rights law "because it is the

law" is unlikely to solve the issue for those who consider the human rights edifice to be Eurocentric.

Second, it makes little sense to counter an ethical debate with a purely legal argument: the discussion is not about whether many ratified human rights treaties exist in this world—they clearly do exist—but rather whether their content is sufficiently reflective of international diversity of thought and belief to be legitimate. This is a philosophical or ethical debate that cannot easily be settled with positive law arguments.

Third, even legally, the famous assertion in the 1993 Vienna Declaration and Program of Action that so clearly stated "all human rights are universal, indivisible and interdependent and interrelated" was followed by a much less often mentioned line: "the significance of national and regional particularities and various historical, cultural and religious backgrounds must be borne in mind" (art. I.5). As Peter R. Baehr says: "the precise meaning of this addition, which was obviously the result of a political compromise, has remained unclear" (Baehr 2000, 8). Hence, even from a strict legalistic perspective, there remains some uncertainty about the meaning of and possible limitations on universality. Deep divisions *within* Amnesty International about the rights of gay and lesbian people and about female genital mutilation, for example, demonstrate how unclear the legal statement of universality in reality is (Baehr 2000, 11). Baehr's conclusion is that "notwithstanding the lipservice being paid to the universal nature of human rights, the issue of what exactly that universality means is bound to remain with us. This is as it ought to be" (Baehr 2000, 11). I agree. We need more to solve the universality problem than simply declaring it does not exist because the law says so.

Weak Cultural Relativism

A second path out of the relativity conundrum can be called weak cultural relativism (Donnelly 1999b, 83ff.; Nyamu-Musembi 2002, 4). It essentially argues that the human rights edifice allows space for culturally and socially sensitive variations *in implementation*. The approach posits that the human rights edifice has been designed deliberately in such a way as to allow for culturally adapted modalities of implementation. The specific laws, institutions, and procedures that states adopt to implement human rights standards are their own business, and will—rightly so—be influenced by their value systems, cultures, histories, political constellations, and resources. Reference is often made to advanced democracies, which display significant divergence in fields such as criminal justice, social safety nets, labor policies, religious laws, access of citizens to public information, and the like, yet all respect human rights standards. Human rights, in short, can be respected in forms that are culturally appropriate. This position is weak relativism, for, while it does not doubt the universality of human rights, it does accept that the concrete implementation of universal human rights will be culturally specific.

There is no doubt that human rights instruments have been designed with such a weak relativist approach in mind, creating at times significant explicit allowances for local adaptation. Article 29(2) of the Universal Declaration on Human Rights, for example, allows for "such limitations as determined by law solely for the purpose of securing due recognition and respect for the rights and freedoms of others and of meeting the just requirements of morality, public order, and the general welfare in a democratic society." Various articles in the International Covenant on Civil and Political Rights make allowances for "the protection of national security or of public order, or of public health or morals" (art. 19; arts. 18, 21, 22 contain similar provisions), while article 4 allows for the suspension of most rights in case of "public emergency." The International Covenant on Economic, Social and Cultural Rights exhorts states to take "appropriate" measures, to the maximum of their "available resources," to realize "progressively" the rights described in the covenant (art. 2)—all of this clearly being the sort of language that presents major opportunities for local judgment about priorities and appropriateness. In essence, then, the legal language of major human rights instruments constitutes a nice instance of the weak culturally relativist position. There is significant room for countries to develop a differentiated practice based on context and local particularities (Perry 1998, 82ff.).

Yet, this approach poses many problems, both as a matter of theory and practice. For one, the weak cultural relativism approach is deeply state centered. The language creating allowance for social values like public morals, public order, or national security applies to *states*. It is their policies that may need such allowances; it is also they who will make the determination if and how the allowances shall be invoked. People themselves cannot do so, nor can they make such claims for differential treatment. But more important, the weak relativist case cannot deal with the hard cases. The cases that challenge the universalism of human rights are not really about arguing the evident fact that Sweden, Japan, and the United States are all democratic and respectful of human rights and yet display significant disparities in the way they organize their political systems. These are the easy cases. The weak cultural relativism solution collapses when we start debating the tough issues: Should women have full inheritance rights? Is the death penalty acceptable? Should all religions be practiced freely? Are all sexual orientations legally protected? Can all political ideas be expressed? Is clitoridectomy acceptable? Should certain civil and political rights be curtailed in order to achieve rapid economic growth? All these debates are not matters of how to implement rights in a culturally adapted manner, but rather whether these contested practices are allowed or not, whether they are just or not. Many of these hard cases seem binary: either you practice clitoridectomy or you don't; there is no compromise position. Either you allow the state to kill criminals or you do not; there is no in-between position.

The Affirmative Position

A third answer to the charge that human rights are Western and thus not relevant to the non-Western world lies in the adoption of an affirmative, strongly anti-relativist position. Essentially, to the Eurocentrism charge this position simply answers "so what?"; it denies that Eurocentrism poses any problem at all. Sure, the human rights edifice originated in the modern West, and yes, it is deeply imbued with the values of Western liberalism if not Judeo-Christianity.[3] But none of this, strong affirmativists would argue, decreases its relevance for the rest of the world. Jack Donnelly represents this position perfectly when he writes that "this [Western] history does not make these rights any more irrelevantly 'Western' than the origins and initial spread of both Newtonian and quantum physics makes them 'Western' physics inapplicable to Asia" (Donnelly 1999a, 69).

Donnelly and others move on from there to state that there is little in the supposed values of sovereignty or nonintervention or tradition that justifies passivity in the face of human rights violations, oppression, discrimination, and exclusion. Human rights violations, wherever they occur and however they are justified, whether inspired by fascism, communism, religion, tradition, or the free market, are not acceptable and ought to be ended—period. When the question is posed the opposite way, the point becomes clearer still: "Why shouldn't a country withdraw aid if it objects to a recipient's human rights practices? Why must it loan money to tyrants?" (Donnelly 1999b, 70).

This unashamedly non-postmodernist, non-relativist argument understandably has a strong appeal to human rights advocates. The human rights edifice is indeed all about protecting individuals from oppression, whatever its justification and whatever the social system within which it occurs. If people are uncomfortable with that because they are afraid of seeming Western-centered, neglectful of local and traditional modes of governance, or accusatory, then that is their problem.

Nonetheless, even if an individual or an agency proudly affirms its position, it will preach successfully only to those who are already converted. Affirm as I may that human rights are universal, this does not by itself convince others that I am right and/or that their behavior is wrong. It may make me feel happy, proud, and principled, but it does not necessarily do much for those suffering from the violations. In addition, Donnelly's analogy of human rights (a value system and a political practice) with quantum physics (a scientific model of the natural world) seems rather doubtful upon closer inspection. The same rules of evidence clearly do not apply to both.

The Empiricist Strategy

A number of scholars have sought to develop extralegal ways of grounding human rights and of developing arguments to support their universal validity. One such approach is empiricist: scholars attempt to identify, in various world cultures, religions, and value systems, those elements that concur with, resemble, or accommodate human rights norms. The idea here is that one can empirically demonstrate the universality of human rights by demonstrating a sort of moral organic match between human rights and key elements in cultures and religions worldwide. Fascinating work by Abdullahi Ahmed An-Na'im (An-Na'im 1992; An-Na'im 1990), Charles Taylor (1996), and theologian Hans Küng (Küng 1996; Küng 1998; Küng and Moltmann 1990) cannot go unmentioned here. These authors seek to demonstrate that Islam, Buddhism, and indeed *all* major religions contain principles and norms that are essentially locally specific formulations of key human rights standards. Similar arguments have also been made for democracy (Dalai Lama 1999; Filali-Ansary 1999). To the extent that one can do this convincingly, one may be laying a solid empirical foundation for claims to universality—and one that does not depend on prior acceptance of legal modes or reasoning.

The problems encountered by this method are many. For one thing, it requires a fair deal of cultural arm-twisting to force norms, concepts, and practices that are often inspired by and imbued with totally different values into the mold of individual, secular, liberal, universal human rights (Donnelly 1999a; Yasuaki 1999, 121). According to sophisticated defenders of the empiricist position (Bell 1996), it is not necessary to demonstrate identical justification for the rule, as long as the rule is similar to a human right. However, many scholars, and none more than Donnelly (1989; see also Seligman 2000), have strongly argued that the justification is an absolutely crucial aspect of the concept, or the existence, of human rights.

Take a hypothetical example of a community with a strong and principled practice of not torturing its members, justified on the grounds that torture of tribesmen would upset the social balance or that its Deity disproves of torture of clansmen. As the group lives in a remote area and never encounters non-kinsmen, it consequently never engages in torture and thus has a practice that conforms to human rights standards. This is not at all the same, however, as demonstrating the existence of a locally specific notion of human rights, for the justification of the behavior is what counts. The specificity of human rights is the granting of rights to all humans *because they are human*—not because they belong to a certain group, because they have the right religion, because the ruler does not like it, or because the act is too risky. Hence, the justification for human rights is a crucial and constitutive element of their existence. If that is so, the empiricist position is almost always doomed to fail.

Second, it is one thing to demonstrate that certain values, concepts, or practices in, say, Islam or Buddhism are compatible with human rights, albeit possibly justified on different grounds. It is quite another to say that these values and practices demonstrate that all or even most currently affirmed human rights are organically rooted in *all* cultures (Perry 1998, 72ff.). The decision necessarily needs to be made to drop quite a few rights for some cultures, which, as Donnelly has convincingly argued, is the beginning of a slippery slope toward reasserting the precedence of culture over rights (Donnelly 1989).

Third, traditional cultures and religious systems are neither fixed nor monolithic. They change over time, and they often contain very contradictory texts within them (Thede 2002, 24; Ibhawoh 2000, 841). As Mark Gopin demonstrates, Judaism and Islam both have texts and interpretations that are what he labels "pro-social" (respectful of outsiders, peaceful) and "anti-social" (Gopin 2000) . For scholars to pick and choose those pieces that fit with the notion of human rights—an enterprise that is indeed possible, as all systems in all likelihood contain at least some such elements—is ultimately meaningless; other pieces could have been chosen as well, and none of this is fixed. Indeed, much of this is often contested, as different visions and interpretations of tradition and religion confront each other and as marginalized people draw on different strands than mainstream ones. In short, this may be a strategy of significant practical utility, in terms of establishing a basis for communication and persuasion; it is not, however, a strategy that will yield a serious theoretical/conceptual answer to the relativity charge (Seligman 2000).

Note that this empiricist approach, in fact, has been tried only very rarely and that only a small trickle of theoretical work is being done along these lines. Among human rights *practitioners*, there are, as far as I know, no attempts to take such an approach seriously.

The Philosophical Approach

Another approach to rebut the relativist charge is the inverse of the previous one: starting from a theoretical position, grounded in ethics, religion, or philosophy, one affirms the existence of a universally fixed and identical human nature, from which it follows that human rights practices are indeed universally desirable. If the existence of a fixed human nature can be posited—some feature of humanness that is essentially identical for all humans qua humans—we can then "confidently identify some things that are good for every human being" (Perry 1998, 63).[4] This approach works especially well on the negative side, that is, when describing great evils that we all intuitively feel cannot possibly be deemed good for any human being in this world: murder, enslavement, genocide, rape (Perry 1998, 71).

The most famous recent scholars to work along these lines are John Rawls, Martha Nussbaum, and Amartya Sen. Rawls talks about "primary goods," which all rational individuals, if they were free to choose, would desire as prerequisites for carrying out their lives (Rawls 1971). The broadest such list includes a full list of basic rights and liberties; freedom of movement and free choice of occupation; prerogatives of offices and positions of responsibility in the political and economic institutions of society; income and wealth; and finally, the social bases of self-respect (Rawls 1996, 181). Nussbaum talks about "capabilities" that should be respected and supported by the governments of all nations as a bare minimum of what respect for human dignity requires. Her list is lengthy as well and includes life; bodily health; bodily integrity; senses, imagination, and thought; emotions; practical reason; affiliation; other species; play; and control over one's political and material environment (Nussbaum 2000, 78–80; Nussbaum 1997, 287ff.). Sen's work is very close to Nussbaum's. Talking about entitlements, capabilities, and human functionings, he too focuses on people's capacity to lead life as they see fit, but, unlike the two others, he has not proposed anything like an exhaustive list (Sen 1993; Nussbaum 1997). It must be noted that in all these cases, the authors deliberately adopted a non-rights language because they accuse rights language of certain deficiencies.[5] Their intellectual aims are very much in tune with those of rights scholars, however; that is, they all seek to specify universally valid conceptions of what human beings, qua humans, deserve.

This work has serious defects, though. First, it requires acceptance of the strong and contested assumption that human nature is genetic and not a social product (Donnelly 1989, 16–17, 112). Indeed, Nussbaum and Sen explicitly argue that people's own perceptions and desires are *not* a basis on which to rest such a theory—participation of the people concerned, then, is to be avoided in the definition of the universal goods this approach seeks to achieve.[6] If one were to disagree with this strong position and believe that human nature is at least partly social, this would undermine the universalism claim. Second, as the above examples show, this position seems to lead to lengthy lists of desirable things that are of very different natures: liberties, needs, opportunities, powers, attitudes, possessions. Third, as Lars Osberg observes, "Their writings ultimately represent the reasoned opinion of the author alone, which may or may not be persuasive to others. It is unclear what percentage of the population needs to be convinced of the merits of a philosophical argument, or whether the criterion for acceptance is popular or academic opinion" (Osberg 2001, 27). But should participation by the people concerned be at least part of any rights-based argumentation? Fourth, this mode of reasoning is by definition of a highly theoretical nature. Even if there were general agreement that a core of human values exists, it may well be impossible to go further and agree concretely on what values should be put on the final, universal list and especially what these broad values concretely mean in practice.[7] Beyond lists at high levels of abstraction, then, these exercises provide little basis for grounding human rights universality (Thin 2002, 46). Hence, Noam Chomsky identifies "intellectual development, the growth of moral consciousness, cultural achievement, and participation in a free community" as crucial (Chomsky 1973, 404), while Christie considers "security, well-being, self-determination, and identity" the core (Christie 1997, 316), and Burton talks about "physical needs, such as for food and shelter [and] shared needs for social recognition as individuals and as members of identity groups within a society" (Burton 1997, 2, 17) (see also Gil 1996, 78; Gil 1986, 127–29; Foot 1981). Thus, much of what authors conclude about the basic human needs or "goods" that are universally valid is essentially vague, unverifiable, circular, and declaratory. This criticism is in no way meant to suggest that the above values and ideas are unimportant to human dignity or to processes of social change; on the contrary, I have in the past written strongly in favor of a vision of development that includes many of these dimensions of dignity (Uvin 1998; Uvin 2001). Rather, my argument is that such a listing cannot act as a solid basis for claims to universality of the entire human rights edifice. The above values certainly may be crucial to a dignified life, but they are also contested, always in process of being remade and redefined, deeply political and social and local in nature.

Incremental Change

A final solution advocated by some human rights scholars is an incremental position, advocating internal change that avoids a "brutal break" from the past and seeks a "sympathetic understanding" of local social, political, cultural, and economic constraints (Taylor 1999; An-Na'im 1999). In other words, the approach aims to achieve respect for and promotion of human rights within the culture on the basis of local beliefs and dialogue with local actors (Ibhawoh 2000). Michael J. Perry talks about an "internal critique," defining it as follows:

> An internal critique draws on, it works with, premises and experiences authoritative not just for those whose critique it is, but also for those in the culture to whom the critique is addressed. . . . The critique can be advanced primarily by those inside the culture to whom the critique is addressed, those who have begun to object to the practice in question—perhaps, though not necessarily, because they themselves, or those dear to them, have been victimized by the practice. (Perry 1998, 76–77)

The aim is to find an "unforced consensus" on the norms while possibly disagreeing about their justification (Taylor 1999, 124). External actors can play a role by supplying a language, opportunities to network and exchange, access to information, protection, and occasional financial resources. They will succeed, however, only if they do so respectfully and leave the power of conceptualization and initiative to internal actors.

This approach is intellectually close to the empirical strategy described earlier. There are two main differences. One is that it is evidently more participatory, more action oriented. The other is that this approach never explicitly declares the universality of human rights. Rather, it focuses on how to bring about change in conformity with human rights, how to reduce the gap between (presumably still universal) human rights norms and (particular) current beliefs and practices (see Filali-Ansary 1999 for democracy). As such, its language is very close to the development enterprise when the latter talks about participation and capacity building, for example. It is hard to do more than speculate about how the human rights community might concretely implement this approach, however, as it has hardly been practiced.

Critics—including many human rights scholars—argue that the problems with this strategy are twofold. First, it risks acquiescing for too long in violations of human rights, with unacceptable occurrences that degrade their victims and cause serious suffering. After all, Ibhawoh talks about "compromise" resulting from dialogue and persuasion (Ibhawoh 2000, 854)—processes that are bound to leave quite some human rights violations intact. Second, there are serious doubts about how representative those who speak for tradition and local belief are. Indeed, the appeal of the incrementalist strategy is seriously harmed by the fact that those who may participate in the mediating exercise may often reflect narrow and particularistic positions themselves,[8] or, more broadly, that there are major differences of power and preference within communities, and opinions about human rights may well be divided along these same lines. From the work of Robert Chambers (1986) we have learned that those who are heard by development experts are almost always men (not women) who are older (not young), better off (not the poorest), close to roads (not living in remote areas), better educated, and not minorities or other excluded groups. How do we know if those who engage in these internal human rights dialogues are truly representative of the breadth of society? In societies where certain groups are excluded, is it not likely that whatever internal critique takes place will continue justifying or condoning the exclusion of these groups? Think gender here, or sexual orientation: in societies where women or gay people are excluded, where their voices are silenced as a matter of ordinary routine, any unenforced consensus is likely to allow these exclusions to persist. The incremental change approach thus faces a basic conundrum: a respectful, sympathetic approach to human rights change will often occur within structures of power that may be inimical to much of the necessary change; if one ensures that the viewpoints of minorities or excluded groups can become dominant, one has often already gone far beyond working "respectfully" within that culture.

The easiest way out of the conundrum occurs when strong voices or preferences for change already exist within dominant groups (possibly allied with non-dominant segments of the community). At that point one can simultaneously promote human rights change *and* respect traditional patterns of social organization.[9] In other words, coalitions between local progressive elements within powerful groups and those employing a human rights language may be possible. But what if such progressive groups cannot be found or are very marginal? Will no change then occur?

The human rights edifice provides us with little support to deal with any of these questions. Its language is one of absolutism, neither allowing much room for choices and trade-offs nor providing much in the way of specific operational tools for social change. This may well explain why the human rights community has dealt so little with these matters; supporting incremental change dynamics in local communities, for example, is something no major human rights organization has taken seriously in half a century of work. The human rights community has an attractive, empowering language connecting all forms of social change ("all rights are indivisible"). Yet, perhaps precisely because of the purity of its language, the human rights community lacks the tools to do much with such language and has historically neglected much of its potential. Human rights organizations have mostly preferred to stick to the safe moral high ground and to focus on exposing a limited number of widely accepted civil and political rights, leaving all the other struggles for social change to the level of discourse—or to the development community.

The development community has dealt much more with operational matters of local ownership, attitude change, and cultural adaptation— indeed, one could argue that these issues are at the very core of the development practice. However, the development community has been too willing to overlook issues of principle in the name of incremental change and has neglected the realm of CP rights. Hence, we are back to where this book started: is it possible to integrate these two worlds, or at least make them learn from each other?

Conclusion

At the end of the day, there is probably no perfect solution to the relativity conundrum, no answer that will once and for all silence the doubters. Human rights standards being normative aims rather than descriptive facts, it is impossible to ground them with uncontested certainty in a universal manner. This stuff is about dreams, about visions for a better world, about political aspirations, and these will always be contested and to some extent unprovable. They are not a matter of universal fact but rather constitute a language to make claims with, to conceive of and fight for social change. It is not the only such language in the world. It is a language that, for historical reasons, has become rather strongly codified in international law, which brings with it certain strengths (such as the existence of legal mechanisms to which increasing numbers of states subscribe) and certain weaknesses (the neglect of nonlegal and non-state mechanisms of change).

The "Western-centrism" debate can never be resolved. This is probably not such a bad thing. Constant debate obliges us to come down from the moral high ground and question ourselves. It forces scholars and practitioners to reach out, to develop new ways of seeing things and talking about things, to moderate their claims, to build bridges. At the end of the day, all of that, while making their lives more difficult and their concepts possibly less pure, is rather a good thing for practitioners.

Relevance of this Overview for the Development Community

Our discussion of the strategies adopted by the human rights community to deal with the charge of Eurocentrism is highly relevant to the development community. Historically, the latter, like the human rights community, has acted as if "development" is not contested, not Western, not culture specific, but instead so blatantly universal as to be beyond discussion. The necessity and nature of development, in this understanding, are self-evident, simple revealed knowledge, untainted by matters of history or origin, free of power and particularism. This is akin to the strong affirmative position à la Donnelly described above.

Still, this assumption is being increasingly challenged from various perspectives. The most fundamental challenge has been launched by radical intellectuals, often inspired by postmodernism (for example, Escobar 1994; Ferguson 1990; Rist 2002). These people argue that the entire development discourse is Western created and imbued with the usual dichotomies of Western superiority. These critics like to talk with disdain about the juxtaposition between development practitioners (developed, aiding, modern, active, happy, rich, knowledgeable) and their developing country clients (underdeveloped, receiving, traditional, passive, unhappy, poor, ignorant). These assumptions, they add, are deeply at odds with local perceptions of reality and local social dynamics of change. This development discourse justifies the existence of an interventionist and disempowering bureaucracy.[10] At its most radical, this critique argues that the entire development edifice—the concepts, the language, the institutions built up around it—*causes* the problems it supposedly seeks to solve (Escobar 1994); that is, it creates underdevelopment. Ignacy Sachs states succinctly: "It is not the failure of development which has to be feared, but its success" (Sachs 1992; see also Esteva 1997). No human rights criticism I know of goes as far as arguing that the promotion of human rights standards actually undermines human rights.

A second line of relativist criticism against the development ideology and practice is less radical. It does not deny that a general desire for "development" does exist as a largely universally shared aspiration (especially if development is defined very broadly, as it usually is), but rather it argues that the *specific way* the development enterprise has gone about implementing its mandate has been wrong, culturally unadapted, often exploitative, unsustainable, unjust, and gender biased. For many, this *mal*-development is no accident; rather, it is related to the fact that those doing the defining and the funding are privileged, male, Western, outsiders, racist, self-interested, ignorant, and/or economists—create your favorite combination (Marglin and Marglin 1990; Kothari 1989; Kothari 1993; Shiva 1988).

A third argument, less radical still, comes from development practitioners on the ground who recognize that for many different reasons at the level of daily practice people seem not to participate enthusiastically in the projects and programs implemented by aid agencies. This holds both at the level of national governments and at the level of local communities and individuals. Somehow, the way development practitioners set priorities and define solutions seems not to match with what local people are doing with their lives. Policies of conditionality, ownership, participation, capacity building, and partnership have all been developed to cope with this problem, but for those inclined to self-doubt, this does pose an uncomfortable question regarding the extent to which the development enterprise is altogether external, non-local, non-universal, and inappropriate.

In short, the universality of the development mandate is often contested, just as is the human rights edifice. The fact that the development discourse has been widely adopted may simply mean that, in a world of Western dominance, governments and people are willing to conform to dominant discourses, especially if such conformity brings with it large inflows of money and opportunities. None of this, however, necessarily implies real adherence or real ownership. Note that this is not simply a North-South or "the West vs. the rest" matter. The development ideology may well be deeply subscribed to by many (often Western-educated) third-world leaders as well, while their own populations may have different aspirations, dreams, and values (see, from different perspectives, Chatterjee 1993; James Scott 1999; Kabou 1991).

Faced with these criticisms, the development enterprise has adopted some of the same responses as did the human rights community, but with some major differences in emphasis. Interestingly, the second three approaches listed above (the empirical, philosophical, and incremental solutions), which are the roads far less traveled by the human rights community, have been the ones most widely adopted by the development community. This may be because the first two options preferred by human rights practitioners—both of which essentially consist of referring to the conventions and treaties as sources of inspiration—are much less available to development practitioners; development work is not premised on, or governed by, legal texts. There exists, of course, a growing body of declarations and plans of action (and even "development decades") coming out of a large number of development-related conferences, but these texts have not acquired anything remotely like the constitutive importance or the moral force of the 1948 Universal Declaration on Human Rights or the 1966 covenants. Most development practitioners have never read these declarations or plans of action—and wear this proudly as a badge of honor. The third approach (the affirmative solution), which was very popular in human rights circles, is equally popular in the development world; it by and large denies there is a problem, and, as we all know from our own lives, that is always a stance well liked by many!

A few more words about the three approaches preferred by the development community. For the past two decades or so the development enterprise has begun investing significantly in attempts empirically to ground development programs and projects in other cultures and value systems (path four above). This has led to a lucrative job niche for applied anthropologists, who try to understand local cultures' perceptions of the sort of issues development workers engage in: health care and prevention, gender, natural-resource management, or even the nature of deprivation (for good overviews, see Booth et al. 1999; Moore et al. 1999). The idea here is to understand what different cultures have to say about these issues; how they perceive them; what the values are, the taboos, the power structures, the dynamics of change. Armed with that knowledge, then, development programs can be adapted to local circumstances so as to increase their relevance and impact. Recently, more conceptual work has been done along similar lines: the World Faiths Development Dialogue, for example, is an organization supported by major donors that seeks to involve people from all religious traditions in identifying common definitions of development. Even the World Bank (2000a), with its recent work on poverty as voicelessness and vulnerability, has sought to redefine the meaning of development from the empirical perspective of those concerned. This work has been neither easy nor mainstream, especially in operational practice, but at least there is a history of trying.

The development world also has a long tradition of starting from a theoretically derived vision of human nature and deriving from that legitimacy for its existence and activities (path five above). This appears most clearly in the "basic needs" vision that came to dominate the practice of development from the 1970s onward and that still provides *the* major (albeit usually implicit) conceptual foundation for the enterprise. All human beings, it is argued, have basic material needs for food, water, and shelter, and all development activities and policies should first of all promote the satisfaction of these basic needs; only after that is done should more social and psychological needs be addressed. More recently, the human development paradigm has created a more holistic vision, also including social needs such as dignity and community. The United Nation Development Programme's (UNDP) annual *Human Development Report*

Six Paths	The Argument	Popularity in human rights community	Popularity in development enterprise
Legalistic	States are obliged by international law to do this.	Very popular	Not at all
Soft relativist	Existing human rights law and development declarations allow for locally specific forms of implementation, so it is not Eurocentric.	Very popular and deeply embedded	Not at all
Affirmative	So what if the concepts of human rights and development come from the West? That doesn't make them any less important or less objectively true.	Very popular among practitioners	Very popular among practitioners
Empiricist	All cultures contain elements of human rights and development in their value systems (albeit in other words), and hence human rights and development are universal.	Some rhetoric, no action	Some action, to make projects work better
Philosophical	Human nature everywhere demands or automatically leads to human rights and development.	Some rhetoric, no action	Very popular, but only rhetorical
Incrementalist	Slowly people can be brought to uncover the importance of human rights and development in their lives and to act on this insight.	Some rhetoric, no action	Much action, to make projects work better

Table 1

is the best illustration thereof. This sort of broad vision of the needs of humankind is probably the most important ethical justification of the development enterprise and its prime answer to any challenge to its legitimacy: Don't all people need food? Don't all people want to escape or avoid poverty?

The incremental change approach (path six above) is the other strong path the development community has followed. Over the last decades development practitioners have developed a multitude of techniques to ground their work in local communities, seeking to ensure local participation, ownership, adaptation, initiative, and control. This also includes serious attempts to work with and strengthen the capacities of local organizations—both public and private—on the assumption that the projects they initiate will be more locally rooted and therefore more sustainable than those conducted solely by external agents. At the level of daily practice the development community has gone much farther in this direction of incremental change than has the human rights community. At the same time, doing so has been extremely hard for the development community; its work involves far more money, which induces deeply perverse dynamics. Let me explain.

The human rights community has rather few monetary resources and therefore cannot exert its mandate without significant local voluntary support, initiative, and leadership. Many people risk their lives on a daily basis in the fight against human rights violations. The development community, on the other hand, by and large needs only itself to do its work. Development organizations often pay salaries that are significantly higher than those paid by local organizations, and they have more resources in almost every imaginable way than those for whom they work: access to information, housing and cars, travel, education. Poorer people—whether in the public sector or in NGOs—know that in order to access the manna of aid, they need to talk the talk and walk the walk of the aid agencies. As a result, in the poorest countries it is never clear to what extent local capacities are being built or an elaborate show is being staged in order to get access to money (Uvin 1998; Kanbur 2000; Plank 1993, 419). This is not the fault of the development practitioners as people; they are usually no less intelligent or sensitive than their human rights counterparts. Rather, the fault lies in the nature of the development enterprise and the dominance money plays within it. The empirical extent of this problem depends on the general level of poverty prevalent in the society concerned. In countries with significant and wealthy middle classes and thriving private economies, for example, working with a development NGO or a UN agency may be a demonstration of commitment, while in very poor countries with few well-paid jobs, employment in the development enterprise may stand out as a great opportunity for personal gain.

Note that throughout the world there are a great number of people who are engaged in struggles for social change and empowerment which they wage *without* the support of the development community—and indeed, in too many cases, *against* parts of the development community, foremost the World Bank (Roy 1999). Popular struggles for access to land or against forced resettlement, cooperative action seeking just and fair prices, social movements fighting for access to services that ought to be available to all, new forms of self-organization by women or indigenous peoples to protect cultures and ways of living or gain access to instances of decision-making, campaigns for debt forgiveness—the world is replete with struggles and dynamics that take place independently of the funds and actions of development professionals, and independently of the human rights movement as well. Some—but rather few—of these struggles have used human rights terminology at times. Organizations opposing water privatization, for example, or coalitions in favor of cheap essential medicines and better treatment of people with HIV/AIDS, have used the right to water and the right to health respectively as tools in the struggle (Nelson and Dorsey 2003). And yet, nobody could deny that these dynamics and struggles are about the intersection between development and human rights in the broadest sense. One of the great weaknesses of the development enterprise has been its incapacity to forge alliances with these local dynamics and struggles. Apart from a few of the more radical NGOs, most of the professional development community (including most NGOs) is indifferent if not outright antagonistic toward these local forms of social struggle. There are many reasons for this: a strong focus on the state (partly forced on aid agencies by the institution of sovereignty), a preference for problem definition as technical rather than political or social, the general low visibility of many of these struggles and dynamics to outsiders and power holders, the distrust of many people involved in these dynamics and struggles for the official representatives of the development community, and so on. For some institutions—the World Bank immediately comes to mind, but most major bilateral aid agencies are in the same boat—this problem is close to unsolvable; their mandates, institutional constraints, and dominant ideologies pose enormous constraints on their capacity or willingness to make meaningful alliances with these local dynamics and struggles. For many other agencies, however, such as the more progressive bilateral agencies and many NGOs, a human rights approach to development could provide a basis to connect to these local struggles. We will come back to this later, when we discuss the rights-based approach to development. Achieving this connection could be one of the major ways the addition of human rights could benefit the practice of development.

The Contested Nature of Second- and Third-Generation Rights

Before we continue with our discussion of the way human rights have become internalized in the practice of development, it is necessary, I believe, to focus once more on two categories of rights often invoked in debates about development. These are economic, social, and cultural rights, on the one hand, and the right to development, on the other. A brief discussion of the origin and nature of these rights is important to the development practitioner.

Economic, Social, and Cultural Rights: Mere Aspirations?

There are two major reasons for neglect of ESC rights in the practice of the human rights community. The first is political: the economic rights agenda is deeply connected to interventionist, social-democratic, and possibly even anti-individualist approaches to social change. This approach was, and remains uncomfortable for many powerful people and governments in the West (Scott 1999, 644). This tension was reinforced by the Cold War politics, when ESC rights—and *all* human rights, really—became deeply politicized. ESC rights were championed by all communist and most third-world countries, who used them as weapons in the fight for a New International Economic Order (NIEO) and against US/Western hegemony. Western countries, in the meantime, focused exclusively on CP rights, using them as tools against communist countries (Donnelly 1999a, 614). The end of the Cold War profoundly changed the nature of the competing blocs and the strength of their ideological discourses, and as a result this vehemently partisan and partial interpretation of human rights has lost its sway. Indeed, the "universality, indivisibility, interdependence and interrelationship of all human rights"—in the language of the 1993 Vienna Declaration and Action Plan—are now only rarely explicitly challenged, except by a handful of Asian countries (Forsythe 1997; Craig Scott 1999, 643). Yet, another major barrier against giving due prominence to ESC rights remains.

There has long existed a sense that the nature of ESC rights is fundamentally different from, and more difficult to implement than, CP rights. The latter, it was argued, are "negative" rights, meaning that governments need to abstain from certain behaviors (arbitrary imprisonment, torture, limitations on free speech), whereas the former are "positive" rights, meaning that the government has to undertake often costly action. As such, many organizations have found it more compatible with their free-market ideology to push for the former. At the conceptual level, this separation has been dismantled over the last two decades, and human rights declarations nowadays always refer to the indivisibility and complementariness of the two categories of human rights. In practice, however, most people still treat them very much as separate.

The human rights community has developed two answers to this marginalization of ESC rights. First, the relevant treaties contain language that makes the duties as realistic as possible by taking into account resource constraints. The goals are thus not as idealistic and unrealizable as they may at first seem. Article 2 of the Covenant on Economic, Social and Cultural Rights, for example, states:

> Each party undertakes to *take steps* individually and through international assistance and cooperation, especially economic and technical, *to the maximum of its available resources*, with a view to *achieving progressively* the full realization of rights recognized in the covenant, by all *appropriate means*, including particularly the adoption of legislative measures. (emphasis added)

In 1994, the United Nations Committee on Economic, Social and Cultural Rights defined these vague terms more stringently, giving them some additional intellectual and practical bite. The so-called Maastricht principles define the "maximum of its available resources" clause—which could easily be interpreted as removing all pressures from third-world countries on the grounds of their general state of poverty—as imposing a *minimum core obligation* to ensure the satisfaction of the minimum essential levels of rights; states must demonstrate that every effort has been made to use the resources at their disposition in an effort to satisfy, as a matter of priority, these minimum obligations. Similarly, the terms "achieve progressively," which could be used to justify indefinite postponement of state obligations, has been defined to mean (a) that states must move as expeditiously as possible, and (b) that retrogressive measures are not permissible, not even if justified by progress on the realization of other rights (CESCR 1994; Craven 1995, 114ff.). Note also that the Covenant on Economic, Social and Cultural Rights contains two rights whose obligations are unconditional: the right to primary education and the freedom to establish trade unions. In other words, these rights are not

Cool!

subject to progressive realization but are immediately mandatory (de Feyter 2001, 264).

The human rights community's second strategy to combat the marginalization of ESC rights is to define the nature of state obligations regarding ESC rights along a continuum that blurs the distinction between commission and omission (in other words, between so-called negative and positive rights). Scholars now argue that each human right, including ESC ones, entails the obligation to *respect* (states ought not take any measures that deprive people of their rights; states ought not interfere with the enjoyment of a right); the obligation to *protect* (states must provide protection against deprivation by a third party; states must prevent other individuals from interfering with the enjoyment of a right); and the obligation to *provide* or *fulfill* (states have to ensure that everyone in their territory enjoys the full rights; states must take the necessary measures to ensure the satisfaction of the needs of the individual that cannot be secured by the personal efforts of that individual).[11] Henry Shue argues the same point. According to him, the duties imposed on others by the right-bearer are of three kinds: the duty not to deprive; the duty to protect from deprivation; and the duty to aid the deprived. In the case of subsistence, for example, the first duty implies that "one must refrain from making an unnecessary gain for oneself by a means that is destructive to others"; the second one means there must be "some provision for enforcing this duty"; and the third that "resources be transferred to those who cannot provide for their own survival" (Shue 1980, 158–60).

These three categories, then, as applied to each individual right, can be the basis of a fine-tuned human rights analysis regarding ESC rights. The right to food, for example, is then about (a) abstaining from diminishing people's existing access to food, refraining from discriminating between people in their access to entitlements, and protecting people's capacity to continue providing themselves with food; (b) protecting people against those who would deprive them of their access to food; and (c) in last resort, providing food to those in need (and this provision is, of course, subject to the progressive clauses outlined above, meaning that this obligation depends on resource availability). Such an approach seems also extremely useful for the development community, for it immediately suggests a multitude of (legal, social, economic) strategies to address food and hunger issues, as well as indicators to measure progress.[12]

The Right to Development

Development as a concept first entered the human rights edifice through the debate on the right to development. The idea was launched by the

Senegalese jurist Keba M'Baye in 1972—a period of radical debate about the NIEO and the Charter on the Economic Rights and Duties of States.[13] During the first half of the 1970s, third-world countries used their numerical majority in the United Nations to try to negotiate reforms in the global political economy of trade, finance, investment, aid, and information flows.[14] This effort was led by well-known nationalist third-world statesmen, who were emboldened by the success of the OPEC embargo, which was widely perceived to have been a victory of the Third World over rich countries, and which many thought had profoundly reshuffled the world's economic cards. The notion of a right to development fit well within this struggle, providing a legal and ethical basis for the Third World's request for international resource redistribution. In addition, it acted as a counter-argument against rich countries' exclusive insistence on enforcement of CP rights (Rosas 1995, 248; Marks 1999, 340; Hamm 2001, 1009). Acrimonious discussions about the NIEO persisted for years but led to no concrete results, apart from the signing of a few international commodity agreements. By the early 1980s, these negotiations, and any thought of a NIEO, were unceremoniously dumped after the election of conservative leaders in the main Western countries (Ronald Reagan, Margaret Thatcher, Helmut Kohl), the near destruction of OPEC, and the onset of the third-world debt crisis. By 1985, the intellectual and political pendulum had swung dramatically to the right, and structural adjustment had replaced international reform.

Surprisingly, though, the notion of a right to development did not die altogether—partly because the developing countries had learned that, in the words of Ian Brownlie, "it had become evident that the political futures market was in the area of human rights and it was therefore prudent to pursue policy goals under that banner."[15] After much legal wrangling, the Declaration on the Right to Development was adopted by the UN General Assembly in 1986 (a resolution, not a treaty, and hence without binding force), stating that "the right to development is an inalienable human right by virtue of which every human person and all peoples are entitled to participate in, contribute to, and enjoy economic, social, cultural and political development, in which all human rights and fundamental freedoms can be fully realized" (art. 1.1).[16] This was the kind of rhetorical victory that diplomats cherish: the Third World got its right to development, while the First World ensured that the right could never be interpreted as more of a priority than CP rights, that it was totally non-binding, and that it carried no resource transfer obligations.[17] Demonstrating the extent to which rich countries found even this non-binding and weakened compromise unacceptable, the United States voted against the resolution, while ten other OECD member states abstained. Hence, even in its watered-down form, the right to development amounted to a rich country *vs.* poor country debate, as it had been from the beginning.

Human rights, once set down on paper, never die, even if no one cares much about their survival. Rather, they mutate into working groups, commissions, and expert panels, each of which produces reports that are occasionally the subject of discussions in low-level meetings. It becomes more work, even for those who oppose them, to seek their destruction than to passively go along, and so these human rights stay alive, albeit barely. Sometimes, however, out of this patient work, contested or marginal rights can obtain a second lease on life. At the 1993 Vienna World Conference on Human Rights the right to development was readopted, this time with unanimity, as part of the broader Vienna Declaration and Program of Action:

> The World Conference on human rights reaffirms the right to development, as established in the Declaration on the Right to Development, as a universal and inalienable right and an integral part of fundamental human rights. . . . While development facilitates the enjoyment of all human rights, the lack of development may not be invoked to justify the abridgment of internationally recognized human rights. (art I.10)[18]

Note that, as in the 1986 declaration, the latter sentence was inserted at the insistence of Western countries. Still, the Vienna Declaration and Program of Action was adopted with unanimity, and it thus allowed advocates of the right to development to claim that it reflects a global legal consensus—a hollow victory, but a victory nonetheless. In 1997 the right to development was honored with its very own "independent expert," whose mandate was (barely) renewed by the UN Human Rights Commission in late 2000. The expert, Indian economist Arjun Sengupta, has by now produced five annual reports, followed by annual discussions in the appropriate subcommittee of the Human Rights Commission. Given that essentially nobody cares what he writes and that he is a smart and nuanced man, he has been able to put together a set of very interesting reports over the years.

In retrospect, the right to development process displays contradictory features. Legally, it has been a milestone, but politically and practically, it has been a total failure. Indeed, from the perspective of international law, the 1986 declaration was chock-full of innovations that have led to a voluminous literature. First, it was a key instance of the then emerging collective or solidarity rights approach. Second, it spelled out the link between the different categories of rights (CP rights and ESC rights) more clearly than had been the case until then. Third, it seemed to create duties for the international community (admittedly a vague construct, but supposedly referring to all individual nations, as well as, possibly, international organizations) as much as for the developing states themselves. Finally, the declaration made specific reference to a slew of things that came out of the development world but were back then in international law circles still very much cutting edge, such as disarmament and the rights of women and vulnerable groups. Hence, from a legal perspective, it can be understood that the Declaration on the Right to Development provided major fodder for debate for those legal scholars interested in social change in the Third World (often scholars from the developing world themselves) and could possibly be argued to be a harbinger of revolutionary new ways of thinking in international and human rights law.

At the same time, the Declaration on the Right to Development was, from its inception onward, politically very weak. It was politically engineered as bad law: vague, internally contradictory, duplicative of other already clearly codified rights, and devoid of identifiable parties bearing clear obligations (Slinn 1999, 304; Rosas 1995, 251; Perry 1996, 228; Obiora 1996, 376–86; Bunn 2000, 1425, 1435). It has been devoid of any real impact (Rosas 1995; Obiora 1996, 357). It was perhaps the very last product of the NIEO years and suffered from the political weakness of its promoters. In 1986, as in 1993, it was so watered down that it became meaningless. Affirming that all people have the right to development, and that such development consists of and is realized through the realization of every existing category of human rights, adds nothing to our knowledge. It adds only verbiage. This quality is nicely exemplified in the following quotation from the UN Working Group on the Right to Development, which describes the right as being "multidimensional, integrated, dynamic and progressive. Its realization observes the full observance of economic, social, cultural, civil, and political rights. It further embraces the different concepts of development of all development sectors, namely sustainable development, human development, and the concept of indivisibility, interdependence, and universality of all human rights" (approvingly quoted in UNDP 1998, 3). No wonder it has never been invoked by a social movement or by a major organization promoting social change (Welch 1995, 275). No wonder, as well, that it became buried in some obscure subcommittee. In this book, we will not come back to it.

Part II

Human Rights in the Practice of Development

3

The Basics

Historically, development and human rights have existed entirely separately, at the levels of both discourse and practice. The problem originated from both sides, an act of choice, not a necessity. As a result, practitioners and policymakers have missed great potential for the clarification of mandates, mutual learning, and collaboration on the ground.

The human rights community—especially in the rich countries, which dominate the global human rights movement in resources, visibility, and impact—has focused almost exclusively on CP rights in isolation from their economic and social contexts. With the exception of a few academics and some marginal UN committees, it has totally neglected ESC rights, not to mention collective rights. No major human rights watchdog organizations exist for ESC rights, which are generally relegated to obscure UN subcommittees whose work never makes newspaper headlines.[1] Beyond routine declarations about the indivisibility of all rights, for all intents and purposes most ESC rights have not been part of human rights practice for most of the last half century. As a result, the rights community has yet to build any bridges to the development community. It has collaborated only rarely with the tens of thousands of NGOs and grassroots organizations (GROs) working for social and economic change throughout the world. And it has failed to learn from the development community's experiences with the challenges of fostering participation and capacity building.

The development enterprise has clearly returned the favor. As I wrote this book, I was surprised at the amount of skepticism, if not outright hostility, that still prevails in much of the development community toward human rights; many (although certainly not all) practitioners have told me that, in their opinion, the whole human rights issue is a diversion, a complication, and unnecessary fluff. More generally, the total neglect of the ESC rights framework seems rather astonishing, given that it seems to provide a clear ethical and legal basis for the work of the development community, as well as a network of scholars, advocates, and organizations that could be tapped into. The neglect of the CP rights framework is equally surprising, for many development practitioners' engagement is motivated by a vision of human dignity and seeks to counter the effects of exploitation and social exclusion. Yet, somehow, the development enterprise has stubbornly refused to let human rights enter its agenda, preferring to conceive of development as a combination of good will and technical knowledge.

One perfect example: There exists a longstanding debate among development specialists whether autocratic regimes or democratic ones are more conducive to development. An enormous amount of scholarly work has been written on this question, and it is still hotly debated among practitioners (for good overviews, see Johnson 2002; Rueschemeyer 1991). Back in the early years of development, most people believed that authoritarian regimes would be most able to stick to pro-growth policies, as they are most capable of overcoming dissent from those who stand to lose from challenging the status quo. In more recent years, the intellectual tide is turning, and democracy has made a comeback, the arguments being that the legitimacy of free-market policies and the accountability of governments to implement such policies correctly are greater when governments are democratically elected (for syntheses, see Sen 1999, 328; Sorensen 1998). Whatever the outcome of the debate, the interesting point is that its existence depends on the fundamental acceptance of the notion that development is entirely unrelated to democracy. In other words, the concept of development does not include the many crucial civil rights that are bundled in the practice of democracy (for a recent example, see World Bank 2000b, 113). Clearly, the whole debate would become methodologically and conceptually void if development were not defined in terms that steer clear of respect for human rights (Sen 1999, 5).

This situation is partly due to the workings of sovereignty, especially in the case of international organizations, whose charters contain explicit prohibitions against interference in member states' political matters (Tomasevski 1995, 404–6). However, let's face it, these prohibitions never stopped development agencies from being overtly political in their work with member states when it came to economic policy. The issue, then, is in all likelihood more a philosophical or an attitudinal matter than a purely legal one. It is about differences in professional backgrounds, traditions, criteria for success, and professional ethics; it is also about avoiding the "hot potato" of rights, which is bound to lead to more confrontational relations with (member) states.

All this began to change slowly from the early 1990s onward for three main reasons. One was external to the development world: the end of the Cold War. This greatly affirmed the intellectual victory of liberalism as a system of political and economic organization—no other system seemed possible anymore, the "end of history" had been reached, as a famous book proclaimed tongue in cheek. The end of the Cold War also meant that many developing countries suddenly became a lot less important, as the one remaining superpower cared much less for third-world dictators' sympathy or their vote in the United Nations. Second, a number of intellectual changes took place in the development community during the same period. To address the deep economic crises that hit many poor countries from the 1980s onward, the economist types in the development community had massively invested in structural adjustment programs. Many of these programs failed, to no small extent because they were inconsistently implemented. Increasingly, both the economic crises and the weak policy responses to these crises were seen as caused by a lack of government accountability, leading development specialists to begin a major push for good governance and even democracy. Third, more radical people in the development community (who often did not like structural adjustment very much) continued their old quest to redefine development as being about more than economic growth. They looked for broader, more holistic definitions of development, which often came to include human rights (Mukasa and Butegwa 2001, 4; UNDP 2001, chap. 1). Thus both the Powerpoint presenters and the dirty fingernails folks converged around some acceptance that human rights ought to play a larger role in development.

Ten years later, though, there are few actual experiences that integrate human rights and development concerns in the field. The largest share of development practice has continued, it seems, without much influence from human rights, notwithstanding quite a bit of rhetoric and goodwill. As two observers noted: "Human rights [have been treated] as the cherry on the development cake—and very often the development cake was indigestible and at odds with the small human rights and democratization cherry" (Frankovits and Earle, 2000, 13). As a result, we still have very little in the way of systematic, pragmatically grounded knowledge on how best to integrate human rights and development (Frankovits and Earle 2000, 8, 10). This book intends to remedy that.

In the rest of this book I discuss what it means, intellectually and operationally, to integrate human rights into the practice of development. I present four levels of integration, ranging from the most status quo–oriented approach to the most radical departure. In reality, of course, these different levels occur jointly, often within the same organization. Still, it makes sense to separate them out for analytical purposes, because they have different historical origins and operational implications.

At the lowest level of integration—the level that most maintains the status quo—I describe the purely *rhetorical incorporation* of human rights terminology into a classical development discourse, which is not challenged at all. There is not really much to say about this subject, and so, in order to avoid an oddly short chapter, I include this level in this section, starting at the end of this paragraph. The next three levels of integration, however, constitute major fields of development cooperation and hence are each treated in a separate chapter. The next level of integration (Chapter 4) consists of *political conditionality*, that is, the threat of cutting off aid to countries with poor human rights records. The development mandate is still not redefined here but rather is made instrumental to another agenda. At the next level of integration (Chapter 5), human rights objectives are added to the range of goals of development agencies, and new projects and programs are designed that seek to provide *positive support* for specific human rights aims. At the highest level of integration (Chapter 6), agency mandates are redefined in human rights terms, seeking to create a more structural and more holistic approach to development and social change. Here we face a fundamental rethinking of the entire development practice: its ideology, its partners, its aims, its processes, its systems and procedures. This level can be called the *rights-based approach* to development.

Rhetorical Incorporation

During the 1990s bilateral and multilateral aid agencies published a slew of policy statements, guidelines, and documents on the incorporation of human rights into their mandate. An enormous amount of this work was little more than thinly disguised repackaging of old wine in new bottles. As André Frankovits rightly says:

> With an increasing demand for economic and social rights to be a major factor in development assistance, donors have tended to reformulate their terminology. Beginning with the World Bank's statement at the 1993 Conference on human rights in Vienna, followed by frequently heard assertions by individual donor agencies, the claim is made that all development assistance contributes to economic and social rights. Thus agricultural projects—whatever their nature—are

claimed to contribute directly to the fulfillment of the right to food. (Frankovits 1996, 126; see also HRCA 2001, secs. 2–3)

A few quotes get the point across easily. How about the following affirmation? "[The World Bank's] lending over the past 50 years for education, health care, nutrition, sanitation, housing, environmental protection and agriculture have helped turn rights into reality for millions" (Lovelace 1999, 27; World Bank 1999, 3, 4; see too Shihata 1991, 97). This one is nice too: "[UNDP] already plays an important role in the protection and promotion of human rights. . . . Its program is an application of the right to development" (UNDP 1998, 6). NGO representatives sometimes adopt the same rhetoric as well (Benoit et al. 2000). What these statements essentially do is colonize the human rights discourse, arguing, like Molière's Bourgeois Gentilhomme, who discovered he had always been speaking prose, that human rights is what these development agencies were doing all along—case closed, moral high ground safely established (see also Tomasevski 1995, 409; Uvin 2002a and the reply by Slim 2002). Or, as Mark Duffield argues regarding the rights-based approach to humanitarian aid: "It is not a case of the NGO reforming to address human rights but the reverse: *it is the aid agency reforming its concept of human rights to bring it in line with the work that it already does.* . . . It is as if aid agencies have suddenly discovered that the selfsame . . . model of development that they have been pursuing since the 1980s is a human right as well" (Duffield 2001, 222–23).

A more benign interpretation, of course, is that these verbal changes constitute the first steps toward a true change of vision. Indeed, much political science scholarship argues that discourse changes have real impact; that is, they slowly redefine the margins of acceptable action, create opportunities for redefining reputations and shaming by transnational normative communities, change policymakers' incentive structures and the way interests and preferences are defined, and influence people's expectations (already observed by Claude 1966; for an overview, see Abbott and Snidal 2000). The same notion is also a key proposition of all international law; even in the absence of enforcement mechanisms, international law *does* matter, for it reflects and affects actors' norms, expectations, perceptions, and reputations. Hence, the rhetorical incorporation discussed in this section, while it changes little in the immediate actions undertaken, may make a real difference in the longer run. There exists some hope, then, that the rhetorical posturing described above constitutes the beginning of a new learning curve.

At the same time, there are also some serious problems with this particular incorporation of human rights into the development rhetoric. Typically, this rhetorical sleight-of-hand overlooks the tensions between the logics of human rights and of development (Sano 2000, 744). As Jack Donnelly argues convincingly, referring to the UNDP's work on human development:

> Human rights and sustainable human development 'are inextricably linked' only if development is defined to make this relationship tautological. "Sustainable human development" simply redefines human rights, along with democracy, peace, and justice, as subsets of development. Aside from the fact that neither most ordinary people nor governments use the term in this way, such a definition fails to address the relationship between economic development and human rights. Tensions between these objectives cannot be evaded by stipulative definitions. (Donnelly 1999a, 611)

To work out the relations between development and human rights requires more than simply stating that one automatically implies, or equals, or subsumes the other. This is a rhetorical move only, a mere relabeling rather than an honest attempt to come to grips with complicated issues or to devise innovative solutions. Michael Windfuhr, founder of the world's foremost human rights organization devoted to an economic right (FIAN, working on the right to food), describes the problem this way:

> Besides the general misconceptions related to ESC-Rights—that they are costly to implement, that implementation can only be done progressively and that they are therefore not rights at all but rather political objectives—one additional basic misunderstanding often comes up in discussions on how to integrate ESC-Rights into development cooperation, the concept that development cooperation automatically implements ESC-Rights because it is oriented to improve health or food situations of groups of the population. A rights-based approach means foremost to talk about the relationship between a state and its citizens. (Windfuhr 2000, 25)

In other words, a positive result in a field—say, increasing food production in one region, or building houses for poor people in a town, or providing a grant to a village health committee for the purpose of buying medicines—does not automatically promote respect for the right to food, housing, and health respectively (CESCR 1990, par. 7). After all, a right is about a long-term guarantee, a set of structural claims, particularly for the most vulnerable and underprivileged or excluded. It is not simply the result of a gift, an act of charity, or even of a smart policy blueprint. As Henry Shue says: "Are people's subsistence rights being respected if they simply happen to have enough? No: They must have a *right* to security and to subsistence—the continued enjoyment of the security and the subsistence must be *socially guaranteed*." This means that "people will make arrangements so that one will be able to enjoy the substance of the right even if—especially if—it is not within one's own power to arrange" (Shue 1980, 16).

There is a real danger, then, in this kind of rhetorical repackaging. Far from constituting the first step toward a fundamental re-conceptualization of the practice of development cooperation, it may merely provide a fig leaf for the continuation of the status quo. By postulating that development projects and programs—limited, one presumes, to those that are at least successful—by definition constitute an implementation of human rights, the important difference between a service-based and a rights-based approach to development is obscured.

The prime reason that development agencies adopt such language with its deliberate obfuscations is to benefit from the moral authority and political appeal of the human rights discourse. The development community constantly needs to regain the moral high ground in order to fend off criticism and to mobilize resources. As the development community faces a deep crisis of legitimacy among both insiders and outsiders, the act of cloaking itself in the human rights mantle may make sense, especially if doing so does not force anyone to rethink or to act very differently. We will come back to this at the beginning of Chapter 6.

I must admit that my argument thus far, despite being one I feel spontaneously most comfortable with, can be solidly contradicted. Does it not condone another status quo—the one, this time, of failing to decrease people's suffering *now* because we are too busy laying the structural groundwork for the enjoyment of rights later? Radical scholars and activists—in university campuses as much as in Latin American politics—usually speak with disdain about service-based development assistance; *charity* is a term of affront to them, for it suggests that one fails to get at the structural issues that cause suffering, choosing the "feel good" path of individual acts that fail to get at deeper issues of discrimination, inequality, social exclusion, and the like. Yet, is this purist position not setting the bar too high? Is it not looking away from the ravages of deep individual suffering in the name of abstract, long-term ideals—valuable ideals, for sure, but certainly not superior to decreasing suffering now? Would a true human rights approach not entail relieving the pain of those who suffer right now?

This is the position recently adopted in a fascinating and important article about the right to health by Paul Farmer, who argues that "an exclusive focus on a legal approach to health and human rights can obscure the nature of violations, thereby hobbling our best responses to them" (Farmer 1999, 1487; see also Farmer 2003). He bases this argument partly on simple practical reasons: as human rights laws have systematically been flaunted for decades, and as denunciations of violations often do not reach their aim, it is necessary for those who care about the right to health to do more, have a broader range of actions than simply naming and shaming, to provide care to the sick. But his position is also grounded in an ethical argument: because "those who talk about human rights violations are not those who suffer from them," it is too easy for the former to neglect the immediate needs of the poor and sick and hungry in the name of long-term, legally based change. This argument for what Farmer calls "pragmatic solidarity" clearly has relevance: if one works with the poor and excluded, as Farmer does, and one asks them what sort of support they seek, it is certain that many will privilege better health care and access to certain basic services. To them, it is irrelevant whether such services are socially guaranteed or not. If their kids are dying, they care little about the legal basis for services—they want, and deserve, them right now.

Farmer reminds us of a very important point: the reason we are interested in human rights is not because we are lovers of social guarantees or fetishists of legal texts, but because we think that human rights (and development) work will help improve people's lives. At the end of the day, that remains the litmus test of effective change. That said, Farmer overstates his point. First, while there is no doubt that Farmer's "pragmatic solidarity" is important, there is no reason to call it human rights work. Farmer essentially advocates a model of humanitarian aid, which can produce major benefits, but which we know is not very sustainable; it too often depends on the continued presence of foreigners and foreign money, and it sometimes unintentionally ends up disempowering local dynamics of social change. NGOs and other development agencies have provided services for decades now, and in doing so have made amazingly little structural difference (although they have saved lives). The fields of humanitarianism (which is historically exclusively service based) and development (which is evolving toward a deeper integration with human rights) are simply not the same. Second, and linked to the former, there is place for both of these modalities of work. There is no reason why *all* international aid or engagement should be only of a rights-based development nature— nor, for that matter, why the opposite should be the case, and we should cease all rights-based development work in favor of an exclusive focus on charity programs. There should be a balance between the immediate relief of the suffering that comes from human rights violations and long-term work on the structural prevention of these same human rights violations. Third, not only are these two strategies complementary, but they may be mutually reinforcing. As Farmer's own work with Partners in Health shows, it is precisely when human rights campaigning and organizing for long-term political and economic change is linked to field work that the strongest impact in terms of creating rights-based social guarantees can be achieved.

To conclude this discussion: Good development or humanitarian work does *not* automatically constitute human rights progress; that requires legal and social guarantees, especially at the level of the state. At the same time, the quest for such guarantees should be accompanied by, and grounded in, attention to people's immediate needs and aspirations. Development agencies, more than others, are capable of working at both these levels.

4

Political Conditionality

When people first consider the relation between development and human rights, most spontaneously begin by thinking about conditionality. They argue that donors should threaten to cut off development assistance—and execute that threat—to recipients that consistently violate human rights. How can donors develop policies that employ their aid resources to put pressure on human-rights-violating recipient countries and make them mend their evil ways? At what point should countries be threatened with the withdrawal of aid in order to oblige them to respect human rights? It is in these terms that ordinary people—including human rights groups—usually approach the problem; the same holds for most scholars. During my last five years of work in Rwanda, for example, the need for political conditionality (with many diplomats and aid experts opposing it and others seeking much more of it) has constituted *the* key issue in any discussion about the relation between human rights and development there. Note that this debate, in Rwanda as everywhere else, is in practice exclusively concerned with CP rights, and most particularly those rights related to democracy. Only under the rarest circumstances—the fate of the Ogoni people in the oil-producing regions of Nigeria comes to mind—has political conditionality been discussed for ESC right violations.

There are understandable reasons for the popularity of political conditionality. First, donors have a longstanding de facto policy of providing development aid to regimes regardless of their human rights practices. According to some data, until recently countries that were heavy human rights abusers received significantly *more* aid than others.[1] As a result, people opposed to human rights abuses have historically and politically couched the debate in terms of ending aid to dictators or using aid to force dictators to change their behavior. Second, most people, including scholars, spontaneously assume that aid is a powerful lever for policy change.

This seems evident: how could massive amounts of foreign aid to weak and poor countries *not* lend major power to the donors? Why not use this power to force policy changes in the direction of greater human rights compliance?

In addition, the big nongovernmental human rights organizations such as Amnesty International, Human Rights Watch, Fédération Internationale des Droits de l'Homme, and Helsinki Watch have historically campaigned for a greater use of political conditionality (Chandler 2001, 700). Their prime method has been the exercise of pressure through what has been described as the mobilization of shame: the documentation and publication of ongoing human rights violations, with the aim of creating sufficient counter-power to force the offending government to cease and desist. The pressures may be direct (reputation, legitimacy, access to resources, and the like are at stake) or indirect (through other governments and international organizations that will in turn put pressure on the offender). Margaret Keck and Katherine Sikkink call this the "boomerang effect" (Keck and Sikkink 1998). All of this work is of a confrontational, arm-twisting, threat-based nature, which is close to conditionality. One of the boomerang actions human rights NGOs typically push for is precisely that offending governments be threatened with the withdrawal of development aid.

History of Conditionality

When the political margin for maneuver increased at the end of the Cold War, there was a concerted push for conditionality among scholars, activists, and politicians alike. Most of the focus was on democracy (Sano 2000, 736), but some of it was also related to specific human rights violations. During the first half of the 1990s, almost all bilateral donors added language about the importance of democracy and human rights for development. While talking about human rights, most bilateral agencies applied conditionality by and large only to democracy, with the latter typically defined simply by the requirement to hold elections. Dozens of countries were told they would receive no more aid if they did not organize multiparty elections. A double reduction had therefore taken place—from human rights to democracy, and from democracy to elections.[2] This process still occurs in many places.

The reason for this reduction is that elections are in many ways the easiest human rights–related aim to agree upon for donors. Donors tend to be divided in their assessments of the situations, their aims for the immediate future, and their willingness to engage in confrontational relations with recipient governments, but they tend to agree that elections—the end to authoritarian regimes—are a good thing. In post-genocide Rwanda, for example, the need to hold elections is the only human rights–related condition the donor community has managed to agree upon during the last fifteen years, with both the pre- and the post-genocide regimes. Not only are elections universally seen as an uncontested good, but they are also the sort of thing donors feel they know how to deal with: they can help write laws, distribute ballot boxes, organize civic education programs, and send monitors to hang out when the beautiful day comes. Elections seem simple and straightforward, backed up by domestic public opinion, and beneficial under all conditions. As we will see in the next chapter, however, nothing could be further from the truth.

This may be the moment to make the following point: much of this and the next chapter deals with democracy. The reasons are multiple, and they include foremost those mentioned in the previous paragraph. It is true that a functioning democracy does constitute a bundled instance of human rights; the right to vote, to free speech, to assembly, and the like are all bundled in the notion of democracy. For that reason, it is both popular among policymakers and has been the subject of quite some research—vastly more, certainly, than the literature on human rights per se. In our attempt to learn from experience, therefore, the lessons learned from democracy conditionality—and in the next chapter, democracy promotion—must figure prominently.

As much as we tend to think of Washington when we think of conditionality, it is actually within Europe that democratic conditionality has been most aggressively advanced. This is the case for relations among European countries and relations between Europe and the Third World. Within Europe, for example, countries can only become members of the European Union and the European Bank for Reconstruction and Development (EBRD) if they are democracies—strong carrots, indeed (Olsen 2002, 137). Both the EBRD and the Organization for the Security and Cooperation in Europe (OSCE) also have the promotion of democracy among their explicit aims. The European Union has also gone furthest in integrating human rights conditionality into its development relations with the Third World through the conventions that govern its relations with developing countries. In 1991 EU members adopted a resolution stating that a transition to democracy would be one of the conditions for receiving EU aid (Olsen 2002, 131). From 1990 onward, the Conventions of Lomé and Cotonou, which govern EU relations with so-called ACP countries,[3] defined human rights, democratic principles, and rule of law as the three essential elements of all development cooperation, whose breach may, ultimately, lead to suspension of relations (Holland 2003, 166). And indeed, since 1992 all trade, aid, and investment treaties with third-world countries contain a human rights clause—120 EU cooperation agreements, for example, now contain a "democracy as an essential element" clause, with an associated "suspension" clause (EU 2001, 4, 9; Santiso 2002, 16). EU aid has been suspended at least eleven times for failure to respect this democracy condition (Santiso 2002, 37).

Difficulties

The use of conditionality to promote democracy and human rights, however, presents many difficulties. Some stem from the behavior of donors, others from the behavior or characteristics of recipients, and still others reside at the systemic level. Here we organize these arguments against conditionality into four categories: (1) conditionality is unethical (it ought as a matter of principle not be employed); (2) conditionality is never fully implemented (even if it were ethical, it is never really employed); (3) conditionality does not produce the results it aims for (even if it is employed, it does not work); and (4) conditionality destroys that which it seeks to achieve (not only does it not work, but it causes more harm).

Conditionality Is Unethical

For some, conditionality poses questions of principle. It is considered unjust, or unjustifiable, and consequently it ought not, or only very rarely, be undertaken. The most invoked argument is that aid conditionality (and its stronger cousin, trade sanctions) hurts the poor and vulnerable, who are thus made to suffer for the sins of their rulers. The rich and well connected, it is argued, have many ways to escape the ill effects of aid sanctions, while the poor lose the benefits aid brings them. What we have here, then, is supposedly a situation where the means used to achieve respect for human rights is contrary to human rights standards, since it hurts the weakest and therefore, one could argue, deprives them of their rights. It is for this ethical reason that most of the practice of conditionality has exempted humanitarian assistance, the idea being that humanitarian aid is of a life-or-death, emergency nature and thus ought not to be withdrawn, even to achieve otherwise desirable aims.[4] Addressing this claim has both empirical and ethical components.

The empirical question is simple: Before we can conclude that the suspension of aid hurts the poor, we have to prove that current aid helps the poor. Clearly, if the benefits of aid never reach them, then suspending aid cannot hurt the poor either. This is an argument that was often made by economists in defense of structural adjustment: as the old policies never benefited the masses of the poor, we cannot blame the (conditionality-induced) cessation of these policies for the poverty of the masses (Sahn 1997). While this is a dismal, possibly even counter-intuitive argument, it is possibly correct as well as empirically solvable.

The ethical question is a complicated matter, however. For one, what we are weighing here is a situation wherein one human right is violated and the attempt to remedy that may involve the (supposedly temporary) violation of another human right—a trade-off, in other words, possibly justified by considerations of strategy. A widely used solution to this problem has been a humanitarian exemption, whereby humanitarian assistance—supposedly life-sustaining assistance supplied to the most needy—is exempted from the conditionality or sanctions. This is more or less standard practice today. The Committee on Economic, Social and Cultural Rights (CESCR) endorses this exemption but argues that the collateral infliction of suffering of many sanctions regimes is still unacceptable and that states ought to design and monitor sanction in such a way as to minimize such suffering (CESCR 1997).

The most evident solution, of course, is to determine if there are *other* tools available that may achieve the same result (cessation of the current human rights violation) without the cost (creation of an additional human rights violation). In that respect, promise may lie in *targeted* sanctions or targeted aid suspension that, like guided missiles, only hurt leaders and inflict minimal collateral damage. (I wrote this during the war in Iraq and have clearly been influenced by the ambient military jargon.) But such innovative sanctions—travel bans, bank account freezes, reductions in those aid programs that provide direct benefits to senior civil servants, suspension of military cooperation—have not widely been used until now and fall in large part outside of the realm of development actors.

Another ethical limitation to aid conditionality is the fact that it is much less likely to be tried, and less likely to work, with larger, richer, or more strategically important countries than with smaller, poorer, and unimportant ones. Scholars have documented how the United States and the European Union, for example, avoid conditionality with politically and economically important countries, while other, often less egregious, offenders are punished or threatened (Tomasevski 1989, 18; Smith 1998; Laakso 2002; Olsen 2002, 131; Crawford 1997). This tendency holds also for multilateral institutions, whose performance on the matter is highly erratic because of the pressures they receive from powerful member states.[5] This creates a perception of injustice that undermines the legitimacy and political acceptability of conditionality. Clearly, donors displaying a partial and inconsistent commitment to democracy lose much of the moral high ground when they try to force some countries into line with human rights standards and not others. As I wrote earlier:

> Given donors' past record of inconsistency in applying principled standards of behaviour, attempts at conditionality are widely seen as illegitimate. . . . As one senior person observed, "when we talk about universal principles but we do not apply universal mechanisms (i.e. the United Nations), there is a problem: it looks like unilateral imposition." The charge of neo-colonialism is more than hollow rhetoric for many in the Third World, and it is deeply felt. (Uvin 1999a, par. 54)

One could, of course, argue that conditionality still remains desirable, even ethically: while a more consistent policy would certainly be more desirable, conditionality does not suddenly become bad because it is not always applied. If that were the case, truth, love, and understanding would be unethical too.

Another ethical argument often employed against conditionality is that it constitutes a form of forceful interventionism, violating a country's sovereignty, or worse, a people's right to determine its own path of change (Kapur and Webb 2000). Who is to decide on this sort of issue? What is the value of national borders, of sovereignty?

The entire human rights edifice, of course, is built on the notion that sovereignty is not in and of itself a protection against judgment and interference; indeed, by their very design human rights constitute probably the foremost battering ram into the thick walls of sovereignty. Scholars and some politicians have recently tried to reformulate the notion of sovereignty to include a duty, a responsibility, to protect one's citizens, arguing that if a state fails to do so, the benefits that flow from sovereignty—nonintervention, foremost—cease to exist as well. (ICISS 2002; Deng et al. 1996) Hence, bemoaning a violation of sovereignty as an argument against human rights–inspired conditionality does not seem to constitute a strong charge, for human rights are precisely developed to render previously purely domestic matters subject to limitation and possibly international intervention. Still, on a more practical level, problems remain with the forceful imposition of constraints.

The degree of principled objection to conditionality might depend on the nature of the government. In the case of democratic governments, it seems much more ethically and legally difficult to use conditionality than in the case of nondemocratic ones. This, to some extent, is simply a statement that in democratic countries fewer human rights are violated than in nondemocratic ones (where the right to free speech, association, and vote is at least violated, in addition to whatever else may be). The opinions of the people directly affected by conditionality ought to matter as well. André Frankovits argues that popular acceptance ought to be a precondition for the exercise of conditionality: "Suspension or reduction of the country program or of individual projects will only be done in consultation with the affected parties" (Frankovits 2002, 11). The most famous such case is undoubtedly South Africa under the apartheid regime, where the ANC supported sanctions even though they imposed costs on many black South Africans. But mass-based political movements in Myanmar, Indonesia, and Nigeria have also at times asked for conditionality against their own governments. From a human rights perspective, explicit acceptance by the affected parties of the use of conditionality against their rulers is an ideal situation, and it may well be fulfilled more often than we think. Indeed, in conversations throughout Africa, people have told me they would be willing to contemplate ending aid if that action were to ensure a change in the status quo of human rights violations they endure. The practical problems are, of course, that there will never be a situation where *all* people are willing to do so and that there are many situations in which it is difficult to know *what* the parties affected think or want; in addition, it is not certain that cutting aid would bring the benefits people expect (all of them hoped that if aid were cut, the regimes in power would collapse and be replaced by more representative people, committed to the public good. I am not at all convinced that cutting aid would produce these outcomes).

So, what are we to do in the many situations where regimes are not democratic and we are not sure of the affected parties' opinion on the matter (or perhaps they are deeply divided)? My answer to this is influenced by current events, which have changed my mind on this matter. The very day I am writing this is March 20, 2003, and the United States has just launched an air and ground assault on Iraq in order to restore democracy and bring down a dictator—in short, to ensure a human rights agenda.[6] (Admittedly, the Bush administration also used other arguments, including that the Hussein regime and its weapons of mass destruction constituted a threat to US security.) This brings to the fore once again that sovereignty is not only a legal construct required for the smooth functioning of international relations, but also insurance against abuse by foreigners.

Compare the US intervention in Haiti to restore democracy to the same country's intervention in Iraq for the purportedly same purpose. As one who was happy with the former and deeply troubled by the latter, I must admit that, upon closer inspection, there seems little difference. In both cases a powerful outside government, backed by a significant number of its own citizens as well as a vocal community of refugees from the target country, argued that forceful and unilateral intervention was required to achieve major benefits in terms of democracy, human rights, and peace. I happen to like one and not the other, but structurally there is little difference. Sovereignty is a practical protection mechanism against all intervention—the ones I dislike and the ones I do like. Sovereignty basically says it is *never* the business of outsiders to make such decision, not because they are always wrong, but because without sovereignty we live in a world where the powerful—who have always been remarkably good at wrapping themselves in the mantle of progress and values—can use force against others (Rieff 2002a, 61).

Where do we end up standing, then, on the ethics of conditionality? It is a tough decision, and one that has caused development practitioners great professional doubt. Clearly, a key function of the human rights edifice is precisely to be able to break through the defense mechanism of sovereignty: what a government does with its citizens is nobody else's business. Sovereignty as a value could hardly as a principle outweigh human rights without fatally undermining the latter. Massive and continued aid given to consistent human rights violators seems like an act of acceptance, if not of encouragement or of complicity. And yet, many of us feel uncomfortable with much of the one-sidedness and the power politics behind conditionality, that is, its ability to provide a justification for policies undertaken for other reasons and the ease with which it can act as the proverbial stick with which to hit the dog. In the end, an ethically acceptable, nuanced practice of conditionality might look something like this:

- it should be designed so as to not impose costs on vulnerable groups.
- it should seriously seek to build on internal debate in the country concerned: if significant proportions of the population, or groups that can reasonably be held to represent them, are in favor of the use of conditionality, its legitimacy is greatly strengthened.
- the more government policies are backed by their populations (among others, but not exclusively, as a result of democratic elections), the stronger the burden of proof against conditionality. The use of conditionality against democratic regimes is not impossible—serious violations of minority rights, for example, may occur in democracies, and

may warrant the use of conditionality—but must be subject to much more rigorous criteria.

- it should be done in a graduated manner; there is no reason to cut *all* aid, suspend *all* actions, drop *all* programs at once. One can even continue working cooperatively with the same government for the rest. It is not all or nothing.
- it should try to build on existing laws within the country concerned: even if these are imperfect from a pure human rights view, if they constitute steps forward, it is better to push for their implementation.
- it should be based on multilateral procedures and institutions.

Conditionality Is Never Fully Implemented

A second line of arguments against conditionality holds that, even if it is ethical, it can never be fully implemented. It will be applied only to some countries and not to others, or only by some countries (or multilateral agencies) and not by others. As a result, both its legitimacy and its effectiveness suffer dramatically.

We have already discussed the well-known fact that on the donor side, economic or political interests intervene, rendering conditionality policies highly inconsistent. In addition, donors have found it extremely difficult to coordinate their conditionality pressures and their aid policies more generally (OECD 1997; Uvin 1999a). Competing interests, struggles for influence, unwillingness to invest in coordination, and the like partly cause this problem. There are more legitimate reasons for the difficulty of coordinating as well, since donors may reasonably come to different assessments regarding the nature of any particular situation and the most desirable approach for moving forward (Uvin 1999a; Uvin 2001). Differences in political systems and ideologies at home also make coordination more difficult.

Others argue that threats by multilateral institutions hold little bite, for the multilaterals are as dependent on the continuation of the money-moving system as are the borrowers; without continued lending and granting to a maximum of countries, their raison d'être would disappear (Mosley et al. 1991; Morrissey 1998; Hibou 2002, 179; Easterly 2001). As Ravi Kanbur describes, drawing on his experience as World Bank country representative in Ghana during the structural adjustment period, there is enormous pressure for aid to continue, even to recipients who clearly violate the terms of adjustment agreements, for donors are as dependent on aid as recipients (Kanbur 2000). Some of the causes he identifies include fear of economic meltdown, pressures to release earmarked funds within a specific fiscal year, demands from both the foreign and domestic private sector to keep poorly performing governments flush with cash so that they are able to pay out on their contracts, and concerns from aid agency personnel who rely on government counterpart funds. But the problem is not only that multilateral organizations are under pressure from their member states to continue business as usual even when it violates the agreements they signed; strong institutional factors also exist *within* these organizations that push in favor of continued aid at all costs, thus effectively undermining any possible impact of conditionality. Indeed, the very raison d'être of these institutions would come into question if they had to engage in the difficult, politically charged, self-critical sort of activity that effective conditionality requires (Mosley et al. 1991; Hibou 2002, 179). They, even more than bilateral agencies, need continued working relations with everyone, for fear of extinction. Nicolas van de Walle, writing about sub-Saharan Africa—and talking about both bilateral and multilateral aid—perceptively adds the lack of accountability by donors for results: they are only in charge of following bureaucratic procedure but not of producing results, and thus they have a strong built-in disincentive against the sort of critical and confrontational analysis required for effective conditionality (van de Walle 2001; Easterly 2002).

All of this poses not only an ethical problem, already discussed above, but also a major efficiency problem: conditionality will lose its bite and fail to work if there are always donors who will not go along. When one donor withdraws, another takes over. Some may decrease their aid eventually but will cite other reasons (budgetary limits, typically), thus decreasing the impact of their action. In short, an uncoordinated, ad hoc policy of conditionality is currently the best the world seems able to produce; it is also basically useless.

Conditionality Does Not Produce the Intended Results

A third line of criticism against conditionality is that it simply does not work. It does not produce the desired results, because (a) it deals with the symptoms and not the causes, and (b) the recipients possess too many tools for evasion. These problems, then, relate to features on the recipient side of the relation, unlike the previous ones, which were situated at the donor side.

Negative conditionality only attacks the symptoms but not the causes, of a problem. Sanctions and conditionality "only scratch the surface of much deeper issues" (Simma et al. 1999, 575) related to attitudes, interests, distribution of power, the nature of institutions, deficient knowledge,

and the like. Bad behavior often has profound causes, and merely imposing sanctions against it does not always durably change it—whether with
our own kids or with rights abusers.

In addition, there is currently a general sense that if the governments
and civil societies of recipient countries do not agree with the policies and
politics being promoted by aid conditionality, no amount of arm-twisting
will produce sustainable results. Results, to the extent they occur, will be
artificial and/or temporary, lasting as long as the foreign assistance is available or as long as the donors are watching (Uvin and Biagiotti 1996).
Conditions may also be easily subverted—after all, what can be done with
one hand can often be undone with the other. Recipients can also fake
fulfilling adjustment conditions while simply postponing the problem and
cutting into future growth (Easterly 2001, chap. 6). Donors are in practice
unable to change this situation (Killick 1998); at best they can buy what
has been called "financially-driven tactical compliance" (Wood and
Lockwood 1999, 1).

Take democracy, for example. Recipient countries may be forced to go
through the motions of organizing elections in order to maintain access to
international aid, but they also possess many ways to ensure that these
elections will be neither free nor fair. They can use public resources—
funds, patronage, media attention—to outspend and divide their opponents. They can foment ethnic conflict to ensure chaos (or to turn populations against moderates). They can adopt constitutions that serve the status
quo, stack electoral commissions with cronies, allow very little time for
opposition parties to organize, administratively harass opponents, threaten
sympathizers with the suspension of clientelist benefits, and the like. Indeed, in many countries forced elections have led to ethnic violence, as
powerful groups who favored the status quo employed violence to achieve
their aims. Rwanda may be considered the most dramatic case of this, but
there are many others, such as Kenya. Recent aid evaluations have more
or less explicitly acknowledged this unexpected outcome (de Feyter 2001,
58; Klingebiel 1999). Perhaps because of these challenges, proponents of
the practice often say that political conditionality works best when there
are strong internal forces in favor of democracy (or whatever other aim is
being sought). The argument, in short, is that conditionality works best
when it is least needed (Panday n.d.; Heinz, Lingnau, and Waller 1995;
Ghai 2001, 29).

In February 2001 the International Monetary Fund's Policy Development and Review Department published a major study on IMF conditionality, talking about the IMF "over-stepping its mandate and core area of

expertise," "short-circuiting national decision-making processes," not taking "adequate account of the authorities' ability to muster political support for a multitude of policy changes at one time, as well as their capacity to implement these reforms," and establishing conditionality "on policies that were unlikely to be delivered, calling into question the realism of program design" (IMF 2001, pars. 12–13). The review concludes:

> Finally, there are concerns that overly pervasive conditionality may detract from implementation of desirable policies by undermining the authorities' ownership of the program. . . . Policies are not likely to be implemented in a sustainable way unless the authorities accept them as their own and unless the policies command sufficiently broad support within the country. (IMF 2001, par. 14)

These are serious words. They have been written by what may well be the most powerful international organization in the world, one that basically invented conditionality, applying it rigidly to purely economic factors, and one that is also backed by the combined pressure of the world's commercial banks and powerful governments. If such an institution admits that conditionality does not work, how much weaker must it be for other development actors who don't even remotely possess the IMF's resources?

Conditionality Is Counterproductive

A final, stronger version of the previous argument goes even further: not only does conditionality not achieve its purpose, but it actually undoes what it seeks to promote. There are three reasons why this might be the case. First, heavy-handed external pressure can lead to a backlash that actually undermines the desired aim. Domestic groups may become suspect if they are too cozy with foreign agencies. In the many countries where nationalism is one of the main ideologies, it certainly is easier to discredit opponents and their ideas on the grounds that they are mere puppets of outsiders—especially if that outsider can be construed to be an ex-colonial power, or, in much of the world, the United States, and especially if that outsider uses heavy-handed pressure tactics. This is certainly to some extent what happened with UK pressure on Mugabe's regime in Zimbabwe.

Second, while the aim of conditionality (especially in the structural adjustment variant) is to place limitations on the economic and political power of incumbent regimes, these same incumbent regimes are de facto in the driver's seat to implement conditionality; indeed, the programs are negotiated with these incumbents, who also are charged with implementing them and who receive the concomitant financial rewards for their good behavior. For that reason, contrary to aims, incumbent power elites are typically strengthened rather than weakened, even by economic and political liberalization programs that seek to place limits on their actions (Hibou 2002, 185).

This brings us to the third and most fundamental criticism, namely, that conditionality by its very nature destroys the very domestic accountability and social transformation it seeks to achieve. Panday writes:

> What donor activism is doing in my country, Nepal, is that it is diluting public accountability, the enforcement of which is precisely and rightly what the donors wish to emphasize and ensure. Perhaps a greater danger is that donor activism may crowd out the energy and integrity of domestic pressure groups that alone can provide long-term sustenance to governance reform. (Panday n.d., 5)

Former World Bank chief economist Joseph Stiglitz writes eloquently along similar lines:

> Rather than learning how to reason and developing analytic capacities, the process of imposing conditionality undermines both the incentives to acquire those capacities and confidence in the ability to use them. Rather than involving large segments of society in a process of discussing change—thereby changing their ways of thinking—it reinforces traditional hierarchical relationships. Rather than empowering those who could serve as catalysts for change within these societies, it demonstrates their impotence. Rather than promoting the kind of open dialogue that is central to the democracy, it argues at best that such dialogue is unnecessary, at worst that it is counterproductive. (Stiglitz 1998, 10–11)

Conditionality thus reinforces a system in which "approval or disapproval by the international community may well be more important to a state's prospects of survival than any criterion relating to its domestic power or legitimacy" (Clapham 1996, 15). Governments are not made responsible for their development, nor do they need to negotiate the terms thereof with their citizens; all they need to do is to continue the international game in which promises are broken, ideas are parroted and "adapted," and money flows are maintained—a reactive game at which elites in many countries have become most adept. The development of a local social contract is short-circuited, and sovereignty is transferred to outsiders (Collier 1999, 319). This is, of course, rarely the best way to create sustainable political change (Uvin and Biagiotti 1996; Uvin 1998; Kanbur 2000; van de Walle 2001; Santiso 2001a; Santiso 2002).

In sum, there is a growing sense among policymakers that political conditionality, contrary to expectations, is ineffective.[7] In scholarly circles there is close to unanimity on the ineffectiveness of both economic and political conditionality (Stokke 1995; Burnell 1999; Burnside and Dollar 1997; Gwin and Nelson 1997; Collier 1997; Crawford 1997; Morrissey 1998; Uvin 1999a).[8] As a recent synthesis of the literature on aid conditionality concludes: "Conditionality emerges as at least ineffective and at worst counterproductive as a lever of policy reform" (Morrissey 1998). The title of the previous study in the same series also says it clearly enough: *Donors as Paper Tigers: Why Aid with Strings Attached Won't Work* (Killick 1997). So, where do we go from here?

Beyond Aid Conditionality

As a result of the general sense that conditionality does not work, there has been much thinking about what to do instead. Different paths are currently being discussed, ranging, as usual, from minor tinkering at the margins to fundamental rethinking of issues of ownership. We will discuss three recently adopted solutions here:

- improved conditionality design: more targeted, limited, fine-tuned versions of the old policy;
- selectivity or post hoc conditionality, based not on countries' intentions and promises, but on their demonstrated records; and
- comprehensive development framework (CDF) or process conditionality, in which a broad process of consultation is supposed to bring about ownership of the desired policy.

Improved Conditionality

The IMF has recently sought to rethink its policy of conditionality. Its solution is threefold:

- Establish far fewer conditions (only those that are truly critical for the achievement of macroeconomic stability) and thus allow for broader local discussion on program design, especially in noncritical areas (something that allows for "giving maximal scope for national owner-ship," in IMF parlance [Sugisaki 2001, 2]);

- Monitor these conditions in a more flexible manner, with broad gov-ernment participation;
- Distinguish IMF conditionality as clearly as possible from other agen-cies' conditionality, foremost the World Bank.[9]

This constitutes a rather minimal rethinking of conditionality; in simple political terms it means the IMF will still be inflexible on the core goals that it *knows* are good for a country. It then leaves the country free to decide how to get there or how to design its overall program, especially in those economic areas that are not crucial to the success of the adjustment program, and it makes sure that its conditionality does not get confused with that of other agencies, so that the IMF will not share the blame if things go wrong.

Selectivity

Another rethinking of conditionality (but employing a completely differ-ent discourse) is currently coming from the World Bank in the form of the new policy of selectivity. Starting from the twin (and rather radical) as-sumptions that all aid is fungible[10] and that all conditionality is ineffective, a 1998 World Bank study, *Assessing Aid* by David Collier and David Dol-lar, argues that aid resources should only be allocated to countries whose governments have demonstrably adopted a "good policy environment" (Collier and Dollar 1998; see also Devarajan et al. 2001; Tsikata 1998). This selectivity policy is at first sight a total departure from traditional conditionality, and it has some significant advantages. It ends attempts to twist unwilling governments' arms, suggesting instead that donors respect-fully and programmatically work with those partners who have the right policies. For governments that adopt bad policies, the selectivity policy suggests very limited involvement: no more than the provision of training and the promotion of national dialogues, but again, without conditional-ity. Essentially, the heavy-handedness so unpalatable in traditional condi-tionality all but disappears in the selectiveness approach; either we work in partnership with trusted governments, or we work minimally with those we don't trust, but we are no longer twisting anybody's arm.

The approach is currently intellectually popular in aid circles—indeed, it had been discussed in European aid circles for some years prior to the World Bank publication. Tony Killick, for example, author of the above-mentioned *Donors as Paper Tigers* review of conditionality, proposed the following alternative strategy in 1997:

A new model of donor-recipient relationships is urged, based upon four principles or pre-requisites, viz:

- an ownership principle requiring that donors take their own rhetoric on this theme more seriously, and desist from using financial levers to obtain policy vows which borrowing governments do not believe in
- a principle of selectivity, requiring that programme aid be limited to governments that have decided for themselves to introduce policy improvements
- "support" refers to conventional financial support for adjustment programmes, extended to improved contingency financing and debt relief for reforming governments, and to technical assistance (also unshackled from conditionality) for governments requesting it to raise their own policy capabilities
- a "dialogue" pre-requisite means donors must redirect their efforts toward exerting influence, and to maximise the number of channels through which non-coercive influence might be expressed and applied.

The selectivity approach holds the promise of allowing donors to move beyond conditionality and engage in more respectful and less confrontational relations with those recipient countries they choose to work with; it may also overcome some of the ill effects of conditionality on the quality of governance (Brautigam 2000, 54ff.). Of course, at the end of the day, from the recipient's perspective, selectivity is a form of conditionality as well, for it implies that aid will not flow to those recipients that do not behave in ways the donors deem correct. For that reason, many scholars call it ex-post conditionality[11] or allocative conditionality (Nelson and Eglington 1993). Some even argue that selectivity actually *extends* the reach of conditionality, for now the entire government budget and policy are subject to debate, whereas in the past at least some segments were beyond donor debate. Finally, a selectivity policy still poses the ethical issue discussed earlier: are poor people being punished for the sins of their rulers?[12]

The actual implementation of a selectivity policy has made far less progress, however, mainly because the donor-side constraints on conditionality have not disappeared (Ostrom et al. 2002, 17). Multiple political imperatives, the need to move money, differences in assessment, unwillingness to coordinate policies, unwillingness to rock the boat—all these make a true selectivity policy hard to achieve. In addition, such a policy would require rigorous and consensual indicators and monitoring mechanisms to determine countries' status on the selectivity criteria—an extremely difficult task, for most countries will not lie at the extremes of either perfectly good economic policies or totally awful ones. The same would hold for political selectivity; most countries will be neither full, nicely functioning democracies nor absolute total dictatorship, but will rather lie in gray zones between these two extremes (Santiso 2002, 27; Carothers 2002; Schmitter and Brouwer 1999).

Comprehensive Development Framework (CDF) and Poverty Reduction Strategy Papers (PRSPs)

Since early 1999, the World Bank has also been trying to develop another "post-conditionality" approach, namely, the creation of a large, broad process of soliciting input and discussion around liberal policy strategies. The idea here is that "ownership," the crucial missing link, can be created as a result of broad consultation and discussion. Originally this was called the comprehensive development framework and consisted basically of a giant national discussion process involving government, civil society, and the private sector, seeking to create locally owned good policies.[13]

In a joint note the Bank and IMF describe the Comprehensive Development Framework as:

> a means by which countries can manage knowledge and resources to design and implement effective strategies for economic development and poverty reduction. It . . . is centred on a long term vision—prepared by the country through a participatory national consultation process—that balances good macroeconomic and financial management with sound social, structural and human policies. The CDF, however, is not a blueprint. It is voluntary, and each country must decide on, and own its priorities and programs. In order to ensure the most effective use of human and financial resources, the CDF emphasises partnerships between government (at the national and local levels), civil society, the private sector, and external assistance agencies. (SGTS 2002, no. 1.6)

The CDF philosophy, then, is explicitly designed to overcome the weakness of conditionality, namely, the difficulty of achieving the elusive "ownership"; this, in turn, should bring about the equally elusive "partnership" approach.

Eventually, under the leadership of the DFID, the CDF morphed into the PRSP process, and it has become mainly known and implemented under the latter name. PRSPs have become very popular; as of 2003 they dominate international development practice, especially in Africa. The OECD, the G8, and the European Union all have declared that their aid policies will be based on PRSPs (Santiso 2002; Booth 2001, 41; SGTS 2002, no. 1.5). It must be noted as well that a major part of the PRSP process consists of a detailed collection of data by recipient government agencies on the incidence, nature, causes, and perceptions of poverty.

In the vision of its promoters, the PRSP is essentially or ideally a giant, broad-based process of national dialogue around economic and social (and political) policies and the use of the national budget. The resulting policies should be locally owned; if they truly are, the need for further conditionality of the arm-twisting type should disappear. This should allow aid agencies to take a much more hands-off position in their assistance program.

> The main principle is that we will work in ways which support the PRSP principles with the aim of building capable states. This includes helping to build accountability of governments to their domestic stakeholders, and to enhance the government's own systems or resource allocation, performance management and internal accountability. . . .
>
> Supporting a PRSP . . . means . . . buying into the priorities and accountability mechanisms that the government is determining for itself in dialogue with its own national stakeholders. . . .
>
> A key change in donor behavior is a change in our attitude to accountability. Governments should be held accountable by their own parliaments, legislatures, civil society organizations, press and public. For as long as governments feel that they are mainly held to account by donors, this reduces the influence of domestic stakeholders, undermines the growth of sustainable systems of domestic accountability, and distorts government priorities. Donors should tie their accountability requirements to the Government's domestic accountability framework, which in turn is buttressed by the PRSP process. (DFID 2002, 1, 4, 12)

The idea, then, is that the process of the PRSP will create the required social and political ownership, upon which can then be built a contractual support relationship between donor and recipient. David Booth calls this "process conditionality" and describes it thus:

Traditional IMF and World Bank conditionalities have been associated with a low level of national ownership of poverty-reduction efforts, which has reduced their effectiveness and sustainability. This suggests the hypothesis that a "process conditionality" in which recipient governments are expected to follow certain procedural steps, rather than accept specific policies, might work where other forms have not. . . . The PRSP initiative provides an opportunity for addressing some of the most notorious contradictions and dilemmas of development aid. It could be the solution, in particular, to the chronic tendency of much aid for poverty reduction to undermine the conditions of its own success, by weakening the capacities of governments and other national institutions to act for themselves. (Booth 2001, 7, 12, 14)

What emerges here is a fascinating story of "democracy lite." Basically, donors try to create so-called national dialogues in the many countries whose institutions are not democratic—a very complicated balancing act. PRSPs are supposed to reflect widespread participation by the population at large, but they take place in political environments where significant parts of that population are habitually excluded from debate, have little access to the necessary information, and are not represented by strong and legitimate institutions. In addition, in the name of ownership and sovereignty, the donors allow the government to lead the dialogue process. What, then, is the chance that a true national dialogue will occur? All independent empirical studies until now point out the lack of participation in PRSPs (SGTS 2000; Dembele 2003). It seems that without additional conditionality (that is, without arm-twisting the governments to ensure that all groups' voices are truly heard), this supposed post-conditionality approach is doomed to fail.

An additional ambiguity resides in the fact that the PRSPs (like the selectivity policy, for that matter) are clearly embedded in the standard neoliberal policy prescription package; indeed, their execution is mandatory for highly indebted countries to get "expanded HIPC" debt relief from the World Bank and new adjustment loans from the IMF (Booth 2001). Hence, strong margins exist on the population's—and, for that matter, the government's—participation in this dialogue; each PRSP process has to lead eventually to the adoption of a structural adjustment–like policy framework (SGTS 2002, no. 1.10).

A report written for DFID bemoans this close link between the PRSP and the HIPC in terms of timing: the HIPC process is organized along a clear and relatively rapid schedule, of which the PRSP is a part, and this *d history Major?*

may affect the dynamics of local dialogue, which may need more time and flexibility (SGTS 2002, no. 1.31ff.; Guttal et al. 2001, 4). This is correct, but the real issue is one of substance, not timing. Indeed, with the PRSPs acting as necessary steps on the road to modern structural adjustment, they could hardly arrive at policies that go against the tenets of this ideology. The whole process, then, remains designed to ensure at least acceptance of an existing policy package—the rest can be locally designed. Admittedly, this does include the possibility of adapting the package to local circumstances (like adding grape flavoring to children's medicine!), as well as of adding some additional locally inspired elements to the package, provided they do not contradict the core tents of structural adjustment. It may even be that these policies are objectively the best policies available and in the recipient countries' best interests. Still, what is created is neither ownership nor even dialogue but basically gentle imposition, acceptance, conformity, swallowing the right medicine (Wood and Lockwood 1999, 2). As a result, old-style conditionality continuously lurks in the background of the PRSPs. In practice, this plays itself out through the strong influence of the World Bank on drafting the discussion documents; the pressure the World Bank brings too bear on the senior people in ministries of finance, planning, or economics to ensure that documents remain within the guidelines set by itself; the fact that the World Bank—and the local governments—often fail to make available the relevant information on a timely basis, in a local language, or at all; the fact that completed PRSPs must be submitted to the World Bank and IMF boards for approval; the fact that other conditionalities exist in other Bretton Woods mechanisms that in many cases preempt the consultative process undertaken in the PRSP (Booth 2001, 32; Guttal et al. 2001, 2–4; Cheru 2001), and so on.

It is not all bad news, however. One could argue that the constraints imposed by the functioning of the international political economy will never disappear; that is, with or without the PRSP, with or without the World Bank and the IMF, no country can escape from the dominance of neoliberal thinking. Whether one views these constraints positively or negatively, it serves little purpose to blame the PRSP process, which neither created the constraints nor can single-handedly address them. To the extent that change in these global political-economic parameters is possible, it will result from social movements both within the countries concerned and across borders (Booth 2001, 40–41).

The PRSP process, within its limitations, *does* begin investing in a conversation within governments, within civil societies, and between them. It makes more information available than before, sometimes in local languages, and as a result it provides some fresh opportunities for civil society organizations to begin reflecting on these matters—something that until a decade ago was almost impossible for them. Even though it is still a far cry from a real dialogue, in poor and often closed societies it may provide one of the first opportunities for local citizens to get access to macroeconomic policy documents, to discuss them among themselves, to take a position and express it in public—especially where a civil society is already present (CRS 2003, 3–5). PRSPs have also typically included good-governance types of aims and policies, allowing citizens to see that these issues are also on the table, albeit in the odd language of the development enterprise. In the short term, none of this will challenge the powers-that-be in Washington D.C. or in local capitals, but there is no saying what the impact may be in the longer run.

It also seems reasonable to argue that, from a human rights perspective, PRSP-like approaches are superior to regular conditionality to the extent that they involve significantly greater amounts of transparency and participation. That said, PRSPs are still fundamentally rights-devoid conceptual frameworks. While they often contain some language setting out democracy or rights-related policy aims, they are not inspired by, couched in, or conceived of in human rights terms. This is not simply a matter of semantics. Rights language provides stronger claims to participation and access to information than the technocratic language of ownership and civil society consultation; the PRSP *process* would benefit from that. In addition, *substantively*, PRSPs could be encouraged actually to set out rights-based frameworks as well as the policies to get there and the benchmarks to measure progress. PRSPs outlining rights to education, health care, or employment guarantees, discussed with civil society and backed by long-term donor commitments, for example, could constitute much more powerful tools for sustainable social change than the current technocratic poverty focus. There is none of that in the current PRSP process. Although they all contain some references to human rights, they usually do so in a general, formulaic manner. The reasons for that lie both with governments, which do not usually like to include such specifics, and with the Bretton Woods institutions, who, contrary to their rhetoric, do not possess any understanding of or commitment to a human rights approach.

Conclusion

Human rights organizations, politicians, and pundits of all sorts constantly clamor for conditionality against dictatorial, oppressive regimes. It seems that for most everyone, from the person in the street to the typical aid worker, conditionality is the first tool that comes to mind when discussing the relation between development aid and human rights: *Stop giving aid to those governments that don't behave well*. It has, consequently, been a quite widely used tool. While conditionality has been used much less often than many critics have asked for, one can also say that, within the constraints of the normal diplomatic and strategic functioning that prevails in the community of states, it is actually amazing to what extent aid conditionality, often specifically invoking human rights, *has* been employed.

Yet, conditionality is beset with problems. Some are ethical and legal: On what grounds to employ conditionality? Who shall make these decisions? What if conditionality is applied bilaterally, inconsistently, and incompletely, as is bound to be the case in the current world order? What if its effects mainly hurt the poor, who typically did not create the contested behavior? (In the cases of Iraq, Haiti, and Burundi, for example, all of which were under both trade and aid sanctions to punish their rulers, there exists significant evidence demonstrating a great human toll.) But the main problem is that conditionality has a track record of not working, of not producing the desired results, and even, possibly, of creating dynamics that undermine the desired results.

Whether one regrets or applauds it, current donor understanding is that aid conditionality does not work and should not be employed. I share this understanding. Conditionality is about shortcuts and absolute power, the at-first-sight attractive idea that "our" money can function as a lever to force change in favor of the things we care about, such as respect for human rights and democracy. This is a dream—and probably not even a good one either. No simple ways exist to "buy" human rights in other societies; the required sorts of political and social change do not come about through one-directional, outside-generated pressures. One cannot push buttons to make human rights happen—not even in societies where one invests a lot of money. As a matter of fact, the risks are enormous that the opposite will happen. Conditionality may weaken the quality of governance, the domestic accountability of governments, the legitimacy of opposition groups, and the capacity to develop internal processes of change.

Yet, clearly, that does not make the initial problem go away: what *should* aid agencies do when confronted with significant human rights violations in countries in which they work? Simply accepting them on the grounds that conditionality does not work seems hardly the ideal policy. Quite apart from the moral imperative, the impact of aid is bound to be smaller under these circumstances. Some form of action that goes beyond passive acceptance and that is not traditional conditionality (since it does not work) thus seems required.

Donors have struggled with this matter as well. One solution, adopted mainly by the IMF, consists of a retrenchment, limiting conditionality only to a few, important, purely technical criteria, on the assumption that these are easier to enforce and monitor than the large packages of yore. In essence, this is still the standard conditionality, but with the implicit assumption that striving for perfection is bound to fail; a minimum of enforced technical change suffices, and the rest must be left to local dynamics. One could apply a similar strategy to political, human rights–related conditionality: reduce it to a bare minimum, as technical and objective as possible. Such a minimum conditionality would not seek to reform entire governance systems but simply set a few basic criteria, lack of respect for which would automatically lead to the suspension of aid. Organizing genocide supposedly is one of these already (although the case of Rwanda demonstrates that it was not upheld), and overthrowing democratically elected governments seems to be another emerging trigger point. I believe that there remains an important role for such a function of conditionality; that is, the drawing of a minimum level, a threshold below which recipient government behavior cannot fall.

This can be called principled behavior, which I discussed in an OECD report on how aid can be used to create incentives and disincentives for peace:

> There are points at which it may be necessary to contemplate suspending or withdrawing aid without expecting policy changes—not so much a case of conditionality as of principled behaviour. Setting up 'bottom line' conditions is necessary, not because it will directly change the disputed policy, but because it signals a moral stance, an unwillingness to become complicit. It seems that until now, the sole clear bottom line has been when donor citizens are victimised in conflicts. An emerging bottom line seems to be the overthrow of legitimately elected governments, as happened in Myanmar, Algeria, Burundi, Niger and Haiti, among others. A broader foundation for a bottom line could be where parties in conflict deliberately and massively target civilian populations. (Uvin 1999a, 15–16)

This strategy, then, differs from regular conditionality only in that it makes no claim to be able to change the offending behavior. It simply states that donors will not engage or work with governments that violate certain standards. We probably cannot change the offending behavior with the tool of aid conditionality,[14] but we do refuse to support the situation, and we hopefully send a strong signal of disapproval. This is an important

and unjustly neglected policy choice. It has been unjustly neglected because all forms of suspension have been equated with conditionality and
thus have been discussed solely in function of their capacity to change the
offending behavior. But even if such change seems unlikely, shouldn't donors, out of principle, refuse to be engaged in certain situations?

There are, of course, some problems with this approach, as with all
others. First, by definition such thresholds need to be set at a very low
level, both in order to ensure that there will be sufficient unanimity among
the donors and in order to avoid tendencies toward the micro-engineering
and constant confrontation that would emerge with more maximalist
thresholds. This approach, then, is not very satisfactory for those who
want to see major improvements in human rights outcomes; it sends signals when very low levels are reached but does not create many incentives
for achieving top performance. Second, it basically carries with it all the
ethical disadvantages of conditionality in terms of who makes such decisions, who gets hurt by them, and what partial implementation means—
without even pretending to achieve the benefits of conditionality, namely,
behavior change. It may thus consist mostly of a moral high ground for
donors, who can say that their hands are clean, while not offering much of
a path out of the dismal situation for the rest. In the long run, if consistently applied, such a principled policy might come to constitute a form of
ex-post conditionality (in a way similar to the selectivity solution of the
World Bank); that is, all coup plotters or potential human rights violators
in the world would come to realize that there is a price to pay for the
behavior they are considering, and at least some of them might be deterred
by that cost.

The two other alternatives to conditionality we discussed in this chapter go further, seeking to build less confrontational relationships with recipient countries while still employing aid to achieve aims of traditional
conditionality. In other words, they seek to achieve their aims by infusing
the practice of conditionality with elements of partnership while at the
same time decreasing the arm-twisting component. One solution, selectivity, does so by working only with countries with demonstrated track records
in implementing the "right" policies; the other, embodied in the PRSPs,
does so by setting in motion a supposedly broad-based and participatory
process of discussion that constitutes the basis for partnership.

From the perspective of our discussion on human rights, it is clear that
human rights could easily be part of both these mechanisms; they could be
a criterion for selectivity, and they could be dealt with in the PRSPs. (The
PRSP has the advantage that, in addition, as a *process* it seems to conform
more to human rights standards, as it is based on broad-based and inclusive

consultations. Supposedly, it would allow as well for more locally specific and culturally appropriate packages of human rights-conforming policy prescriptions upon which conditionality could then be based.)

In actual practice, no such thing has happened. Both these alternatives to conditionality, to the extent they have been implemented, are impregnated with the free-market orthodoxy of the Bretton Woods institutions; they reward, or discuss, free-market policies much more than human rights concerns. Whether one esteems free-market prescriptions to be the correct ones or not is not the point I wish to make; rather, the point is that these prescriptions have tended systematically to trump human rights concerns. This, then, is a limitation not of these methods but rather of their implementation; it is perfectly possible to implement these methods with a strong human rights focus.

A final alternative to regular conditionality is for donors to adopt a more collaborative strategy, one based on pragmatic objectives and support rather than arm-twisting for large-scale change. In contrast to the threat-based, so-called negative conditionality ("you'll get *no* money if you don't behave"), this has been called positive conditionality ("I'll work with you to help you do better"). To be clear, this is not really a form of conditionality; it is just an instance of a nice rhetorical/conceptual twist. The differences, after all, are major: with conditionality, democracy/human rights are a *condition* for aid relations, whereas here they are the *object* of these relations; conditionality seeks *immediate* or short-term change, whereas this approach is a medium to *long-term* venture. I propose, thus, to name it clearly, labeling it positive support as opposed to (negative) conditionality. This brings us to the next chapter.

But before we move ahead, there is another point I wish to make, and it applies to individual aid professionals and the organizations that employ them. Aid professionals need to stop their habit of self-censorship, of obfuscation of rights issues, of silence and looking the other way when it comes to matters of human rights abuse. This holds especially for the expatriates, and the senior ones, among them. To be sure, this is not easy, especially in highly repressive countries. Aid professionals risk the suspension of their visa or the non-renewal of their contracts. These things do happen, no doubt. But by and large, international aid professionals are free from risk; their political mortality rate is close to nil worldwide. The exceptions to this relative safety are humanitarian workers and local aid staff. Humanitarian workers run much greater risks; in the conditions of war and massive violence they typically work in, any public position can cost them their lives. Too many humanitarian employees have died in recent years, including in my region of specialization, Central Africa. A more open and thus probably more confrontational stance may also entail risks for the safety of the local employees and partners of aid agencies; the latter must thus make sure not to needlessly endanger these people. They should discuss what they can do with their employees and create mechanisms that insulate them.

But beyond these constraints I strongly believe that most development professionals fail to use fully the influence they do possess. It is amazing to what extent in most countries the entire official aid rhetoric and all the written documents tiptoe around the key human rights challenges, preferring silence, insinuation, self-censorship, and gentle neologism to any frank mention of the stakes, the problems, and the unfulfilled challenges. It can be argued that in many countries this self-censorship is necessary because of the repressive nature of the government; that is, if one were to mention things by their real names, the government would not like it and there would be repercussions. In other words, that argument goes, aid managers and experts do know that the way it is written down in their documents and studies and evaluations does not reflect reality, but they "clean up" their texts so as to not endanger their projects or their relations.

This is mostly nonsense. Governments cannot and will not clamp down on all critical analyses, especially not if they are well done and shared among agencies. Governments cannot end up kicking out *all* foreigners, refusing visas to *all* technical assistants, and antagonizing *all* potential donors. The internalized fear for negative repercussions in the donor community is based much more on passivity and habit, on a general desire not to rock the boat, than on a realistic assessment of the scale of negative repercussions. Aid workers get socialized in the art of whispering, of gently brushing under the table, of looking the other way, and in so doing they jointly create the very silence they individually decry. I believe that if all or simply most agencies adopted a more honest and explicit style, there is little most governments could do about it, and doing so could contribute to a situation where local people might be pulled into these debates. This means that donors—bilateral agencies as well as NGOs—must be more willing to face up to these issues in their work, to discuss them formally with other agencies and arrive at joint positions, to check these positions with local partners so as to ensure the relevance and validity of their insights, to convey these to the offending parties—foremost, typically, the government, but possibly also non-state actors—and to plan their interventions in explicit acknowledgment of these facts.

After all, the risk is simply too great that the sanitized versions of reality will become the real ones. Indeed, as development practitioners repeat the same "cleaned up" statements and obfuscations, even if they don't really believe them or for that matter verify them, these fabrications become real. They become the intellectual framework in which people conceptualize and judge their actions, leading to passivity and, equally bad, cynicism.

5

Positive Support

Positive support represents the next step in the integration of human rights into the practice of development. Rather than trying to force countries to respect human rights, the aim here is to create the conditions for the achievement of specific human rights outcomes. Conditionality seeks immediate or short-term change, whereas the positive support approach is a medium- to long-term venture. Positive support, then, is a weak tool when seeking rapidly to affect major ongoing crises; its potential lies in the long run, not in the here and now. Conditionality is essentially a practice available to large donors (the major bilateral agencies and the Bretton Woods institutions) who command sufficient resources to inflict pain; it is hardly a tool available to NGOs, whose threats of aid withdrawal would not create more than an amused smile on the faces of rights-violating dictators).[1] Positive support measures, however, can be—and are—undertaken by all kinds of aid actors, including NGOs. As a matter of fact, especially in the earlier years of positive support, NGOs played the main role, partly because some of this work, such as political party development, is politically sensitive, and consequently governmental donors prefer to subcontract it to specialized foundations and NGOs.

Positive support has been one of the fastest growing fields of international development assistance during the last decade; from next to nothing, it now consumes more than 10 percent of aid budgets, and in some countries much more (in a post-conflict country such as Rwanda, for example, governance-related activities account for one-third of all aid). Much of what human rights organizations ask for falls within the domain of positive support as well; indeed, over the years, agencies have moved beyond calls for conditionality, requesting that human rights–violating governments, and their international donors adopt improved laws, implement those laws, ameliorate the quality of justice, investigate past abuses, organize elections, free the media, and so on. But while professional human rights organizations lobby for these changes, they are not often involved in making them happen on the ground; that job, if anyone's, seems to have fallen to the development community. And thus a tacit division of labor seems to have come into being in which human rights organizations push for major changes from the moral high ground, while development organizations (more or less enthusiastically and competently) are muddling through, trying to get (more or less willing) governments to implement these changes. Little or no explicit dialogue takes place between these different organizations on strategies or combinations of approaches, though.

Positive support projects seek to achieve a broad variety of goals, including but not limited to strengthening civil society or legislative bodies; improving the legal and institutional underpinnings of the rule of law; strengthening the media or human rights watchdog organizations; creating electoral mechanisms; instituting human rights training for policemen, soldiers, and NGO leadership; and bringing about judicial reform. These projects involve a wide range of political units including administrations, courts, local governments, people's organizations, journalists, policemen, political parties, NGOs of all kinds, and the population at large. The overarching impression one derives from these projects, however, is their strict degree of separation from "traditional" development practice. These projects typically stand alone; that is, they are exclusively devoted to human rights or democratic governance goals. What Hans-Otto Sano observes for the Danish bilateral aid agency (Danida) holds for all donors:

> Complementarity rather than integration seems to characterize Danida's practical efforts in relation to human rights and development activities. Danida's 1996 annual report stresses that human rights and democratization are important elements in the effort to fight poverty in developing countries. However, in the list of activities that follows (carrying out elections, building an independent judiciary, instituting an ombudsman, and decentralizing), it is quite difficult to confirm the establishment of this relationship. Danida conveys the impression that it prefers to work with human rights as a complement to the other aid efforts. It provides support for elections or strengthens the judiciary, or it works with more traditional capacity-building and resource transfers within sectors such as health, education, or infrastructure. (Sano 2000, 742)

While there have been regular evaluations that have stressed the need to move beyond stand-alone projects and integrate human rights and democracy components in sectoral programming, little of this has happened.[2] Positive support to human rights, democracy, and governance remains a sector by itself, with separate funding lines, specialists, and activities. It is only at the next level—the rights-based approach to development, discussed in the next chapter—that human rights concerns will permeate *all* development cooperation rather than being an add-on.

This is the first level we examine at which aid money is actually being *spent* on human rights concerns. Indeed, at the previous levels, no actual changes in resource allocation took place—all that changed was either the discourse or the criteria by which recipient countries were selected (or deselected). In addition, *human rights* here, as in the previous level, only refers to CP rights related to democratic systems of governance; ESC rights, such as the right to education, do not figure in this agenda.

Note that donors use this approach for goals that tend to fall under the terminology of human rights, good governance, or democracy—clearly overlapping concepts, but ones with significant differences as well. Most experience to date has been acquired with democracy-promotion projects, which have been much more numerous than specific human rights projects. The reason for that is, I believe, that democracy acts as an easily recognizable and highly legitimate aim. Nobody is opposed to it, and all donors think they know what it looks like. It is thus easy to support, both intellectually and politically. Strictly speaking, of course, democracy promotion is not the same as the promotion of human rights, even if the latter are only limited to CP rights. On the other hand, it *is* true that democracy basically constitutes a bundle of human rights—to free speech, to free assembly, to vote, and so on (UNDP 2001, 56), and thus when we analyze democracy promotion, we are also getting to understand human rights promotion, at least a subset of CP ones. In addition, because of the relative popularity of democracy promotion, there have been many more evaluations and studies and scholarly analyses of its record so far, and so we can draw on a rather voluminous, and relevant, literature here. For all these reasons, the following pages deal mainly with democracy, but what is said holds for human rights as well.

The Practice of Positive Support

During the last fifteen years or so, positive support to democracy, human rights, and governance has become a major sector of development cooperation, accounting for up to 10 percent of overall aid flows, and more for some recipient countries. (Post-conflict countries, for example, typically receive much more of this sort of assistance because there is a general sense that the (re)construction of institutions of governance and justice is crucial for peace to stand a chance.) For all donors a positive support approach has become the favored way to promote democratic development; unlike negative conditionality, it is very popular in aid circles. The opposite holds for human rights organizations, for whom such "technical assistance" work constitutes only a small part of their work, far secondary to conditionality-type reporting and the mobilization of shame. A few specialized NGOs dealing with democracy or transitional justice are the exceptions.

The agency that first added democratic governance to the traditional development agenda in a significant manner was USAID, and it has remained the biggest player in this domain. In 1990 it rephrased its mandate in terms of six major policy objectives, including the "establishment of sustainable democracies." This is to be achieved, according to the USAID website, through "establishing democratic institutions, free and open markets, an informed and educated populace, a vibrant civil society, and a relationship between state and society that encourages pluralism, participation, and peaceful conflict resolution." There exists a strong consensus in the United States on the desirability of promoting democracy (although not on the means to do so), which relates to the US's perception of itself as a beacon of freedom, as well as to a longstanding idealist tradition in US foreign policy (Cohn 1999, 1; Rose 2000, 186). Under the Clinton administration, promoting democracy became one of the three pillars of the US security policy and under the George W. Bush administration, the invasion in Iraq was justified by the overthrow of a dictator and the creation of a democratic state in the heart of the Middle East.

After the collapse of the former Soviet Union, the number of projects exploded—and a large number of these democratic governance projects were precisely in the republics of the former Soviet Union. According to much-quoted figures from Thomas Carothers, the United States spent as much as $700 million a year on governance in the latter half of the 1990s (Carothers 1999; see also Cohn 1999, 1). The European Council created the European Initiative for Democracy and Human Rights in 1994 and, through this and other mechanisms, spent 550 million euros in 1996–98 (Santiso 2001b, 155; Santiso 2002, 10; EU 2001, 14), and the Canadian International Development Agency (CIDA) has invested over $350 million (Cdn) in good governance and democratic development programs since 1992 (Brown 2002). While these are significant sums, they still constitute no more than about 10 percent of all these agencies' aid.

From Human Rights to Democracy to Elections

The World Bank entered the fray early on as well (in 1989, according to Hibou 2002, 173), with the concept of good governance, invented as the apolitical equivalent to the democracy and human rights agendas of bilateral donors. During the 1980s the World Bank had become involved in public administrative reform as part of sectoral adjustment loans; this included foremost public-sector downsizing, but also training, reorganization, support for budget management, and the like. In most countries this approach was a total failure (Schacter 2000, 6). The good-governance agenda was designed as the next step forward, looking at the deeper institutional issues embedded in the fabric of governance. The World Bank identified "four areas of governance that are consistent with the Bank's mandate: public sector management, accountability, the legal framework, and information and transparency" (World Bank 1992). As such, the good-governance agenda was explicitly designed to be the complement, the political extension, of structural adjustment (Hibou 2002, 174). Good governance is not, then, as many argue, a pro-democracy agenda but rather an emptying thereof, a reduction and de-politicization of democracy to good liberal management (Thede 2002, 26–27; Ghai 2001, 26).

The good-governance agenda also fulfilled a rhetorical-political function. It allowed the World Bank to discuss the reforms it proposed as economic and not political matters. It allowed it to combat corruption by invoking economic arguments only. In short, it constituted an attempt to de-politicize the concepts of democracy (and a fortiori human rights) in order not so as to appear to be infringing on sovereignty, as well as to benefit from the widespread acceptance that economic thinking enjoys in the development community. This appearance of political neutrality and noninterference is crucial for the survival of international organizations in a world of de jure if not de facto sovereignty.

Indeed, as has oft been mentioned, Article IV, Section 10, of the World Bank's Articles of Agreement reads: "The Bank and its officers shall not interfere in the political affairs of any member, nor shall they be influenced in their decisions by the political character of the member or members concerned." The IMF's charter similarly states that it should "not be influenced by the nature of a political regime or a country, nor should it interfere in the domestic or foreign policies of any member" (IMF 1997). This presentation of politics as limited to its purely economic incidence, beyond actual political judgment or discussion, is absolutely crucial for the survival of these organizations.[3]

More recently, as already discussed in our earlier section on rhetorical incorporation, the World Bank has officially converted to human rights, and its discourse on governance has subsequently become less technical, at least in documents aimed for public consumption. This produces interesting results. "By helping to fight corruption, improve transparency, and accountability in governance, strengthen judicial systems, and modernize financial sectors, the Bank contributes to building environments in which people are better able to pursue a broader range of human rights" (World Bank 1999, 3). As this quotation suggests, and as we discussed already in Chapter 3, much of the human rights conversion still amounts to little more than rhetorical repackaging; that is, policies that were once justified by their potential to improve investor confidence are now justified for their human rights benefits, at least in brochures destined for the human rights community. Nothing else, however, changes. It takes more than a few ideological leaps to see how strengthening financial systems is a human rights activity. One feels sure that the framers of the Universal Declaration on Human Rights and the two covenants were not thinking of shoring up banking reserve requirements, improving accounting standards, or current account liberalization—useful as these are for a variety of important purposes—when they were building the human rights edifice.

In statements like these, the many faces of power, and their associated discourses, come together. Human rights, free trade, good governance, the ideology of globalization (what the French so aptly call *la pensée unique*, the "sole way of thinking"), democracy, and the willingness to let rich country multinationals buy national assets become conflated. All amount to restatements of the liberal world view by the powerful. They are decreed from above, morally self-satisfying, and compatible with the status quo in the centers of power. Northern countries' over-consumption, history of colonialism, environmental degradation, protectionism, dumping of arms in the Third World, history of shoring up past dictators, wisdom of structural adjustment and globalization, alternative religious and ethical value systems—all of these are off the agenda. No wonder so many people resent the human rights agenda.

The Tools of Positive Support

It is very difficult to analyze positive support projects and programs in practice. First, it covers such an unusually wide range of sectors and activities, in a wide range of countries, that general lessons, valid across cases, may be impossible—or little more than truisms (Adapt to local culture! Be flexible! Know the context!). Second, most of this work has not been well evaluated. While many reports certainly are written about specific projects, there is little in the way of systematic, comparative, or critical independent research on the practice. Third, evaluating these sorts of projects and programs is exceedingly difficult, posing major methodological issues of data and attribution, and fitting badly within standard project-management procedures (Poate et al. 2000). Fourth, given that the field is new and has been subject to hostile criticism from the beginning, most managers of such programs are wary of publicly admitting to any failure, hiding behind general optimistic statements—as is typical in the aid community in any case (Mendelson 2001, 74; Hyman 2002, n. 4). Finally, the scholarly literature on the dynamics of democratization is deeply divided as well, with significant disagreement on things as fundamental as the definition of democratization, the methodology for measuring change, the role of structures *vs.* actors, the weight of economics *vs.* politics, and the like.[4] As a result, what Carothers wrote a few years ago still holds: "Despite thousands of democracy projects carried out in dozens of countries, billions of dollars spent, and endless reports by aid providers, there is surprisingly little conventional wisdom on the utility of democracy aid" (Carothers 1999, 303). In this chapter I will not be able to remedy that; it would take a book to do so, if it is possible at all. Rather, I wish to discuss a few strategic and conceptual issues involved in democracy promotion and their relation to the role of human rights in the practice of development. Note that I focus foremost on democracy promotion, because this sub-field has been studied the most and the insights gained here hold for broader programs to modify human rights and governance outcomes as well.

It may be useful to begin with some systemization of the wide range of activities and sectors involved in positive support. Carothers divides democracy assistance into three fields that have not changed for the last two decades: elections, state institutions, and civil society (Carothers 1999). In the early days, elections were the prime focus; nowadays, in financial terms, support to state institutions is highlighted, but civil society programming is growing the fastest (see Santiso 2002, 12). These are indeed the typical choices: investing in organizations (human rights commissions, ombudsmen, supreme courts, and so forth), processes and procedures (ratification of treaties, drafting of laws, education of people, citizenship and democracy campaigns, media), and structures (civil society strengthening, government capacity building).

A related way of systematizing the potential range of actions can be found in a report I authored for the OECD that sought to synthesize a three-year process of learning by all the major development actors on "incentives and disincentives for peace"—concepts inspired by the work done in the Carnegie Commission for The Prevention on Deadly Conflict (Cortright 1997). While the large extract below deals with dynamics of peace and not human rights as such, it is highly instructive of the type and range of actions current aid managers can conceive of, and it organizes these in a framework that serves a discussion about human rights equally well.

Incentives for peace refer to all purposeful uses of aid that strengthen the dynamics that favour peace, by influencing actors' behaviours; by strengthening pro-peace actors' capacities; by changing the relations between conflicting actors (ethnic groups, the state and civil society), and by influencing the social and economic environment in which conflict and peace dynamics take place. Disincentives do the opposite: they weaken and discourage the dynamics that favour violence. Incentives and disincentives can occur in a conditional or in an unconditional manner (i.e. with or without reciprocity requirements, with or without an expected immediate response).

EXAMPLES OF INCENTIVES AND DISINCENTIVES FOR PEACE		
	Non-conditional	**Conditional**
Incentives	Providing human rights training to the police and judiciary sectors.	Engaging grant budget support or debt relief upon reaching specified and agreed-upon political goals.
Disincentives	Sending human rights observers; providing material support and international networking to local human rights NGOs.	Threatening to cut (or actually cutting) ODA unless the government improves its human rights record.

. . . .

Schematically, donors seek four broad categories of objectives as they employ ODA in a framework of incentives and disincentives for peace: influencing actors' behaviours; modifying actors' capacities; changing the relations between actors; and influencing the social and economic environment in which conflict and peace dynamics take place. The order in which these four types are presented is from those dealing with the most proximate, actor-related, causes of conflict to those dealing with the systemic, root causes level. . . .

Influencing actors' behaviours. Donors employ ODA to encourage actors to behave in a more pro-peace manner, or discourage them from the opposite. Examples include:
- Offering significant increases in overall ODA to governments engaging in peace negotiations or completing them.
- Providing human rights training to military and police forces.
- Assisting soldiers with demobilisation.
- Developing non-partisan curricula and textbooks. . . .

Modifying actors' capacities. In this case, the aim is to strengthen the capacities of actors who already behave in pro-peace manners to do more of the same and to be more effective, or to weaken those that benefit from conditions of violent conflict. Examples include:
- Capacity-building and financial support for pro-peace or human rights NGOs.
- Research on mechanisms to limit the inflow of arms in a region.
- Demobilisation programmes.
- Leadership training to labour leaders or women leaders.
- Strengthening local peace initiatives and creating horizontal linkages between them.
- Monitoring and reducing military expenditures. . . .

Changing the relations between actors. Here, donors seek to modify the nature of interactions between social groups in society—whether between various communal groups, or between the state and civil society—to become more inclusive and less violent. ODA examples include:
- The creation of fora for reconciliation and opportunities for inter-communal collaboration.
- Trauma counselling.
- The creation of neutral spaces for communication and dialogue between different social groups.
- Justice projects, including international tribunals for crimes against humanity.
- Democratic policing programmes.

- Independent ombudsmen offices or civilian review boards for civilian oversight of security forces. . . .

Changing the social and economic environment in which conflict and peace dynamics take place:
- Debt relief to kick-start the economy.
- Support to dialogues on electoral systems and free elections.
- Strengthening the media and access to free information.
- The provision of peace-keeping forces or election observers.
- De-mining and demobilisation.
- The reconstruction of basic social and economic infrastructures.
- The promotion of transparent and accountable mechanisms of governance.
- The promotion of regional dynamics in favour of peace and integration. (Uvin 1999a, pars. 5, 11–15)

As the author of the above extract, I was told not to provide examples that were coercive in nature (this was too controversial, too explicitly manipulative, too interventionist in appearance). As a result, the list above—all actions currently undertaken by aid actors in many of the world's countries—contains only incentive-style examples. So, all the above examples are cases of positive support, albeit in a conflict resolution context, rather than an explicit human rights promotion one. Still, I believe this lengthy quotation gives the reader an excellent idea of the range of available actions in a positive support strategy.

Rereading this quotation, I am amazed at how explicit it is in its political approach. This stuff is about power and counter-power, about overcoming the resistance of those who favor the status quo and strengthening those who seek positive change. It explicitly recognizes that international donors "must confront the underlying interests and power relations in the sector in which they wish to bring about change" (Carothers 1999, 151), and it proposes a list of actions that seek to influence political and power dynamics. Effective positive support to democracy and human rights, this extract says—and many scholars would agree—should be politically savvy and explicit; if it is not, it is doomed to fail. While I believe the above extract reflects what many aid managers (foremost in bilateral agencies, which have the resources and the self-proclaimed mandate to do this) are doing when they think strategically about their work, it is not what any of them are willing to admit publicly. The extract, in short, goes beyond permissible development discourse, precisely because of its explicitness about the interventionist and politicized thinking a "human rights promoting" or "conflict reducing" development strategy can entail; the box above is "X-rated" in a world where political self-censorship reigns supremely. (This is why it was not included in the final, official report.)

The high level of politicized intervention poses two problems. First, it conflicts with the development community's constant tendency to de-politicize and render technical all matters it touches. Second, if done well, it ends up creating a giant interventionist machine, which may be neither desirable nor, ultimately, possible. Let me explain both these points.

First, one of the main features in the practice of positive support—like all other development work—is its technicality: donors intervene in what is increasingly called governance through a set of discrete projects with mostly technical aims.[5] Indeed, the spontaneous tendency in the development community is always to "do" human rights and democracy in ways that are apolitical and technical. The foremost reason for that, as we have already discussed, can be found in the dictates of sovereignty. The myth that nobody is actually intervening in the recipient government's internal affairs must be maintained; instead, a simple process of technical assistance is being undertaken at the request of that government. A variety of other factors are grafted onto this basic structural fact of sovereignty: the fact that the development community has few people on its payrolls with fine skills and knowledge of political science and history of the countries concerned; the fact that it is easier not to rock the boat by avoiding complicated and often confrontational political assessments; the fact that donors often do not agree among themselves, or that they have many interests that are related to neither development nor human rights; and the fact that the local powers-that-be very clearly recognize the political nature of the stakes and do everything to subvert them.[6]

At the end of the day, though, what may have started as actions undertaken to address explicitly political variables—those that create conflict, that perpetuate human rights violations, that close off political and social space—turn into discrete, short-term, entirely technical projects: making lawyers available to assist with the drafting of new legal texts; offering training sessions in principles of human rights for bureaucrats, soldiers, or the population at large; providing computer and logistical support to national human rights commissions; and many other projects of this kind.

While all this may be useful, it tends to avoid the true political issues brought up in a human rights approach to development: Are all people in a society equally included in the dynamics of social change? Do they have capacities for complaint and redress if this is not the case? Are the benefits created by projects sustainable through local mechanisms of control and empowerment, or are they charity-based, reversible at will (either by aid actors' departure or by the action of local powerful people and politicians)?

Admittedly, aid policymakers and practitioners are often smarter than what they are willing to commit to paper would suggest. The apolitical language they employ and the technical projects they create may deliberately obfuscate their true designs—a pretense required by the "organized hypocrisy" of sovereignty (Krasner 1999), or, as I argued earlier, a tendency to avoid trouble by sugarcoating everything (bitter medicines are never popular). However, a major price is paid for this game: key debates do *not* occur; actions are often overly circumscribed and self-constrained; monitoring and evaluation are done on the basis of the wrong criteria; and at some point, as a result of using this obfuscating language all the time, too many people start taking the game for reality and stop asking the tough questions.

Second, what is being described here is a highly interventionist machinery of social engineering, whereby donors seek to understand the social and political machinery that produces human rights violations (or authoritarian governance) and then set out to block certain levers, strengthen certain pulleys, grease certain transmission belts, add a bit of fuel here and a small brake there, and create an outcome that is much more in conformity with human rights standards (or more democratic, or accompanied by less violent conflict—whatever their aims). This image of social engineering, however, is fundamentally flawed. Human rights and democracy, as well as peace, constitute particularly unpredictable and complicated and contested dynamics; they are not machines social engineers can master. In the next pages I look more closely at a number of points that have both scholarly and operational interest, trying to think through the strategic and operational implications thereof for the practice of development. The issues I discuss start from the following widely accepted facts about democratization (and, to repeat, I believe these observations are directly relevant to the concerns of this book as well; that is, one could substitute *human rights promotion* for *democratization* in all these phrases without problem):

- democratization is nonlinear, unpredictable, and sometimes reversible;
- democratization is not a matter of transplanting Western institutions— it is not the form, but the process, that matters;
- democratization requires significant investment in civil society, which will lay the groundwork for meaningful democracy; and

- democratization support projects must use much more flexible and appropriate tools than they currently do.

The very large majority of aid policymakers and practitioners would agree that these statements are correct, I believe, but they may not have fully thought through their implications. This is what I set out to do in the next pages. And, once again, while I use the term *democratization* here, it could be replaced by *supporting changes in human rights observance* or *promoting changed state-society relations* and the resulting insights would still be valid. The basic insight is that the tools and methods and ideologies of the development enterprise are contrary to what is needed to make positive support projects succeed—and consequently, it comes as no surprise that most of them fail.

Democratization Is Nonlinear, Unpredictable, and Sometimes Reversible

There is general agreement in the scholarly literature that "democratic transitions often do not follow a natural, orderly or linear sequence. Democratization is an irregular, unpredictable and sometimes reversible process taking place in a highly fluid and volatile political environment" (Santiso 2001b, 162).[7] This observation has important consequences, which are valid not only for democracy promotion but for the entire positive support approach, whose unfolding then should never be predictable, linear, or identical across cases.[8] And yet, of course, it is.

On a conceptual level we immediately face the question of knowledge, of judgment: If human rights–inducing and democratization processes are nonlinear and reversible, how are we to judge where we are in the process, what the dynamics are, the margins for change, the windows of opportunity, the risks of backsliding, the forces of stagnation? And *who* shall make such judgments? These are more than theoretical questions. If donors seek to promote democratic or human rights change, and if they are aware that such change will never be linear, orderly, or straightforward, than it logically means that in practice they are willing to accept backsliding and failure as part of the process. It means they accept "hanging in there," keeping their eye on the prize, even while human rights violations or authoritarianism increase, for they understand that such backsliding or failure is part of the (learning) process, and they expect these setbacks to be followed by improvements, with the overall long-term trend being forward, upward, onward. As an image, this is all fine, but the judgment calls implied in this approach are stunning. People will definitely differ in these judgments—how could they not? And, of course, some will argue for termination, for conditionality, while others will favor continuation, understanding, treading lightly.

In addition, if we agree that the process is nonlinear and straightforward, this ought to have a major impact on the way development cooperation is organized and implemented. If setbacks always and unavoidably occur, if the path of change is different in each case and impossible to predict, then donors clearly need to behave in very different ways than they usually do when "doing development." They clearly need much more long-term horizons and a much greater willingness to persist with their aims for the long run, notwithstanding the unavoidable setbacks and stagnation; they also need to abandon conditionality. Short-term projects are rather useless, then, unless they are undertaken in full consciousness of the fact that they are merely small steps on a long road. This is not a call for the sort of intellectual laziness that can justify any failed project by the fact that, in the long run, it may do some good. Neither is it a call to continue projects and programs indefinitely, even though they show no signs of success. Rather, it means that there ought to be serious commitments for long-term support, with actions designed in flexible ways to adapt to changed circumstances in full cognizance of where the country stands on the long and tortuous road to democracy and with a willingness to continue collaborating even during setbacks. In my opinion, donors do not possess the flexibility, knowledge, foresight, or persistence for such a policy, and it is highly unlikely that they will develop it any time soon. Indeed, it may be close to impossible to do so. The political judgments involved are too difficult to make, especially in a consensual way, and the political pressure at home for clear results (or for totally unrelated agendas, connected to political and economic donor interests) may make this sort of fine-tuned, intelligent, long-term approach highly unrealistic. In practice, then, this view of the process risks becoming a license for passivity, an excuse for inaction ("You have to expect some backsliding. You can't expect things to move forward the whole time, can you? Given the history of this place, it's amazing they have come this far."). Others, who for whatever reason are more doubtful, less willing to look at the long term, simply never engage on this path ("It's crazy to give this government such a blank check. These other donors are so naive and easily fooled. It's all show anyway. We've got to be much tougher."). I have heard all these comments from ambassadors and senior aid representatives during my last five years of work in Rwanda, mainly related to DFID's ten-year program with the government of Rwanda, which precisely set out a long-term, governance-related agenda. No donor explicitly joined the British in this policy, thus minimizing its impact from day one (although some implicitly behaved in ways similar to it). Clearly, this dissension within the donor community is close to unavoidable and will in all likelihood seriously reduce the impact of DFID's policy.

Democratization Is Not a Matter of Transplanting Western Institutions

Another general lesson from the literature is that it serves no purpose to transplant Western institutions of democracy and assume that democratization has taken place. More generally, it is not the form but the function or the process that counts. Democratic change is not the reproduction of institutional endpoints but the production of political processes. We know that, and it makes intuitive sense. Outsiders only control the form, not the substance, of the institutions they help build. They can, for example, ensure that courts exist, in terms of having buildings to be located in, trained people to staff the desks, cars and fuel to help the people move, computers to help them write and store information. What they cannot ensure—or in any case not easily, and not with the usual tools of the development system—is that these formal institutions also effectively, substantively, act in the way donors expect or desire. Thus one can have a perfectly rebuilt judicial system that produces no justice or a well-equipped parliament that is little more than an empty shell. Infrastructures, training sessions, even operating costs covered—all these may be necessary but do not guarantee well-functioning institutions that produce substantive results. Such results only come into being through deep and locally owned social and political dynamics. These dynamics *are* influenced by the international community, but not through their usual projects and not in easily plannable ways. They require astute and explicit analysis of political and social trends, a close ear to the voices that come from within society, a capacity and willingness to address difficult issues respectfully and firmly with local partners, and a willingness to work with a broad range of social actors for the long run.

The lessons from this discussion include, once again, that fine political analysis is constantly required to bring this endeavor to a good end. An additional lesson is that there lurks a real danger in the sort of technical, de-politicized, short-term approach of much of this work. Even if it were only discourse, produced for public consumption, it still yields political outcomes, and these are likely to be negative. The constant reduction of political choices to technical discourses, the constant self-congratulation that is so common in development work—the photos, the receptions, the ambassadors declaring what a major step toward progress has been made on this day—undermine the ground for explicit and frank political analy-sis, allow all those concerned to hide behind these statements, and ulti-mately benefit most those with power, those who control this machinery of smoke and mirrors. A quotation from a very interesting study of de-mocracy assistance in Russia by Sarah Mendelson states it well:

> A negative, unintended consequence of un-nuanced laudatory state-ments by Western officials—for example, those that categorize elec-tions as "free and fair" when they have many irregularities, or that tout parties as signs of democratic progress when in fact they shun contact with civic groups—is that democratic activists on the ground in Russia are increasingly isolated. Equally serious, the Russian lead-ership may have learned an unfortunate lesson: the generally posi-tive Western response to recently established Russian institutions that sometimes only vaguely resemble democratic ones suggests that the form of these institutions may be more important to Western policymakers than if or how they function. (Mendelson 2001, 76–77)

I argued the same for the case of Rwanda. The sort of self-congratulatory statements and mutual backslapping that occurs whenever a justice, or human rights, or democracy project begins or ends may be more damag-ing than helpful; it discredits true change and the people fighting for it (Uvin 2003a). Fixation with forms, then, to the neglect of substance, pro-duces results that are not only incomplete but also often detrimental.

Civil Society Support

It is increasingly accepted that civil society support lies at the heart of democratization and human rights promotion. For most practitioners, the relationship is clear: for democracy to consolidate, more is needed than writing the right laws, holding elections, and building parliaments. What is required "to turn democratic forms into democratic substance" is civil society, the presence of voluntary organizations that act not only as counter-powers to the state but also as breeding grounds of democratic values (Carothers 1999, 337). In the eyes of most practitioners, the idea that civil society is always a positive force for democracy is unassailable (Carothers and Ottaway 2000, 3). The transition of the communist countries from Eastern Europe to democracy is seen as proof for that idea, and a similar model of social change is projected on the rest of the world.

In the following pages, I make two arguments. First, I discuss the am-biguous political nature of civil society support rhetoric and practice. This argument may be of more interest to scholars than to practitioners. Second, I analyze some operational weaknesses in current civil society support practices.

The Politics of De-politicization

The entire civil society support sector presents a fascinating insight into the dual political/apolitical face of development aid. Ultimately, it also provides insight into the many facets of power and how ambiguous discourses serve the function of not unduly disturbing the powerful. Current civil society discourse and programming, it seems to me, serve three interlocked aims simultaneously:

- to provide moral high ground to aid practitioners;
- to de-politicize donor involvement; and
- to hide major political choices made by outsiders.

All these functions are useful to the development enterprise as it seeks to deal with the challenges of sovereignty and social change on its own terms.

The term *civil society* was seldom used fifteen years ago in the development community, but it is now at the center of all debates. At first, development professionals spoke about NGOs and people's organizations, but now these have all been relabeled CSOs (civil society organizations). This renaming is based on a more or less implicit intellectual premise: civil society is the totality of voluntary organizations between the state and the family (and besides the market) that acts, by its diversity, organization, and dynamism, as a counterweight to the power of the state (as well as, usually neglected, a counter-power to the unbridled power of the market). As NGOs, for example, are part of this totality, they can be called CSOs. The problem with this renaming is that it implicitly transfers to each individual organization the characteristics of the whole, that is, the notion of political counter-power. Of course, there is not the slightest reason why each and every NGO or association ought to act as a counter-power to the state; indeed, most do not remotely desire to do so. Yet, by a sleight of the definitional hand, this is the impression created, and henceforth all donor support to NGOs can be considered a contribution to democracy, human rights, and good governance.

And what is more, according to the dominant narrative, the CSOs contribute to these goals in a way that is not directly political—a truly handy concept in a world in which we desire to achieve political goals in apolitical ways! Indeed, unlike political parties, NGOs and interest groups rebaptized as CSOs are nonpolitical; they do not run for office or "do" politics. They simply defend human rights, the public good, the interests of citizens. As Thomas Carothers and Marina Ottaway point out, this construction

> helps defend the claim that it is possible for donors to support democracy without becoming involved in partisan politics or otherwise interfering unduly the domestic politics of another country. (Carothers and Ottaway 2000, 10–12)

And they add, rightly so:

> Civil society actors, which supposedly seek to make their countries better by influencing government policies but not by seeking power, can thus appear to make up an antipolitical domain, a pristine realm in which a commitment to civic values and the public interest rules in place of traditional divisions, beliefs, and interests. (Carothers and Ottoway 2000, 12)

Nancy Thede adds:

> Civil society has become the catchword of international funders interested in democracy—one has the impression that it is often seen as a "neutral" alternative to funding (corrupt) government agencies or political parties. The latter are often implicitly delegitimated in the discourse of funders, rather than understood as necessary institutions for agglomeration and representation of disparate interests, something civil society per se is rarely equipped to do. (Thede 2002, 22)

Without denying that often courageous people who do behave in this way in each country do exist, and that they deserve all the support they can get, such people are bound to represent in every society only a very small part of the range of available opinions and organizations. Most people and organizations will not fit this ideal-typical construction—and disappointment is thus all but guaranteed (as in the often-heard complaint that "these NGO leaders just use this as a springboard into politics"). What do we expect? That they stay politically untouched forever? In our own societies do NGO leaders not use their networks and prestige as a basis for political careers? Do they not seek political change? This de-politicization of civil society is a weak intellectual construction. It does not ask questions about representativity. Most of these supposed CSOs are small professional organizations, typically almost entirely funded by donors. In whose names do they speak? How do we know they represent the public interest? How do we know that they are not explicitly positioning themselves in highly political ways?

And yet, at the same time as the discourse whisks politics out of sight, the actual practice of civil society support is deeply political. Many of the organizations that receive much support have agendas that are confrontational to governments. It could be that these agendas are absolutely worthwhile and good, but they are surely seen locally for what they are, namely, deeply political. They are also not uncontested: there are other political agendas out there as well. Donors make choices about who will receive that support, and these are by definition political choices. Take the following quotation about US civil society support: "Conservative and centrist, pro-United States and pro-free market forces are strengthened and helped into power, while other indigenous forces are marginalized. Thus the political map of the target country becomes reshaped by US involvement" (Cohn 1999, 2). This author is clearly writing from a leftist perspective and overstating, as is so often the case, the effectiveness of this support, but her general point is valid: all such choices, especially if backed up by significant resources, amount to a deliberate intervention in domestic processes. Cohn interestingly adds, "As the furor surrounding China's contributions to US political parties highlights, the US government does not tolerate foreign interference in American political campaigns or elections." My own experience in Rwanda confirms the conclusion of another study of civil society support in three African countries, namely, that while the sums involved are often relatively small, foreign-aid funded actors can have a large impact on the debates about democratization and economic policy.[9]

To conclude, the civil society support discourse and practice are, like all development assistance, a curious mix of political naiveté and technicality, on the one hand, and deep social engineering and political interventionism, on the other. From the very terminologies in use to the predilection for short-term projects, the enterprise has two goals: to provide a safe moral high ground for the development enterprise, and to avoid brushes with the charge of interventionism. At the same time, ample space remains for the aid enterprise to prod and poke the domestic political system, to influence and manipulate, to pick and choose. Power is exercised here, and it is often done in service of very explicit (although rarely written down) political criteria. I guess there is no way that the exercise of power can be avoided in the business of development assistance, and a fortiori in those sectors that seek to promote changes in human rights and democracy outcomes. What may be most bothersome, here, is (a) the disjuncture between rhetoric and practice, (b) the way the rhetoric makes practitioners blind to their own exercise of power, and (c) the fact that by hiding the act of power, there is so little way to discuss it, to criticize it, to thus ultimately to improve on it. There are, for example, as far as I know, no transparent or objective criteria out there by which these choices are made, and thus critical debate about them, whether public or private, becomes more difficult.

To complicate things even further, *local* actors in recipient countries are well aware of all I have written in this section. The professed apoliticalness and technicality have never fooled them; they know the name of the game is politics, directly and unambiguously. They know that when outsiders pick and choose a number of organizations and put lots of money into them, especially in environments of great financial scarcity, this is politics, end of story. They tend to know much better than us the local context and mechanisms and stakes, and they have acquired over the years a great capacity to repeat the donors' discourses. Formally, their power is small, as is typically the case for those who are on the receiving end of an aid relation. Yet, they enter the game with major resources of their own: a much deeper knowledge of the local dynamics, networks of trust and clientelism and power unrecognized by outsiders, and a long-term and much more politically savvy outlook. As a result, even though their formal power may be small, they play the political game for all it is worth, often subverting the aims of the foreigners without the latter even realizing it. The end result, then, is one of ambiguity, where most of the things that count take place in the shadows of formal discourses and institutions, where the rules are personalized and who you know is more important than what you know, where outcomes are systematically unexpected, unrecognized, and performing under expectations (Uvin 1998)—surely not a context propitious to democracy, civil society strengthening, or human rights promotion.

Disentangling the Mechanisms

There is now a growing realization that such a simple, automatic relation, in which more aid automatically produces more and stronger NGOs, which automatically produce more civil society, which in turns has automatic positive impacts on all kinds of desirable things such as democracy, human rights, peace, and tolerance, is nonsense. Each of the supposedly causal relations—from more aid to more NGOs, from more NGOs to more civil society, and from more civil society to more democracy—is problematic and uncertain. I focus here mainly on the first and second of these relations; the third one has been widely discussed in the scholarly literature (see, for example, Uvin 1998, chap. 6; Carothers and Ottaway 2000; Ndegwa 1996), and is by now widely known.

As to the relation between more aid and more NGOs, civil society support overwhelmingly takes place with the oldest and weakest tool in the development toolbox: project aid. The litany of the deficiencies of project aid has been repeated for two decades now, and yet it still remains painfully relevant. Projects tend to be small, last for ridiculously short periods of time, are devoid of any serious long-term vision, are not transparent in their criteria for support, and are strongly influenced by remote headquarters in the West. They are administratively heavy and costly, with large delays between identification and actual implementation, offer little flexibility, and contain weak monitoring and evaluation systems. While such aid may keep many NGOs and community-based organizations (CBOs) alive—indeed, in the poorest countries, foreign aid can constitute almost the totality of the financial resources of all NGOs and most CBOs—it does so while keeping them dependent, weak, and outward oriented. It also creates tremendous competition among them (Howell and Pearce 2001, 148). In the end, this may well weaken rather than strengthen NGOs. All of this has been known for the last two decades (for an early and influential argument to that effect, see Lecomte 1986), but, apart from some European NGOs, donors have found it nearly impossible to muster the changes in administrative procedures and trust required to fundamentally alter this practice.

In addition, donor support may actually undermine NGOs and CBOs as democratic actors by weakening their mechanisms of accountability and orienting their growth outward rather than inward. This is an argument that is often made regarding the impact of aid on governments, to which we will come back later, but here we apply it to so-called CSOs, who end up tailoring their positions depending on funding agencies' financial resources (or the threat of discontinuation of aid), to the detriment of their relations with their social bases or clients. This is especially so in very poor countries, where a good relationship with an aid agency may mean the difference for individual NGO staff between living in poverty and living well. Note that there is a structural problem here: there are many NGOs in most countries, all competing for funds from donors, who are in the position to pick and choose among them. The pressure on local NGOs is thus enormous to mimic donor behavior and rhetoric.

In short, it often seems as if donors are doing all they can to ensure that their aid will have the smallest possible impact in terms of strengthening

NGOs and promoting dynamics that favor human rights and democracy (Duffield et al. 2001). But there is more. Not only does the project approach to civil society support produce weak and suboptimal results, it may also be fundamentally wrong for promoting a civil society. This argument is made much less often, and yet it is much more crucial. It applies, for that matter, to *all* development aid.

There are two ways in which this happens. First, the current system rewards those who are well connected much more than those who are representative or engaged in grassroots-supported social change. Second, the entire vision underlying civil society support programs fails to get at the crucial levers for collective action and citizenship. It works on the symptoms but not the causes.

Indeed, the scattered, muddled, uncoordinated, and contradictory nature of donor assistance and the myriad of small projects without any common vision, all distributed following other criteria and procedures and goals, are primarily of benefit to the well connected, the insiders. Those who best understand the game, who are best connected to the players in the international community, who can best manipulate discourses and networks of power, ultimately get to sit at the table to divide the manna from abroad. These can be great, courageous, important people, the best a society has to offer, true forces for change—or, as likely, those social entrepreneurs who talk the best, who are in the right spot at the right time, who know the right people, who can suck up to foreigners well. There is really little way of knowing. The fact is that the same incentive structures push all of them to behave in conformity with donor desires, discourses, sectors, and approaches; the people who master this game will end up with the largest slice of the pie. In some ways, then, the donor community strengthens that which it fears most: a lack of accountability, small networks of power, weak relations between society and its leaders. In this system the distribution of benefits across the territory is typically very inequitable; everywhere we find one village in which massive amounts of money are being invested, while down the road in the next village one-tenth of that amount is available. As this system is entirely dependent on the capacity of intermediaries to bring the manna in, it creates clientelism and disempowerment—the very opposite notions to what human rights are all about.

In addition, this strategy of supporting existing NGOs deals with the symptoms but not the causes, the underlying dynamics, of a civil society. Building a genuine civil society is not the same as funding a set of popular or "good" NGOs (even if these NGOs could somehow be objectively proven to be the "best" that money can buy). The kind of civil society that eventually can create rights and democracy grows out of the engagement of people at all levels of society, as they interact in ways that affect and make up the public good. This requires that people engage in collective action, build trust and confidence in their own capacities and the actions of others, and develop the ability to oppose and negotiate and ally themselves with other groups within civil society and with government as required. What I am describing here amounts to a transition from a set of highly personalized relationships between society and the state (as well as within society), in which individuals and organizations seek access to ad hoc benefits as clients (of the state, of local elites, *and of the development aid system*), to much more institutionalized relationships governed by predictable, transparent rules, in which individuals and groups are able to demand access to rights as citizens. This is a fundamental social and political transformation, which historically has been driven by economic change; it is truly the process of democratization and the emergence of citizenship.[10]

Aid agencies can assist this process not by selecting a few of their favorite NGOs and providing them with funding (and least of all with project funding!) but by creating incentives and support for people to organize at the local level, initially, in all likelihood, around (urgent) livelihood interests. When incentives for long-term collective action exist, the resulting organizations, networks, experiences, and confidence could become more institutionalized, becoming the springboard for engagement around more public, strategic issues. A rights-based approach may play a crucial role here, as suggested by the experience of the famous Maharashtra Employment Guarantee scheme in India (Joshi and Moore 2000). Key features were that incentives for collective action were built into the scheme (a minimum number of people need to organize and request employment before work sites are opened); it provided a legal guarantee (a right, in other words) that employment would be available if certain conditions were met; and over time that came to be regarded as a credible right backed by predictable funding, so poor people and politicians and NGOs all saw the worth of organizing to claim that right.[11]

This leads to a radically different strategy for civil society promotion, and, I believe, for positive support to human rights:

> What we can say upfront is that the work will be medium-term and structural, rather than limited to direct support for CSOs; that it will cut across all fields of development cooperation, not only civil society

sector work; that it will focus as much on the state as on existing civil society organizations; and that program design will be crucial. Our focus is on collective action by poor people, since they are in the majority, and are most disadvantaged when it comes to getting their voices heard. But action by other groups, especially if it offers the basis for alliances with poorer groups, is also a critical part of the total picture. (Unsworth and Uvin 2002)

We went on to discuss the country's ongoing decentralization program (especially a major program of providing block grants to the lowest level of decentralized structures), and how donor programs could hook into that to develop alternative strategies for civil society support:

For donor support to decentralization to contribute to civil society building and changed state/society relations, we believe it needs to have four crucial features. It needs to be predictable, pooled, locally accountable, and facilitated.

First, predictable (and long-term) funding. An adequate flow of funds through decentralised structures is essential to meet the enormous needs for investment in productive infrastructure and services in rural areas. But from the perspective of civil society building (as well as, for that matter, "developmental state" building), predictability of funding is as important as volume. Predictable flows create incentives for people to mobilise: confidence that money will be available strengthens those incentives and helps to institutionalise the process. Throughout the world, including in Rwanda, there are plenty of examples of small groups of people getting together to get access to the relatively short term benefits offered by project funding, but all too often those arrangements collapse when the project ends. More predictable funding allows people to acquire the experience to plan for, manage, and monitor resources, to learn from mistakes, to gain confidence in their capacities, and to pass through elections and learn that they can change those people who did not do their jobs well. All this contributes to stronger and more "institutionalised" collective action. . . .

Second, none of this can happen unless donors are willing to pool their funds and channel them in an equitable manner to decentralised structures. This is so not only for obvious ethical reasons (why should one district receive vastly more funds than the neighbouring one?), but because of the distorted incentives separately funded projects create that undermine collective action. If some districts, sectors, or cells receive vastly more support than neighbouring ones for the simple reason that they were lucky enough to be covered by an outside NGO or bilateral agency, the international community is reinforcing exactly the kind of clientelist system to which it so strongly objects when states engage in it. This is a system in which personal contacts, ideology, negotiations between remote powerful actors (donors carving up the territory into their own fiefdoms)—all processes outside the control of the vast majority of ordinary people—can bring about vast flows of money—or nothing. Such projects increase the power of those intermediaries that can access the foreign money—typically people belonging to elite groups that have entries into the international community.

Pooling challenges the whole set of clientelist relationships induced by direct donor or NGO funding of a particular district or set of partners. Assuming it also leads to more predictable funding it can provide the basis for government to start offering some services (for example primary education or a public works programme) on the basis of rights—which can in turn prompt a different quality of long term collective action, as people start to organise to claim them. . . . By contrast, direct funding of projects outside the budget, even if the amounts involved are significant, cannot lead to the creation of universal, credible benefits, let alone rights. Only the state can provide these. Better co-ordination between donors is not an adequate response (though it would be a welcome interim measure).

Third, pooled and predictable funding should reinforce common audit arrangements at district levels and below. Indeed, accountability mechanisms should not be primarily to donors but should be those envisioned by the law: local committees, audit systems, elections, etc. Better public expenditure management is an essential building block for reducing distrust of government, and providing entry points for civil society to challenge misuse or perceived unfairness. If this system is to be accountable primarily to local people, it needs to be accompanied by arrangements for putting out regular accessible information in kinyarwanda.

Fourth, these local structures need to be supported, in order to increase their management capacity, their capacity to deal with unavoidable conflict dynamics, and their degree of inclusion. This support ought to be light, adapted to local needs, and given both to decentralized structures, CBOs, and people's representatives. This is not blanket "sensitisation" but training and support around particular needs—planning systems, financial management systems, tools for conflict transformation, support for leadership, etc. (Unsworth and Uvin 2002)

Anuradha Joshi and Mick Moore make a set of similar points, arguing that

> the environment in which poor people and external organisations interact is frequently inimical to collective action by the poor. It is characterised by so much uncertainty and arbitrariness that investment in collective action is not worthwhile. External agencies should concentrate more on creating incentives for collective action, above all by removing the obstacles that they themselves create. (Joshi and Moore 2000, 7)

They go on to identify four crucial features for the creation of such an enabling environment:

- tolerance: make sure that the political environment is not hostile and punitive to collective action by the poor. . . .
- predictability: the extent to which external programmes are stable over time in content, form and procedural requirement. The more predictable a programme, the more it is worthwhile for politicians and social activists to invest in learning about it and trying to mobilise around it. . . .
- credibility: the extent to which, in their relations with the poor, public officials can be relied on to behave like partners in an enterprise, i.e., to do their job correctly and reliably.
- rights: the extent to which (a) the benefits received under external programmes are recognised as moral—or better, legal—entitlements and (b) there are recognised (preferably legal) mechanisms that the beneficiaries can access to ensure that these entitlements are actually realised. (Joshi and Moore 2000, 7)

These observations lead the authors in some unexpected directions, as when they attack two of the most popular instruments in the development policymaker's toolbox, namely, NGOs and social funds. Indeed, they argue that the use of these two institutions creates a disabling institutional environment:

Especially NGOs that are (a) not strongly rooted in the populations they serve; (b) are oriented mainly to obtaining external financial resources; and (c) are engaged more in service delivery rather than advocacy. These types of NGOs provide pure benefits, not rights in either the moral or legal sense of the term. . . . NGO programmes typically are diverse, fragmented and unstable (they lack programme predictability), and . . . they are not even potentially formally enforceable in the way that programmes run directly by governments may be. . . .

Social Funds . . . are supposed to provide demand-driven, locally adapted development services, . . . and contribute to the mobilisation of beneficiaries. But the reality is very different. While they are characterised by tolerance, they are deficient of predictability, credibility and rights. Communities are presented with their Social Fund opportunity out of the blue; they face what appears to be a once in a lifetime opportunity. . . .

The Social Funds case is very similar to that of the NGOs: a new set of institutional arrangements for delivering public services to the poor are justified through the rhetoric of "community," client demand," localism" and "decentralisation," while little real attention is paid to creating an organisational context that will enable the poor actually to organise to help ensure that programmes work in their favour. Both cases illustrated the main point of our argument: mobilising the poor effectively might better be done by paying less attention to sending emissaries, organisors and propagandists down to the grassroots, and putting more effort into providing the poor with an enabling external bureaucratic and programme environment—one characterised by more tolerance, credibility, predictability and rights than one is used to encountering. (Joshi and Moore 2000, 28–30)

I have quoted more than usual in this section, because these ideas are, I believe, original and important, as well as almost totally opposite to current dominant development practice. Any attempt to create rights-based institutions in developing countries should move away from the multitude of small, often NGO-based projects that currently dominate the field and seek to work on providing enabling environments for people to organize to fight for their own rights. Much development aid currently does not only fail to do that, but it may well undermine any chance of this happening. At the very least, this should provoke a reflection among practitioners as to the aims and procedures of their work.

Does Positive Support—If Not All Aid—
Undermine Governance by Definition?

All the above brings us to a major issue: what if the practice of aid by itself undermines or weakens good governance? This is an argument that has been made both by economists and, more recently, by political scientists. It comes in either a "lite" or a radical version.

The first argument essentially holds that the proliferation of hundreds of donors, managing thousands of uncoordinated projects, with their own bureaucracies, requirements, aims, and ideologies, cannot but amount to a weakening of local governance—whether in terms of bureaucratic performance or in terms of accountability. This argument has been around for two decades or so, since the major evaluations of aid of the late 1980s (Cassen 1986; in 1984 Elliott Morss spoke about "institutional destruction" to describe this dynamic). This sort of argument is also very often made by people in recipient countries. A recent DFID document sums it up nicely in more scholarly language, describing how the behavior of donors can:

- impose *transaction costs* on the recipients, tying up scarce resources in negotiating with donors and implementing and monitoring conditions;
- *marginalise and undermine government systems* (for example budget planning, accounting, procurement, personnel management); this undermines the incentive to reform and improve systems which are vital for the delivery of government services as a whole;
- create *uncertainty,* particularly in financial planning, which makes planning and long term investment impossible; the unwillingness of donors to make longer term commitments is inconsistent with the importance they attach to medium term planning;
- impose *tied aid conditions* which make aid less effective, add to transaction costs, and create a multiplicity of systems and standards in public services;
- make *competing demands* on government, through uncoordinated and inconsistent donor priorities and conditionality;
- divert attention to activities which *are transactional rather than transformational.* (DFID 2002, 3–4)

Ravi Kanbur takes this a step further, arguing that aid recipients spend far too much time and energy interacting with external donors to maintain normal relations with their own population, which is at the expense of their domestic governance (Kanbur 2000). And Deborah Brautigam adds, "Aid dependence also structures accountability as something between the executive branch of government, and aid donors, rather than between state and society, and this may have long-term effects for the consolidation of democracy" (Brautigam 2000, 29). This is the same point we discussed in our discussion of conditionality, arguing that it undermines that which it seeks to achieve. In this analysis, *the way development assistance is provided*—the uncoordinated, bureaucratically demanding, supply-driven, fluctuating ways that are by now so well known—destroys state capacity and legitimacy (see also Harrison 1999). This means that, while aid caused the problem, better aid could solve or avoid it. This is why I call it a "lite" argument: it assumes that better management can solve the problem. Note that this argument mirrors the one I made in the previous section about the outward-orientation impact of aid on civil society organizations.

A more radical version takes this one step further arguing that all aid, *by definition*, structurally, causes these problems—or that the more aid is given, the more these problems will occur, and no improved management can avoid that. In that case, less aid—or, more precisely, *no* aid—is the only way to solve the problems. In its simplest form, this is the old conservative argument that all forms of aid, charity, handouts, or social security take away people's incentive to help themselves and eventually create unintended and counterproductive effects, keeping people in poverty rather than helping them (for critical discussion of this age-old argument, successively invoked against women's rights, civil rights, and social security, see Hirschman 1991). Or it could be the argument that the market is sublimely capable of making decisions about where and how to employ scarce resources productively; any form of aid sends the wrong signals, undermines the functioning of the market, and hence retards development, which is defined as economic growth (Bauer 1983). In this sort of reasoning, as with so much radical thought, everything follows from the strong assumptions: accept these, and the world will conform.

But the argument also comes in a more sophisticated, empirically verifiable form, less burdened by conservative assumptions. Stephen Knack, an economist, has this to say on the matter:

> Good governance—in the form of institutions that establish a predictable, impartial, and consistently enforced set of rules for investors—is

crucial for the sustained and rapid growth in per capita incomes of poor countries. Aid dependence can potentially undermine institutional quality, by weakening accountability, encouraging rent seeking and corruption, fomenting conflict over control of aid funds, siphoning off scarce talent from the bureaucracy, and alleviating pressures to reform inefficient policies and institutions. Analyses of cross-country data in this paper provide evidence that higher aid levels erode the quality of governance, as measured by indexes of bureaucratic quality, corruption, and the rule of law. (Knack 2001, 310; see also Booth 2001, 23; Mick Moore 1998; and especially Brautigam 2000)

Deborah Brautigam states it this way: "The indiscriminate availability of aid creates a moral hazard, where aid availability, by 'insuring' incompetent governments from the results of their actions, allows governments to postpone reform efforts and weakens their incentive to find alternative revenue sources" (Brautigam 2000, 24). Her book goes on to argue that aid dependence weakens the quality of governance.

Many political scientists studying sub-Saharan Africa have recently come to similar conclusions. The argument has been made that in situations where weak states possess significant rents, that is, incomes that are unrelated to taxation of citizens' incomes—foreign aid comes to mind, but diamonds and oil have the same impact—rulers will use these resources to pay off clientelistic systems of domestic support and enrich themselves. As a result of the availability of aid, then, rulers can basically rule without domestic compromises, without social contract (on the absence of social contracts in Africa and how aid reinforces this absence, and how democracy can help overcome some of this, see de Waal 1997 and 2000). On the other hand, the main difference between aid and any other windfall—oil or diamonds—is that aid donors tend to get involved in the management of the resources, which is not the case for natural resources, a difference with both negative and positive effects (Therkildsen 2002). Generally, there is a growing sense in the development community that the capacity of governments to raise taxes—and to negotiate their use with the population—is a crucial measure of, and possibly path to, state strength and accountability (Brautigam 2000; Unsworth 2001).

As we already suggested, there is no reason for this dynamic to apply only to states. Indeed, NGO funding of all kinds can also be said to reduce the accountability of their leaders to the members or clients in much the same way. Especially in the poorest third-world countries, NGOs often seem almost exclusively oriented toward the ever-changing donor whims rather than toward their supposed constituencies or members (see Clayton et al. 2000; Bourque 2002; Brautigam 2000 briefly mentions this as well).

How are we to escape the conundrum that all aid *by definition* undermines governance, even if it seeks to improve governance or human rights outcomes? It seems only profound change could possibly begin to address the severity of the problem; half-measures seem too weak. I discuss two possible such paths for change: a radical capacity building approach and a strong contractual approach.

But before I do so, I wish to point out that the straightforward radical argument is basically unsolvable. This is because the conclusion is solidly embedded in the methodological assumptions. Both Brautigam and Knack, for example, apply economic-type public-choice methods to the study of sociopolitical processes. These models begin from the explicit assumption that all people, including politicians and bureaucrats, seek their own self-interest and nothing else.[12] From that point of departure, we cannot but arrive at the conclusion that development aid—or, for that matter, the very existence of the state—is bound to create moral hazard, for *of course* people will use resources that are not theirs to do self-interested things that by definition do not serve the public good. As shared values, ideologies, sense of community, altruism, social networks, and power and counter-power have by and large disappeared from the analysis, every system that is not the free market is bound to under-perform if not fail. That said, it is clear that self-interested and abusive behavior often occurs in states (as it does in corporations and other non-state actors), and the insights gained in this sort of analysis, while in need of nuance, remain of importance. This brings us back to our discussion of possible solutions.

The first possible path out is a strong commitment to a radical vision of capacity building. An excellent example of such an approach can be found in a text published for the World Bank (but not remotely reflecting mainstream thinking or the practice of that institution). In it, David Ellerman talks about autonomous self-development, arguing that it is based on the idea that true change in knowledge or behavior cannot be imposed from the outside. Even if a person is persuaded, by some means of coercion or reward to change his or her behavior, the change will be unsustainable (Ellerman 2001, 2002). Our discussion on conditionality suggested the same point. Ellerman argues that only learning based on *intrinsic motivation* and internalizing knowledge in a manner consistent with a person's existing beliefs and experience will result in genuine change:

- help must start from the present situation of the doers—not from a "blank slate,"

- helpers must see the situation though the eyes of the doers—not just through their own eyes,
- help cannot be imposed on the doers—as that directly violates their autonomy,
- nor can doers receive help as a benevolent gift—as that creates dependency, and
- doers must be "in the driver's seat"—which is the basic idea of autonomous self-direction. (Ellerman 2001, 2)

A radical capacity building approach, then, almost obsessively assures that aid will be complementary to local action and knowledge but never a substitute for them. It will not act without or in lieu of local actors (Fino 1996, 2001). Indeed, to add complementary resources to local actors the latter need to be investing their own resources, developing their own programs, making their own decisions. The radical capacity building approach is characterized by negotiated and contractual relationships. Such an institution-building strategy scrupulously respects the autonomy of the local institutions, acting only upon request and never directly intervening. It starts from an understanding of capacities and initiatives rather than problems or constraints. It lets local actors, whether public or private, fail and learn from failure. Indeed, one could state that the degree to which local actors are allowed to fail on their own terms is the best measure of the extent to which an aid relation is one of partnership and capacity building. The key working mechanism of such an approach is never to substitute for local action but always to wait for local people to organize and act, and then only bring in complements on demand—whether these complements are of a financial nature, or knowledge and training, or any other.

While I am convinced of the need for such a radical approach to institution building, it does pose a major question: does such a strong capacity building approach conform to human rights standards? The answer is unclear. It could run along the following lines: a strong yes as far as values such as freedom of choice and autonomy are concerned; a maybe for other civil and political rights such as democracy, for it really all depends on the nature of the institutions that are being strengthened; and a rather strong no, at least in the short term, for ESC rights, to the extent that any serious strategy of capacity building is almost always going to take longer to yield results than a delivery- or service-based approach.[13] In addition, there is no a priori reason why a "capacity built" institution would seek to work only for the promotion and protection of human rights. It could use its increased capacity and autonomy for any goal it sets, including choosing to violate human rights standards. If capacity can only be created and used for human rights–conforming aims, then we are clearly moving away from the pure "do not substitute or impose" paradigm into one where outsiders decide what is worth strengthening and what is not. The capacity of local organizations and people to set their own goals, struggle for their own change, and learn from their own mistakes becomes limited. This may be the morally right thing to do, but it does pose clearly the contradiction between a strong capacity building approach and a strong human rights one. It seems impossible to have them both together.

Most people working with a strong capacity building approach will agree that the key element for success is the choice of the partner whose capacity will be built; one needs faith in the partner to be able to work in such a hands-off, reduced-power approach. This means automatically that one will not be able to employ this approach everywhere, with everyone. It also means that one needs criteria to identify such partners. This, then, seems to amount to a selectivity policy as presented by the World Bank and discussed above, and would pose the same ethical problems: are poor people who live in areas where no states or NGOs are deemed worthy of such a capacity building approach being punished for the sins of their rulers? The difference seems to be that a radical capacity building approach can be adopted with a much broader range of actors than the selectivity one, which has a strong a priori liberal ideological and "state-centric" element to it.

The other radical change that may overcome some of the above discussed limitations is some form of what Santiso calls "political pacts for governance reform":

> Second generation democracy assistance should be grounded in political pacts enshrining the shared political objectives of the cooperation as well as the mutual obligations and the reciprocal commitments between donors and recipients in terms of democratization and governance reform. (Santiso 2001b, 170)

The author is clearly talking about a contractual approach to development cooperation, including to governance work. Such an approach is cutting-edge in the development community, and the UK (DFID)—currently the gold standard in development thinking—has taken the lead in implementing it. The already mentioned PRSPs fit in with that vision, for they are, as DFID says should be the case for development partnerships, based on

- a *shared agenda*, based on nationally-led, participative policy process and a credible commitment to poverty reduction;
- *mutual obligations,* which recognise the need for donors to make commitments . . . as well as the obligations of developing countries to deliver poverty reduction for their populations;
- *mutual accountability,* in which partners hold each other to account for their progress in meeting their obligations, possibly facilitated by a neutral third party. (DFID 2002, 4)

Conceptually, the oldest major example of such an approach is the Lomé Convention, which the European Union agrees upon every five years with more than one hundred developing countries, and which contains a broad set of mutual obligations in the realms of aid, trade, investment, and general foreign policy (including, as we discussed in the chapter on conditionality, the obligation for developing countries to respect human rights). These negotiated conventions always had strong partnership language, with all the right buzzwords of "dialogue, contractuality, stability, and predictability" (Santiso 2002, 28; Holland 2003).

How does this work in practice? In 2001, for example, the UK and the government of Rwanda signed a Memorandum of Understanding that commits the UK to ten years of budget support at £30 million a year and contains chapters of commitments in the fields of national unity and reconciliation, conflict resolution, good governance, poverty reduction, sustainable macroeconomic stability (including the very contentious commitment to "continue to reduce the defense spending/GDP ratio"), and human resource development. The funding supplied by DFID is general budget support, not project aid, in order to minimize the institutional destruction and weakening of central state capacity that comes with project aid (DFID 2002, 6; similarly, Kanbur et al. 1999 advocates the use of a "common pool" system).

The strategy contains significant potential and great risks. In the case of post-genocide Rwanda, those who provide significant budgetary support claim to do so as part of a deliberate and respectful strategy in which both sides dialogue to produce a long-term political and economic vision for the future (as opposed to a strategy based on micro-management and arm-twisting). In practice, the Rwandan side gains greater power, partly because of its greater capacities for deception (examples include keeping military expenditures off the budget or paying them through the occupation of parts of the territory of the Congo), and partly because no one in annual monitoring exercise wants to rock the boat and undermine the nice setup. Such a conspiracy of silence, as we discussed before, invariably results in under-performance. Although one part of the strategy—empowering the government by supporting its entire development (and political) strategy—is indeed met, there is little evidence that the other part of the strategy—actually influencing this same overall development (and political) strategy—has produced any results. Admittedly, the UK does not employ such strategies with all recipient countries, but only with those it believes can do it well—an element of selectivity, then, that acts partly as a protection (DFID 2002, 9).

In addition, what is to be done with this prescription in countries that are not democratic? As such contractual relationships are by definition made with governments, will not the key changes that may benefit large numbers of people be kept off the agenda? And, more broadly, what is the cause of the strong external accountability? Patrick Chabal and Jean-Pascal Daloz, in their famous *Africa Works* (1999), argue that aid dependence is carefully maintained by local elites, who benefit from the external accountability it creates, which serves their interests (Bayart 1989 also makes this argument). Nicolas van de Walle, studying sub-Saharan Africa, strongly argues that low government capacity, for example, results in large part from deliberate government policies; the destruction of mechanisms of holding governments accountable and to implement transparent planning is no God-given accident, but serves political functions. Thus it cannot be addressed by capacity building programs (van de Walle 2001). If arguments like these are at least in part correct, then the ideas underlying the PRSP policy and all similar contractual relationships will mostly fail for human rights and governance-related aims. Can accountability (or democracy, or good governance) be given back through donor behavior, or is this one more illusion, and must it be fought for from the inside? And, given the objective fact of external resource dependency for many countries, is any outcome other than weak internal accountability at all possible? That is to say, even if donors sincerely want to limit their importance and set up contractual mechanisms to create internal accountability, are the large amounts of funds they unilaterally bring to the table not automatically generating the outward orientation they seek to avoid? After all, innovative institutional setups and methodologies notwithstanding, the decisions about this funding, and the pockets out of which it comes, remain in Western capitals, not in the slums or the countryside of the countries concerned. In DFID's PRSP policy, for example, which outlines the strongest mainstream vision of contractual aid relations I am aware of, donor power lurks just below the surface. Read, for example:

If the government does not meet its targets, then we will assess whether the government has a credible commitment to poverty reduction. When a government commitment to poverty reduction is no longer credible, we will withdraw from giving financial aid to the government. . . . Our short-term response to underperformance will, for the most part, focus on tightening conditionality over the volume of aid. (DFID 2002, 13–14)

Add to this the general HIPC–structural adjustment philosophy within which the PRSP process is embedded, and it is clear that the internal contradictions remain enormous—between free choice and conditionality, and between external and internal accountability. There is no solution to these contradictions, which are present in *all* aid. Human rights are not the magical solution either. People and agencies need to muster trust and modesty as well as a fine and critical sense of the social and political landscape to struggle with these issues, every day of their practice.

Conclusion

Positive support resembles (negative) conditionality more than may appear at first sight. Given prevailing modalities of aid provision, both tend to have the same low, if not counter-effective, impact. Both may destroy local accountability rather than building it. Positive support programs are caught in ambiguities and internal contradictions: between their strongly politically interventionist mandate and their willingness to be technocratic and short term; between their need to be highly flexible and adaptable and the bureaucratic stifling of the project tool; between their desire to recreate social contracts in poor countries and the outward orientation that seems inherent in their presence. At the end of the day, as with conditionality, positive support to democratization or human rights is bound to produce a very limited impact unless there exists a genuine political will and strong commitment to democracy and human rights within the country concerned (Santiso 2001b, 172).

There seems no easy way out of this low-level equilibrium; tinkering at the margin will not do the job. Radical rethinking is required. It seems that both the radical capacity building and the contractual approach we discussed in the previous section suggest profoundly different ways of approaching the issue. Yet, both of these suffer from major limitations as well. Both present major questions of whom to work with and what happens if the choices made are wrong. In addition, below the surface of both, conditionality rears its ugly head again. It seems that, at the end of the day, all aid relationships eventually revert to conditionality, for it is ultimately donors who decide what countries to support, how long, and with what conditions. If that is true, then the most important way for human rights to have an impact on development may be by acting as minimum criteria for principled behavior by donors.

Post-Script: The Issue of Coherence

In many discussions on negative and positive conditionality, whether by practitioners or scholars, the need for a closer integration between development policies and broader foreign policies comes up (for example, EU 2001, 6). There are many reasons for such a perceived need, and all seem eminently reasonable. Worst of all, there are instances, all too many, where different establishments work against each other rather than with each other, seeking different goals, making different assessments, having different priorities. The European Union, for example, supports Asian and African farmers' cooperatives with its development aid, but its trade policy erects high barriers against these same farmers' exports. It makes little sense to undo with one hand what is being done with the other, and hence coherence—for that is the generic name given to this issue—seems by definition desirable (Box et al. 1997).[14] Less dramatically and much more common, different communities may not be working toward opposite ends but may be simply ignoring one another. Thus development, human rights, commerce, foreign policy, and military establishments may all be going their individual ways, each making its own assessments, setting its own goals, convergent in some cases, divergent in others, but surely producing suboptimal outcomes at the end. In addition, if we accept that development work should be more politically fine tuned, then foreign policy specialists—embassy personnel, country desks in ministries of foreign affairs, intelligence agencies—are just the kind of people one should work with; after all, they possess a vast reservoir of knowledge on these matters that development practitioners ought to tap into. Also, these same establishments possess important resources of dialogue and persuasion; in many countries (albeit not all: there are dozens of unimportant, poor countries, especially in sub-Saharan Africa, where the development enterprise is the big game in town) nondevelopment resources far outweigh those available to the development enterprise, and thus getting these different establishments on board is required in order to have any impact. The sort of highly visible political dialogue that is typically necessary for negative conditionality, as well as for the more positive forms of support we just discussed, all fall within the realm of foreign affairs or cannot be done without their assent and cooperation.

There is no reason to stop with foreign affairs. Defense is, of course, the next logical candidate, but for those seeking to moralize international relations even more fundamentally, ministries of commerce and finance are high up on the list as well. They too possess important knowledge—consider military intelligence, military attachés, defense training institutions, import-export promotion agencies—and have massive resources that can be used in strategies to create incentives or disincentives for change: military aid, access to loans, voting in Bretton Woods institutions, debt rescheduling, trade preferences, and so on. Why leave them out? Why risk that these various worlds, seeking their own interests and making their own judgments, will diverge from or outright undermine the development community's attachment to human rights, democracy, and pro-poor development?

Logical and desirable as the trend toward coherence seems, there are a number of major problems associated with it, both practical and conceptual. The first problem is the contradiction that exists between the search for coherence and the principle of local ownership and control. Let's face it: the development community's search for coherence essentially amounts to donors being able to "gang up" as efficiently as possible on third-world governments by creating a tight front, covering all areas of political and economic life. This is all the more so as the involvement of ministries of defense, commerce, or finance is typically sought for conditionality purposes. These are not exactly the establishments that have long histories or capacities in respectfully supporting the building of domestic constituencies in favor of democracy and human rights! Hence calls for coherence appear as attempts to create tightly interventionist grips on developing countries—success at the cost of voice. To solve this conundrum, two possibilities exist. Either coherence is sought only for aims that are solidly backed by universally accepted principles, such as core human rights standards, or the aims and the content of the coherence policy must be locally anchored, reflecting clearly expressed internal desires for change.

The second problem is one of control, of setting the agenda. Essentially, coherence amounts to the development community getting engaged in business that used to be by and large the exclusive preserve of the foreign policy community.[15] This new collaboration may find the development community in a much more subservient and compromised role than it likes (Atmar 2001; Macrae and Leader 2000). When development actors think and talk about greater political clarity of their mandates and the need for coherence, they implicitly see themselves in the driver's seat, with the other branches of donor government supporting their good works. Development actors are strongly advised not to hold their breath waiting for that moment to arrive. It is doubtful if a coherent agenda will be defined in terms of development or human rights exclusively or even primarily. Will foreign policy and defense become infused with a vision of economic and social justice and human rights—the Blair vision after 9/11, shared by many progressives everywhere, basically amounting to a moralization of all international relations? Or will the US vision prevail, in which development assistance is an adjunct to high politics and security? This is summed up perfectly in the quotation of General Franks, in charge of the war on terror in Afghanistan: "I want an aid worker on every tank." Surely, most aid professionals have the former in mind, but in their quest to get there, they may end up with the latter.

Coherence, then, is a double-edged sword.[16] The end result may be further removed from a human rights conformed development practice than the starting point. Given the imbalances of power and resources between aid and the diplomacy and military establishments in this world, it is more likely that development assistance will be subservient to foreign and economic policy than the opposite—except in those cases where the world of high politics does not care about the outcome. In that case, it is quite possible that the development community can set the agenda, with the small problem that it is not likely to receive much in the way of the desired support from defense and foreign policy, whose attention and resources will be focused elsewhere. Still, though, for these countries at least, if donor country policies could be more coherent, it seems like a step forward.

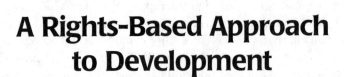

Saliency

6

A Rights-Based Approach
to Development

In the previous chapters on conditionality and positive support, the concepts of development and human rights remained separate; rights were a (usually small) *complement* to development work—either a consideration to be added when making funding decisions or a sector to be funded in addition to other, "regular" development fields. Even though the saliency of human rights had increased, the latter were still considered to be logically distinct concepts, aims, or practices—and, let's face it, from the perspective of most development professionals, clearly secondary.

At a higher level of integration, however, a new paradigm of rights-based development is emerging among certain agencies. At this level, development and rights become different but inseparable aspects of the same process, as if different strands of the same fabric. The boundaries between human rights and development disappear, and both become conceptually and operationally inseparable parts of the same processes of social change. At this, the highest level of integration I discuss in this book, development comes to be redefined in terms that include human rights as a *constitutive* part. All worthwhile processes of social change are simultaneously rights based and economically grounded, and should be conceived of in such terms. This makes intuitive sense, for at the level of human experience these dimensions *are* indeed inseparable (Craig Scott 1999, 635–36).

A story may illustrate the point well. A few months into the refugee crisis in Zaire that began in the summer of 1994 after the Rwandan genocide, a colleague went to Goma for an assessment of the health and nutrition situation in the camps. Upon return, he told me that nutrition intakes in the camps were high, as were vaccination rates and access to health care. As a matter of fact, he added proudly, these rates were better than they had been *before* people fled their homes. As I put down the phone, I realized that my colleague had just described the basic needs and even "human development" approach as implemented by the main development actors: great attention had been paid to health care, nutrition, vaccinations, and the other so-called basic, human dimensions of development. If that is true, then, according to the progressive vision of development then in vogue, people in these camps were "more developed" than before. We intuitively feel that this is nonsense, of course. When people are deprived of their freedom, live in constant fear, cannot move or work as they wish, and are cut off from the communities and the lands they care about, development has emphatically *not* taken place. This story tells us that there is no way to separate human rights from economic and social improvement; the terms mean nothing without each other and can only become meaningful if they are redefined in an integrated manner.[1] Maslow is dead; there are no basic needs. It also tells us, once again, that the *process* by which development aims are achieved is as important as the actual products. Processes can build on, strengthen, neglect, or undermine local capacities, local networks, local knowledge and ways of generating it; they can also fail to respect people and their dignity or their cultures. In that case, the aid given further reinforces the state of deprivation, even though more calories may temporarily be available. The same insight about the fundamental importance and inseparability of both human rights and development also flows from participatory assessments of deprivation and poverty. A few years ago Robert Chambers, father of the rapid, participatory, rural appraisal approach to development research, synthesized decades of work with local communities throughout the world (Chambers 1995). He argued that from the point of view of the poor, what he calls the condition of *deprivation* is about much more than lack of income. Deprivation is characterized by social inferiority, isolation, physical weakness, vulnerability, seasonal deprivation, powerlessness, and humiliation. And the World Bank (2000), after a process of interviewing thousands of poor people worldwide, now describes poverty as multidimensional: poverty, as the poor themselves see it, goes far beyond low income, encompassing also a lack of access to health and education, as well as vulnerability, voicelessness, and powerlessness. Effective poverty alleviation requires that each of these dimensions be addressed. This also strongly suggests the need for further research in each case where outsiders seek to promote social changes—research that need not be heavy handed and time consuming but that at the very least addresses local dynamics and perceptions: What is already being done by local people to address the problems? What do they think they have learned? What are the constraints they identify, that is, what has made their work difficult in the past?

The same sort of point has also been made from a theoretical perspective, and by none better than Amartya Sen, who in *Development as Freedom* synthesizes many of these insights. He defines development as the expansion of capabilities or substantive human freedoms, "the capacity to lead the kind of life he or she has reason to value" (Sen 1999, 87). He rightly adds that "despite unprecedented increases in overall opulence, the contemporary world denies elementary freedoms to vast numbers—perhaps even the majority—of people." He goes on to argue for the removal of major factors that limit freedom, defining them as "poverty as well as tyranny, poor economic opportunities as well as systematic social deprivation, neglect of public facilities as well as intolerance or over-activity of repressive states" (Sen 1999, 1; see also UNDP 2001, 19).

An interesting part of Sen's work is his treatment of the mutually constitutive and simultaneous links that exist between freedom (human rights) and development:

> There is the often asked rhetoric: What should come first—removing poverty and misery, or guaranteeing political liberty and civil rights, for which poor people have little use anyway? Is this a sensible way of approaching the problem of economic needs and political freedoms—in terms of a basic dichotomy that appears to undermine the relevance of political freedoms because the economic needs are so urgent? I would argue, no, this is altogether the wrong way to see the force of economic needs, or to understand the salience of political freedoms. The real issues that have to be addressed lie elsewhere, and they involve taking note of extensive interconnections between political freedoms and the understanding and fulfillment of economic needs. The connections are not only instrumental (political freedoms can have a major role in providing incentives and information in the solution of acute economic needs), but also constructive. . . . I shall argue that the intensity of economic needs *adds* to—rather than subtracts from—the urgency of political freedoms. There are three different considerations that take us in the direction of a general preeminence of basic political and liberal rights:
>
> - their *direct* importance in human living associated with basic capabilities (including that of social and political participation)
> - their *instrumental* role in enhancing the hearing that people get in expressing and supporting their claims to political attention (including the claims of economic needs)

Politics needs ≠ economic needs

- their *constructive* role in the conceptualization of "needs" (including the understanding of "economic needs" in a social context). (Sen 1999, 147–48; for similar arguments, see Nussbaum 1997, 286; Steiner 1998, 30)

Such ideas have made great inroads in international development discourse. Take this statement, for example, from the milestone UN secretary-general's 1994 *Agenda for Development*, specifying the relations between development and human rights:

Democracy and development are linked in fundamental ways. They are linked because democracy provides the only long-term basis for managing competing ethnic, religious, and cultural interests in a way that minimizes the risk of violent internal conflict. They are linked because democracy is inherently attached to the question of governance, which has an impact on all aspects of development efforts. They are linked because democracy is a fundamental human right, the advancement of which is itself an important measure of development. They are linked because people's participation in the decision-making processes which affect their lives is a basic tenet of development. (UN 1994, par. 120; see also UN 1997)

good pnt.

Note that this was written six years *before* Sen's book by an institution that is not exactly a hotbed of philosophical innovation. Hence, we have to at least acknowledge that these ideas have been around in the development field for a long time. Rather than congratulating ourselves on how smart and insightful we have become since we all read and began quoting Sen's work, we ought to ask why we have not acted on these ideas before. And this is where we encounter the limits of Amartya Sen's major contribution to development. Sen does not move beyond the level of broad paradigmatic insight, nor does he try to. He did state and clearly reaffirm important and well-argued conceptual insights, but he did not even begin to talk about their implementation—which is what the present book sets out to do. This is hardly cause for discarding Sen's major contribution; no one person is obliged to do everything. What it does mean, though, is that agencies, by signing up to Sen's vision, remain uncommitted to anything more than improved discourse.

All this begs a question: why the constant barrage of praise for and reference to Sen's seminal contributions to the development field? The reason is deeply linked to the constant search for moral high ground that occupies so much of the development community. Indeed, competition for scarce resources is tough for actors in the development enterprise (Duffield 2001, 223). Yet, contrary to the market, money is never made but only spent (and in the billions of dollars a year, at that); the voices of the users of the services supplied are hardly heard; actions are rarely critically evaluated; and product-quality measures are almost totally unknown. In that world, as in, say, academic fund-raising, the development of attractive visions is the primary recipe for survival and growth. Such visions combine the appeal of science with the moral high ground, and their essential function is just that—providing visions of oneself, markers of identity, trademarks of progressiveness. Many of the ideological changes the development community goes through are traceable to this imperative, and the glorification of Sen's fine work is no exception to this. As said above, with deeply insightful and stimulating conceptual formulations, along with zero practical guidelines or obligations, there is nothing to lose in Sen. Adopting his vision costs next to nothing—it is a pure win-win situation for aid agencies.

But there is one more reason for the popularity of Sen's work, and that is that he has been able to restate well-known things intelligently *in economic-sounding language.* Amartya Sen is an economist by profession, and a good one at that. Over the years he has constructed a body of work that is erudite, methodologically and theoretically sound, empirically rich, as well as—a rarity in his profession—resolutely multi-disciplinary and informed by a deep ethical vision.[2] The fact that he is an economist employed by prestigious universities such as Harvard and Cambridge, and who is therefore, at first sight, certifiably serious and authoritative, speaking in the language of the dominant ideology, *economism,* adds to his appeal—an appeal that has come to border on beatification since he received the Nobel Prize. We, the softies, the do-gooders, the marginal ones, need every economist who comes our way!

Yet, what is the concrete impact of this new thinking? What do development actors do differently when they redefine development along the lines of Sen's ideas? It is interesting here to look at the institution whose discourse has most taken over Sen's ideas, the UNDP. Its excellent *Human Development Report 2001* dealt with human rights, human development, and the relations between the two. The report is full of interesting insights and, indeed, has a very distinct intellectual feeling, much more than, say, your typical World Bank report, or even a UNDP report of a decade ago. This is what the section that describes the practical implications of "promoting rights in development" proposes:

- launch independent national assessments of human rights

[handwritten: Must ccit. Look at each approach]

- align national laws with international human rights standards and commitments
- promote human rights norms
- strengthen a network of human rights organizations
- promote a rights-enabling economic environment. (UNDP 2001, 112)

As we can see, the first four are of the kind we already described under the heading of positive conditionality. These are all potentially useful activities, but they do not reflect any mainstreaming of human rights into development practice; they are simply small, technical add-ons. Only the fifth one seems to offer the potential of going further:

> How to create an enabling environment in which public policy can most effectively provide resources for advancing human rights? First, the public sector must focus on what it can do and leave for others what it should not do. . . . Second, with this division of labor, the state can focus on the direct provision of many economic, social, and civil rights. . . . Third, the major economic ministries, such as finance and planning, need to integrate rights into the economic policy-making process. . . . Fourth, the private sector also has responsibilities in creating an enabling economic environment. Chambers of commerce and other business organizations should contribute to efforts to further improve human rights. (UNDP 2001, 116)

[handwritten: a group that can be acct.ble]

Is this all the new approach amounts to? A standard repetition of the end-of-the-1990s liberal dogma of the sanctity of economic growth and human resource development combined with some pious statements that ministries and corporations ought to integrate human rights into their work? How would this come about, this brave new world in which finance ministries and businesses all work for the promotion of human rights? All this resembles very much what I was writing in my earlier section on rhetorical repackaging. In addition, note that none of the human rights objectives relates to the UNDP itself or to the aid enterprise more broadly. In addition, all the recommendations are to be implemented "out there," in the "Third World," without requiring a critical look at oneself. There is no notion here that a rights-based approach (RBA) to development is something that starts at home or has implications for how aid agencies work.

The rights-based approach to development, then, seems like a lot of rhetorical fluff with little in the way of hard content[3]—and that has also been the spontaneous reaction I encountered when mentioning it to practitioners in the field. Many of them are turned off by what they perceive as the fluffiness of it all: they wonder how the famous RBA will concretely help them to do things better on the ground as opposed to writing nicer documents.

And yet, more is possible. Human rights, when deeply integrated with the practice of development, can be a very powerful addition and correction. Talking about the integration between human rights and development can be much more than adding to the moral high ground. As Hugo Slim states so well:

> Rights-talk can function differently from different mouths. It depends who is speaking about rights and where they are speaking. Human rights can sound and act very differently when they are spoken from what Gustavo Guttierrez [sic] calls "the underside of history"—the muddy side where people pay the price for those walking along the top. The same language of rights that may be rhetorical fluff in one place may be words of extreme courage and radical change in another. The power of speech is the power to name and define things. The use of rights-talk in Washington or Paris might be used piously as new words for the same old liturgy in the cathedrals of international trade and development. This might indeed be "repackaging" of old wine in new bottles as Peter Uvin suggests. It represents the power of re-dressing rather than power of redress. But from another place (a slum or the scene of a rigged election) and spoken from another voice (that of a poor man or a woman land rights lawyer) the same words of rights-talk could function prophetically as a demand for redress to change and challenge power. (Slim 2002)

Anyone who looked at the life or read the writings of another Nobel Prize winner, Burmese political leader Aung San Suu Kyi, will realize that her declaration that "the struggle for democracy and human rights in Burma is a struggle for life and dignity. It is a struggle that encompasses our political, social and economic aspirations. The people of my country want the two freedoms that spell security: freedom from want and freedom from war. . . . Democracy and human rights are indivisible from the culture of peace and therefore essential to sustained development" (Kyi 1995; see also the Dalai Lama 1999, 3–4) is more than fluff. This is a vision for which she and many other people are willing to risk their lives.

In the next pages, I try to tease out what, concretely, a rights-based approach to development entails, and how it would differ from standard

practice. I try to identify "new" things rather than simply repeating ...
I (and others) have already stated. Let me begin by stating that the rights-based approach to development changes the nature of the game not because it edicts rights as fixed properties or legal certainties or because it somehow leads us to discover brand-new actions or services we would never have thought of beforehand. Rather, there are two basic ways in which the rights-based approach to development differs from its predecessors, and they permeate all we do when we "do" development. First, an RBA creates claims and not charity (the *end* of development aid differs, and consequently the whole process of thinking about it, of defining the nature of the problem, changes as well—a new vision emerges). Second, an RBA affects the way development actions are implemented (the *means*, the processes, are different, even if many of the goals remain the same) (Sengupta 2000a, 568).

Vision

The RBA focuses on claims and thus duties and mechanisms that can promote respect and adjudicate the violation of rights (Hamm 2001, 1014). As CARE states, "[Our] human rights focus will mean that we view those we serve as rights-holders, not simply beneficiaries or participants" (Neggaz 2001, 15). This should affect the nature of the response, moving away from charity toward structural change. As Urban Jonsson from UNICEF correctly states, comparing a

> needs-based and a rights-based approach to nutrition, . . . the essence of the differences is that in the former "beneficiaries" have no active claim to ensure that their needs will be met, and there is no binding obligation or duty for anybody to meet these needs. In contrast, a rights-based approach recognizes beneficiaries as active subjects or "claim-holders" and establishes duties or obligations for those against whom a claim can be held. (Jonsson 1999, 49)[4]

A Rights-Based Approach as a Framework for Analysis

A major part of an RBA, then, is that it employs a different lens for analyzing the nature of the problems the development enterprise seeks to address (Jonsson forthcoming). Maybe the clearest statement of this can be found in a recent document by the Committee on Economic, Social and Cultural Rights:

The real potential of human rights lies in its ability to change the way people perceive themselves vis-à-vis the government and other actors. A rights framework provides a mechanism for reanalyzing and renaming 'problems' like contaminated water or malnutrition as 'violations' and, as such, something that need not and should not be tolerated. . . . Rights make it clear that violations are neither inevitable nor natural, but arise from deliberate decisions and policies. By demanding explanations and accountability, human rights expose the hidden priorities and structures behind violations and challenge the conditions that create and tolerate poverty. (CESCR 1998)

The Human Rights Council of Australia states it well too: "Looking at poverty through the human rights lens—as a denial of human rights—enables a richer understanding of the different dimensions of poverty and encourages a more comprehensive policy response to the structural causes of poverty" (Frankovits and Earle 2000, 7).

An RBA draws the attention away from aggregates and averages—from GNPs, average growth rates, numbers of the poor and malnourished—toward individual claims conferring rights and duties. As a result, development practitioners begin thinking more in terms of policy, inequality, exclusion, and discrimination—and not just poverty as a fact of nature or some original state everyone departs from. The switch this entails could be dramatic, going far beyond the mere conceptual (although that in and of itself is an important change already). In the words of the Human Rights Council of Australia, regarding the right to education:

Promoting and protecting the right to education is not simply a matter of increasing the national education budget. The realization of the right to education depends on focusing on issues of discrimination and access to education, especially at the primary school level; of taking into account the degree to which local communities can exercise their right in guiding education and in providing support for their children's education. It is not necessarily about buildings but about the resources and policies to enable all children to enjoy the right, regardless of their geographic location, their gender, race, language or ethnic origin. (HRCA 2001, section 3)

Clearly, then, the rubber of an RBA starts hitting the development asphalt when it leads to a more macro-institutional approach to development work, seeking to empower people through legal and policy reforms that establish key conditions for the enjoyment of their rights—access to land and water, matters of intellectual property, laws and policies that end discriminatory practices of various kinds, and the like. Any organization working within a human rights framework should have a much more automatic predisposition toward legal and policy change that is carried by local communities and individuals.

In the development field this type of legal and policy change has typically been done by the World Bank and the IMF rather than NGOs or even bilateral aid agencies. At most NGOs have worked in a reactive mode, opposing structural adjustment policies of the Bretton Woods institutions, for example. The RBA would change that: *all* agencies, whether multilateral, bilateral, or NGO, would begin to think of their work in terms of policy, law, institutions, exclusion, and nondiscrimination. We will come back to this. First we must discuss some important issues related to rights, claims, accountability, and justiciability (the capacity to get a claim enforced in a court). As we will see, this discussion is not legal hairsplitting but rather very important to bring us to understand the political nature of a rights approach to development.

Accountability

At the heart of any rights-based approach to development are concerns with mechanisms of accountability, for this is precisely what distinguishes charity from claims (Frankovits and Earle 2000, 7; Mukasa and Butegwa 2001; De Feyter 2001, 285; UNDP 2001). As the Human Rights Council of Australia states: "Accountability is key to the protection and promotion of human rights" (HRCA 2001, 2). Indeed, the very move from charity to claims brings about a focus on mechanisms of accountability. If claims exist, methods for holding those who violate claims accountable must exist as well. If not, the claims lose meaning. It is at this level, clearly, that a rights-based approach to development is bound to differ significantly from a basic-needs approach. An RBA will focus more on social structures, loci of power, rule of law, empowerment, and structural change in favor of the poorest and most deprived, as well as mechanisms for reprieve in case of violation. It will work on information and redress. We will come back to this later.

The question of accountability lies at the very heart of development. Many of the governments of poor countries are not accountable to their citizens. This is in part because of their history of colonization: the state was created to extract resources for Europeans rather than be accountable to its citizens, and that model of state-society relations has been continued after independence. It is in part maintained by the practice of development aid, which, as we discussed above, maintains outward-oriented systems of political accountability—all the more so after a few decades of Cold War politics and "blind" development aid. No technical progress is sustainable or beneficial to the poor without improvements in accountability. The RBA has the merit to force this issue onto the agenda—not necessarily because it has anything scholarly to say about colonialism and the like, but because when one begins speaking about rights and claims, one automatically ends up talking about mechanisms of accountability.

In the case of human rights, any discussion of claims and accountability immediately brings us to the thorny issue of justiciability, that is, the capacity to adjudicate a claim before a court of law, or, in another definition, whether the matter is appropriately resolved by the courts. By what means shall violators of human rights be held accountable if, as is so often the case, local legislation that conforms to human rights standards does not exist or local courts do not function well? Most human rights scholars rightly argue that justiciability is not a necessary condition for a human right to exist (Sengupta 1999, pars. 21–23; Sengupta 2000a, 558; Obiola 1996, 380; Eide 1989, 10). As Henry J. Steiner and Philip Alston state:

> The right to political participation . . . will hardly be vindicated by a court within an authoritarian regime. . . . It remains nonetheless a human right, to be vindicated in most instances through paths and strategies distinct from the formal legal system. (Steiner and Alston 2000, 275)

Indeed, if human rights existed only if they were justiciable, then they would lose almost all their bite, because they would by definition amount to no more than positive law (Donnelly 1989; UNDP 2001, 25). So, the absence of justiciability does not mean a human right ceases to exist.

Linked to this is the observation that many human rights are of an imperfect nature, meaning that it is not possible to match each rights claim with clearly corresponding duties and duty holders. This, too, makes life more difficult, for it is evidently preferable to be able to name clearly "who's in charge," so to speak, and whose head has to roll when things go wrong—as would be the case in, say, contract law. Regarding human rights, instead of perfectly linking rights to exact duties or identified actors, it is argued that "the claims are addressed generally to anyone who can help," and the rights become "'norms' of behavior or action" (Sen 1999; UNDP

2001, 24). In short, human rights do not lose their saliency because they are imperfect.

All of the above, however, may make us wonder if human rights—and especially ESC ones—are, indeed, simply castles in the air. Sure, human rights are claims to better treatment, but we do not know from whom that treatment should come or how much better it should be or what to do if no better treatment is forthcoming. Are human rights, then, only nice intellectual or rhetorical constructions, beautiful dreams maybe but, like all utopias, devoid of concrete relevance, especially for the hands-on kind of people who work for the development enterprise? Our answer is a clear no. Human rights are concretely usable tools.

To begin with, it is not true that ESC rights are not justiciable. Justiciability is certainly possible for some rights, or for some aspects of all rights. In addition, other, nonlegal paths for ensuring enforcement of rights exist. As to the point that justiciability is possible for some rights, the Committee on Economic, Social and Cultural Rights argued in a recent general comment that "there is no Covenant right which could not, in the great majority of [legal] systems, be considered to possess at least some significant justiciable dimensions" (CESCR 1998, par. 10, lists many of these rights). In all societies there are laws on the books—or such laws could be written—that render certain aspects of ESC rights violations subject to litigation. Uncompensated expropriation, corruption, outright theft, and unsafe working conditions—all phenomena that frequently occur throughout the world and produce major violations of the ESC rights of the poor—are illegal in almost all countries, with very specific laws applying to these crimes. They are justiciable. This may not happen in practice, because the parties affected are too poor and powerless, or the justice system too corrupt to deal with these case in an efficient, informed, and impartial manner, but that does not mean that they are unjusticiable by nature. It just means that improvements in rule of law are crucial for this aspect of human rights accountability.

In addition, the Committee on Economic, Social and Cultural Rights argued, some ESC rights, such as equal rights for men and women, the right to form unions and to strike, and quite a few others, are immediately justiciable (see Steiner and Alston 2000, 277). Again, such laws may not yet exist or may not be enforced, but that is not a problem of these rights being unjusticiable by nature. Here, too, judicial reform and litigation can be important parts of a human rights strategy, although they are not the only ones.

But the more important point is to demonstrate that there exist many nonjudiciary, nonlegal, and yet effective enforcement mechanisms to ensure that claims can be met, accountability exercised, and violations addressed. Accountability is not only a matter of being able to litigate in courts of law. After all, the impact of human rights on the behavior of states was never exclusively a matter of judicial enforcement; rather, it has always taken place through a variety of mechanisms, including dissemination and internalization of norms, redefinitions of the interests and legitimacy of actors, collective learning about strategies and policies, and the like (Koh 1997, 1999). Similarly, societies contain many nonlegal ways of regulating themselves, and people constantly make claims that are not backed up by courts alone. These include the systematic mobilization of shame and the development of international coalitions mobilizing it; the pressure emanating from the spread of shared expectations and socially acceptable discourses; the mobilization of grassroots and citizen power in favor of certain rights; the certainty that international aid actors will speak out loudly against violations and will extend support to local actors opposing these violations; and the creation of ombudsmen, whistle-blowers, and other administrative complaint mechanisms. All these may be second-best solutions when compared to formal mechanisms of justiciability,[5] but they do suggest that there are many alternative ways by which accountability can be fostered. All these, as well, are part and parcel of a rights-based approach to development.

An important insight, then, is that this is one field where human rights actors and development actors can work together well (Benoit et al. 2000, part IV). The human rights actors tend to be better at the legal matters: influencing legal frameworks and policies, improving judicial systems, and the like. The development actors tend to be better at the on-the-ground stuff: organizing people, creating mechanisms for information sharing and networking, and so on. Both together could work well on innovative domains such as the creation of alternative mechanisms for complaint and redress. Coalitions between these organizations, then, would make eminent sense.

Human Rights Is a Political Matter

At the end of the day, then, notwithstanding the seemingly clear and formal legal basis upon which human rights claims rest, the nature of the duties that are created by human rights claims is a deeply political and constantly shifting matter. What is socially and legally feasible and warranted is never fixed. It is not about merely asserting the existence of legal claims and abstract categories (Craig Scott 1999) but about political struggles, in which codified human rights are tools that crystalize the moral imagination and provide power in the political struggle but do not substitute for either.

There is another reason why an RBA is a deeply political one: when one begins moving beyond charity and technical assistance to the realm of claims and rights, one also begins focusing much more on social structures of inequality, exclusion, and oppression. As CARE's policy paper on the RBA rightly states:

> A rights-based approach deliberately and explicitly focuses on people achieving the minimum conditions for living with dignity. It does so by exposing the root causes of vulnerability and marginalization and expanding the range of responses. It empowers people to claim and exercise their rights and fulfill their responsibilities. A rights-based approach recognizes poor, displaced, and war-affected people as having inherent rights essential to livelihood security, rights that are validated by international laws. (CARE 2001)

There is no misunderstanding the implications of this language: if one adopts a rights-based approach to development, the nature of the job becomes an essentially political one, dealing with power and policy. The struggle may focus at times on the law, but its nature is political. This means that the pretense of technical neutrality falls away:

> A rights approach demands that we be in solidarity with project participants who are suffering human rights violations, whether in the form, for example, of absolute poverty neglected by the government, discriminatory treatment, or unchecked violence. The concept of neutrality, of not taking sides between warring and political parties, is one that CARE has embraced since our earliest days. As an independent humanitarian organization, it is sensible for CARE to aspire to be neutral. More problematically, we have interpreted our commitment to neutrality in many parts of the world as a commitment to be apolitical. . . .
>
> A commitment to the principle of solidarity suggests that we do away, once and for all, with the notion that CARE is an apolitical organization. . . .
>
> A rights approach affirms the importance of systematic identification of the underlying, or "root" causes of vulnerability and of a commitment, wherever possible, to confront such causes in our work. Root causes are often systemic or structural, residing at the societal

or even global level. This requires us to constantly question why people are marginalized. Historically, CARE, in our problem analysis leading to program design, has shied away from examining root causes and considering how we might address them.

The reasons for our traditional reticence lie in the perception, as discussed above, that CARE is an apolitical organization and that our strengths as an organization are in the delivery of supplies, technical assistance, and education at the community level. Regarding the former, the fact is that CARE's interventions are always and inevitably political, in the sense that they effect the local balance of power, and a rights approach challenges us to be more intentional in how we affect political structures and systems. (Neggaz 2001)

Some commentators have described this as a "solidarity" or "social justice" approach to development—a vision that has been on the table for decades. Catholic Relief Services, for example, has for a decade tried to go through a similar conceptual shift, calling it a "justice lens," and basing it on a combination of human rights ideas and Catholic social teaching about justice.

Clearly, a major possible effect of such a political approach to development is that it may put development agencies in a much more confrontational position toward developing country governments as well as social power structures there (and, indeed, other aid agencies such as the World Bank and the IMF, as well as foreign policy establishments of donor countries). This is very difficult to do, for many reasons. One we discussed above: the limitations imposed by sovereignty. These are most evident for international organizations, composed of governments, and often forbidden to engage in politics. But bilateral organizations suffer from similar limitations. Such explicit political engagements carry a diplomatic price. This is what the institution of sovereignty does. It does not—far from it—make international interference in developing country politics impossible; it simply makes it costlier and riskier than had it not existed. Even NGOs, a priori the least committed to sovereignty, feel this cost, for governments can make their lives very difficult indeed (to the point, in certain extreme cases, of kicking them out of countries and intimidating their personnel, especially local employees). Note that it is not only governments that can do this; so can paramilitaries, guerillas, warlords, local ruling families, and robber barons of all kind. These are not actors to whom the rules of sovereignty apply; hence, there is more going on here than merely sovereignty at work. Power at work may be a better image.

In addition, the development community lacks familiarity with as well as tools for analyzing politics. Issues of exclusion, racism, insecurity, discrimination, and representation have historically not belonged to its agenda, and the kind of personnel it employs—from economists to engineers, from agronomists to demographers—are primarily technical in outlook. All these issues are difficult and unclear, and so-called developed countries have hardly resolved them at home. To begin addressing them requires a strong and explicit political analysis—possibly both of issues at home and in developing countries (and, for the former colonial metropoles, of the past and its consequences). This may create conflicts with many current and potential employees and funders, and pose danger for staff in the field. Humanitarian agencies, working under tough conditions of acute violence, negotiating tenuous access to vulnerable populations on all side of conflicts, face this issue most (Minear 2002), but even development actors tend to worry about the loss of perceived neutrality, the risks to personnel, and the antagonization of potential partners or gatekeepers. Adding politics to development, then, makes the job a lot harder.

Process

The second main aspect of an RBA is the realization that the *process* by which development aims are pursued should itself respect and fulfill human rights (Sengupta 2000b, pars. 15ff.; UNDP 2001, 22). André Frankovits thus argues for the need "to apply the human rights practices to the aid program itself and not simply to attempt to assess the human rights implications of aid's outcomes" (Frankovits 1996, 125).

I am deeply convinced that the process is as important if not more important than the product in most development work. There are a number of reasons for this. For one, the dollar amounts of development assistance are much too small and too thinly spread across regions and sectors to make much of a major or long-term material difference in the lives of the poor across the globe. Development aid simply cannot significantly affect poverty and deprivation for more than a lucky few. In most cases, then, that which can last, and which can eventually affect many more people, is the establishment, strengthening, weakening, or destruction of institutions. In addition, development assistance, even if successful in achieving its own technical goals, has often accommodated, contributed, or spawned dynamics of inequality, corruption, and social exclusion.[6] All too often these political, social, and institutional consequences are important, negative, and difficult to reverse—sometimes outweighing whatever the projects managed to produce in terms of roads, vaccines, seeds, credits, or ministry reorganization. In short, good processes are considerably more important for long-term development than good products.

The rights-based approach to development argues that any process of change that is being promoted through development assistance ought to be "participatory, accountable, and transparent with equity in decision-making and sharing of the fruits or outcome of the process" (Sengupta 2000b, 21–22). In other words, it ought to respect the dignity and individual autonomy of all those it claims to help, including the poorest and the most excluded, including minorities and other vulnerable, often-discriminated against groups; it ought to create opportunities for their participation—opportunities that are not dependent on the whim of a benevolent outsider but rooted in institutions and procedures. This means we are talking about a particularly strong and deep form of participation here, one which goes well beyond the standard practice in much development work. Andrea Cornwall and Alice Welbourn state it well, talking about "realizing rights to sexual and reproductive well-being":

> In doing so, we seek to reclaim the transformative potential of participation as a process through which those who are otherwise excluded from the decisions and institutions that affect their lives can exercise rights to voice and choice: as agents rather than as instruments or objects. (Cornwall and Welbourn 2002, 2)

Their book contains many examples of what they believe to be required for such a deep participatory approach, including the "provision of a safe environment for self-expression, discovery, and negotiation, for which good facilitation is crucial," and "building on existing knowledge and practices," including those of ordinary people and marginal groups, and "a shift towards a more equitable power balance between service providers and users" (Cornwall and Welbourn 2002, 13–14).

Note that this is where a rights-based approach to development can go significantly beyond the dominant neoliberal paradigm. While it shares with the latter a refusal to accept the workings of corrupt, authoritarian, oppressive states, it does not believe that unfettered markets will by definition provide the solution; markets do not guarantee participation by the excluded, nor do they concern themselves with dignity. The rights-based approach to development, then, allows one to go beyond the usual dichotomy between ideologies that glorify either the state or the markets (and are unwilling to see the limitations and perversions of either). It argues that the functioning of any system, including a market-based one, is subject to the judgment and limitations that come from the fact that all human beings have inalienable human rights. It argues that processes of accountability, participation, inclusion, justice, and social guarantees have to underlie both the market and the state, and that under all conditions these matters are deeply political.

Nice as this sounds, it still poses the "so what?" question. After all, the insight that all development ought to take place in a participatory manner, with priority given to the poorest and the most excluded and based on institutions of accountability and transparency is hardly revolutionary for the development community—even though it may have been rarely implemented. The same applies to the realization that institutions, laws, policies, and politics matter or that both markets and states can exclude people. In the next pages I try to tease out some practical implications of a rights-based approach to development. What can development practitioners concretely do differently when they adopt a rights-based approach to development? How would they move away from current standard practice or normal professionalism? I outline a series of possible changes, most of which I have seen occur at least once in the field; they are possible, and some agencies have already acquired quite some experience with these changes. It may not be possible or necessary to do all of these things simultaneously, although many of them do go hand in hand.

Some Practical Implications
of a Rights-Based Approach to Development

Knowing the Human Rights Law Machinery

As we have already discussed, and rather unsurprisingly, the actions that come most easily to mind when one introduces human rights into development work are often legal in nature; they are straightforward in their execution, seem directly related to human rights law, and are not too threatening for anybody. Possibly the most popular way of introducing human rights into development practice is by dispensing training—the favorite solution for *all* problems in the development world, for that matter. The need for more human rights training—of aid agency staff, of partner agency employees, of specific target groups (the military, journalists, teachers), or of the entire population at large—is mentioned in almost every document I have seen on the rights-based approach to development (Frankovits and

Earle 2000, 13; Mukasa and Butegwa 2001; Hamm 2001, 1023). In practice, this often amounts to dispensation by capital-based lawyers, employed by a university or a specialized NGO, of rather legalistic knowledge on treaties and articles. It does not do any damage for people to read and discuss the Universal Declaration on Human Rights and the two 1966 covenants; it is also easy, cheap, and can be done on the side.

For other legal formalists, an RBA leads to the possibility for "development policy to be included in the human rights monitoring mechanisms of the UN" (Hamm 2001, 1016) or "the examination [by development actors] of periodic reports by the UN Committee on Economic, Social and Cultural Rights" (Frankovits and Earle 2000, 13). The Geneva-based UN human rights mechanisms constitute some of the most powerless, underfunded, toothless, formulaic, and politically manipulated institutions of the United Nations. Even the human rights NGOs by and large neglect them. For development work to be discussed there, or for development workers to read these discussions, is about as useful to on-the-ground change as knowing the lyrics to "We Are the World" is to ending world hunger.

I do not want to sound cynical—and I realize I do. Knowledge is a good thing. These things will not hurt anyone and may well be part of what it means to live in a society where human rights are deeply respected. It is also possible, even likely, that the spread of these texts, discourses, and associated institutions provides tools for the emergence of counter-discourses, adds legitimacy to new concerns, allows critical local actors to invoke this language, and so on. There is thus no a priori reason not to invest in this line of work. Honesty obliges us to admit that it is also possible that this sort of legalistic work produces negative impacts: it might de-legitimize human rights discourses by rendering them blatantly hypocritical, by coopting civil society human rights activists into meaningless structures, or by reinforcing legalistic readings of human rights texts at the expense of their political meaning. The concrete impact of this sort of formal legal work on social and political change must be studied on a case-by-case basis; it will neither be always good nor always bad. But let's face it, the popularity of this sort of work is primarily due to the fact that it constitutes a safe, legal, technical conduit to avoid the real issues of power and politics. If the RBA amounts only to adding a thin layer of human rights law on top of the development cake (not to reuse the cherry image), not much will have changed.

Capacity Building

Adopting a rights-based approach to development encourages development actors to broaden the range of their potential partners and work with local human rights NGOs. It must be noted that funding local human rights NGOs was also discussed in the previous chapter on positive support, demonstrating once again that the categories employed in this book are not as tight as they at first may seem.

Investing in local human rights NGO capacity building produces a number of benefits. It fits with the general desirability of capacity building and of supporting domestic, internal dynamics as opposed to exogenous ones. It also allows outside organizations to create some distance between the politics of advocacy and themselves; it is not they who engage in explicit political analyses or confrontational human rights work but local organizations, which they happen to fund. Often, to ensure they cannot be burned by the human rights fire, foreign agencies will finance only specific projects of local human rights NGOs, projects that are preferably couched in the most apolitical and non-confrontational terms.

The last decades have witnessed a growth in development funding for human rights organizations; from being nonexistent less than two decades ago, this has become a rather mainstream activity now, especially in post-conflict societies. Where previously local human rights organizations had either no external funding at all or only minimal support from some Western foundations and human rights organizations, nowadays local human rights organizations—who are many more in number, moreover—have routine access to several sources of external support. The amounts are still small, to be sure, especially compared to those available for traditional development activities, but this increase still constitutes a major trend. And it is not only money that is given; support also includes technical assistance and advice, training, and networking. A few more progressive NGOs, such as NOVIB, try to go beyond this technical, arms-length support, identifying more deeply with the struggles of their partners and supporting them programmatically in more visible and political ways. Such an approach clearly is at the outer fringes of standard development practice, drawing much more on models of political solidarity than traditional development assistance.

This work poses many difficult issues. In many countries there is always uncertainty about the quality, independence, and motives of local human rights NGOs. Are they truly independent of the powers-that-be? Are they really nonsectarian and objective? Do they not censor themselves too much? Are they more than vehicles for the power ambitions of their leaders? Are they just coalitions of the loudest mouths? Whom do they exclude? Whose voices are drowned by their noise? What are the relations of power within these organizations? Tough questions to answer—we are lucky that we are not required to ask them of ourselves—because the

interplay of personal motives and severe political constraints is often difficult if not impossible to disentangle.

Questions become even harder to answer when development practitioners question their own assessments and motives, as they should. Why do
they prefer certain human rights organizations and not others? How deep
does their understanding run of local civil society and the range of opinions on trade-offs and proprieties, even regarding human rights? Why do
some donors finance human rights organizations while others fund only
government policy and are silent on human rights violations? After all,
funding decisions here amount to outsiders taking sides in often very contentious and complicated local debates, whether deeply culturally rooted
issues such as women's rights and religious freedoms, or highly politically
sensitive matters such as transitional justice, or economically complicated
issues related to privatization and cost recovery. I am not saying this ought
not be done—indeed, it cannot be avoided, for even not taking sides always ends up benefiting one side more than another—but rather asking
about the quality of analysis underlying these choices.

The going gets really tough when local human rights NGOs are threatened, mainly by governments but sometimes by non-state actors as well.
What are the roles and the responsibilities of development actors funding
part of the programs of local human rights NGOs when the latter are
threatened, imprisoned, and otherwise harassed? How are they to "defend
the defenders"? Aid agencies' *political* support may be more invaluable
than their financial contribution; to speak out when local partners are
harassed or imprisoned is crucial. Bilateral agencies, which are less easily
pushed around, can, and do, bring a certain clout to the table. For many
in-country high-level aid agency representatives (and embassy personnel),
these matters are some of the most difficult ones they deal with.

Hence, while providing funding and capacity building to local human
rights NGOs seems an evident step to take in an RBA, it is also a very
complicated one. As I wrote recently in a paper to aid managers in Rwanda:

> It is important to protect the major independent human rights NGOs
> in Rwanda not because they are the only good or engaged people in
> town, or the most democratic, representative, and well-managed ones,
> but because of the chilling effect their disappearance would have on
> all other organizations. But it must be very clear that this matter is
> emphatically *not* about them only. Civil society in Rwanda is about
> much more than a few human rights organizations, important as
> they may be, and strengthening human rights dynamics requires all
> of them, not only the few specialized ones. Behind them and besides

them there are many other organizations of civil society that may not be so well-connected to a very vocal international pressure group (the international human rights community) but that are equally important to Rwanda's future, composed of committed people, and in possession of a vision of change. An exclusive focus on a few human rights organizations may be even counter-productive, for it antagonizes people against them, distracts from their own weaknesses (thus making them more vulnerable to eventual implosion from within), and allows the destruction of civil society elsewhere to continue, outside of the spotlight directed only to human rights organizations. (Uvin 2003b)

Yet, support to local human rights NGOs remains important work. It is not a magic solution, but it is one that must be part of a rights-based approach to development.

Advocacy

The next step, of course, is for international development actors *themselves* to engage more in advocacy. Note that we refer here to campaigning about policy issues that affect developing countries, and not to the investigation and documentation of specific individual human rights abuses, which we will deal with in the next section. We are talking here, then, about campaigns for arms embargoes; pressures on corporations that invest in war zones or in countries with regimes that are systematically violating human rights; campaigns for rich-country trade-policy reform, for lowered prices on essential medicines, and so on. All these issues have a human rights component, of course, and advocacy campaigns around them may well include human rights NGOs, but they are not the bread-and-butter work done by the specialized human rights NGOs.

For many development NGOs, what the rights-based approach to development boils down to in practice is increasing attention to advocacy. This is so for two reasons. First, to the extent that a human rights lens implies a process of looking at root causes and policies of exclusion and discrimination, advocacy seems a logical consequence; to speak out and to pressure for change would surely be the normal response. Second, advocacy and campaigning are *the* defining features of the international human rights movement and widely seen as synonymous with human rights work.

This equation between advocacy and human rights is simultaneously appealing and scary to many aid practitioners and managers. They fear that they are ill-equipped for the risks and difficulties inherent in advocacy;

t may endanger their relations with the powers-that-be and under-
their traditional development work on the ground; or that it may
alienate their funding sources, whether public or private, and thus endanger the financial survival of their organization.

Indeed, while advocacy is an evident practical step for organizations
seeking to move onto the RBA path, it poses many tough questions as
well, with major unresolved ethical dimensions. One such question relates
to trade-offs in cases where advocacy and more traditional forms of development assistance conflict. Developing country governments may not like
these advocacy campaigns, and neither may funders. If agencies, by taking
on strong public positions, are forced to end their programs on the ground,
are they hurting poor people in order to maintain a principle (even if they
think the principle is to the benefit of those same poor people) or hurting
people in the short run in return for a possible benefit in the long run?
Supposedly, they could ask the poor themselves: do the latter prefer more
advocacy in their name, or more microcredit, health care, and technical
assistance? Agencies shall, of course, do everything they can to combine
both activities—and indeed, research demonstrates that many NGOs are
able to be both confrontational and collaborative with local governments—
but this still does not solve the hard cases where trade-offs do exist.

Most advocacy done by development NGOs takes place in rich countries and is directed toward rich-country governments or major international organizations. This makes sense for two main reasons: first, it avoids
the difficulties on the ground described above, and second, as the famous
UK robber Biggs said when asked why he robbed banks, "that's where the
money is." Similarly, influencing the behavior of the United States or the
World Bank seems logical because that's "where the power is." When the
concerns and interests of poor country NGOs and social movements can
make it to the agenda of powerful actors, this constitutes a potential breakthrough. As a matter of fact, influencing remote but powerful actors (who
can in turn also put pressure on poor-country governments) can constitute
an efficient, indirect strategy for local organizations to affect their
government's policies. But a tough issue here is who sets the advocacy
agenda.

The role of the United States is central in advocacy. First, it is still the
world's most powerful state, and its leadership role, although contested, is
still a reality. Second, the US government is especially vulnerable to NGO
lobbying. This is partly because American politics is imbued with a culture of lobbying and partly because the executive branch is very dependent on Congress. Third, US NGOs are the largest and best funded in the
world, and some are especially skilled in advocacy and lobbying. As a

result, Congressional policymaking provides the Washington NGO community and those abroad with whom it links regular opportunities for influencing the behavior of the most powerful state. Every two years, for example, the US Congress must approve the IDA replenishment; environment NGOs use the occasion to lobby for stricter environmental standards, and development NGOs for more participation. Through this, some critics charge, it is largely US NGOs that set IDA policy. Thus, third-world governments paradoxically are more influenced by the pressure emanating from rich-country NGOs (and often brought to bear indirectly through rich-country governments and international organizations) than from their own civil society.

As a result, the impact of global civil society, as it has been called, reflects the world's imbalances in power and resources to the benefit of actors in rich countries (for case studies, see Jordan and Van Tuijl 1998). First, a limited number of Washington-based NGOs—self-appointed people, at the end of the day—have disproportionate power to influence international outcomes in the name of humanity and the world's poor. One of the privileges of the wealthy and powerful has always been to define the condition of poverty and devise solutions for it, and the trend seems to be continuing in NGOs. Although most of these NGOs honestly seek to speak for the interests of the poor and the oppressed (or for all of humanity), they have no structural obligation to do so—it all depends on their motivations, values, perceptions, and ideologies. Not surprisingly, there have been and are major disagreements between these NGOs and their "partners." For example, many third-world development NGOs differ sharply in their attitude toward the World Bank (and foremost the IDA, the soft loan arm of the World Bank) from American environmental NGOs. The latter, largely critical of the Bank, are willing to curtail IDA resources unless stringent environmental criteria are met, while the former are much less radical (Alexander and Abugre 1997, 13, 20). Similarly, many third-world organizations, including women's groups, sharply disagree with the central importance attached in US NGO circles to family planning and the "population problem."

Second, this situation gives the US foreign-policy establishment—as well as its counterpart in other Western countries such as France, Germany, or the UK—a major opportunity to filter worldwide NGO impact. This happens both because NGOs, to be successful, attenuate their positions according to what is acceptable to the US foreign-policy establishment and because the latter is truly the decision-maker in the matter. For example, the United States has been willing to take on the participation agenda, and push the World Bank on that account, but has been totally unwilling to take on the structural adjustment agenda that is equally, if not more, important to third-world NGOs and poor people (Nelson 1995, 23). The United States has also been unwilling to accept the emerging international antipersonnel landmine regime, although the NGOs lobbying for it are US based.

What we are describing here is simply the basic political dynamic that occurs whenever significant inequalities of power coexist; agendas, priorities, and strategies will be defined by and filtered through the powerful (Uvin 1999b). This dynamic does not simply disappear because the intentions are good or the vocabulary is one of human rights. On the other hand, a rights-based approach to advocacy has the advantage of building on a rather solid conceptual basis and shared language, namely, the large corpus of international human rights law. This is a strength that other campaigns may not have. Yet, as by definition not all human rights violations are being addressed—let alone successfully so—in these international fora, the above described ethical and operational issues do not disappear.

The Violations Approach

When asked what human rights mean in his work, Anton Baaré, a friend and colleague in charge of a human rights and governance project in Uganda (funded by Danida), stated: "The rights-based approach may not clearly spell out what we ought to do, but it sure tells us what *not* to do." In the debate about how to move ahead with ESC rights, a number of human rights specialists have suggested that the most fruitful short-term stance may well be to monitor actual violations of these rights: "While much of the international debate on economic, social and cultural rights focuses on their progressive realization (and thus deploring that resources are inadequate, which leaves matters at the level of arbitrary progress), a fruitful additional approach to monitoring these rights would be to monitor actual violations of rights" (Sano 2000, 746–47).[7]

Clearly, apart from the well-known CP rights violations, activities causing or encouraging forced displacement or the restriction of movement; the loss of land without compensation or the destruction of land rights; corruption and clientelism in the use of donor funds; arbitrariness or systemic bias in employment and promotion; racial and ethnic discrimination in access to education—all of these violate human rights, often right under donors' noses. Development actors adopting a rights-based approach to development could do two things when confronted with such violations:

they could speak out about them, and they could ensure that they themselves do not partake in such policies.

Past development practice shows precious little of either. Many such violations have been condoned or supported, on a daily basis, by development agencies throughout the world, often within the direct realm of their own projects.[8] The reason is not because aid employees are evil or corrupt, but rather because the political and institutional environment within which they act pushes them toward ignorance and/or acquiescence. Part of what facilitates this acquiescence is a development ideology that exclusively focuses on economic growth and social services, allowing many of these political and social processes to continue unchecked. A "violations approach," implemented as part of a move to an RBA, would undermine much of the acquiescence with ESC and CP rights violations that currently prevails in the development business.

A violations approach can also be legally applied to international organizations, which are large players in the development field. The UN Committee on Economic, Social and Cultural Rights summarized the legal human rights obligations of UN agencies as follows:

> In negative terms . . . international agencies should scrupulously avoid involvement in projects which, for example, involve the use of forced labour in contravention of international standards, or promote or reinforce discrimination against individuals or groups contrary to the provision of the Covenant, or involve large-scale evictions or displacements of persons, without the provision of all appropriate protection and compensation. In positive terms, it means that, wherever possible, the agencies should act as advocates of projects and approaches which contribute not only to economic growth or other broadly defined objectives, but also to enhanced enjoyment of the full range of human rights. (CESCR 1990, par. 6)

There has been some enthusiasm in the human rights community about adopting a violations approach to ESC rights, for the work it entails—monitoring and exposing violations—is the bread and butter of human rights organizations. FIAN and Equality Now are unique examples of human rights NGOs that have employed such an approach for more than a decade. Human rights rapporteurs in charge of specific rights—education, for example—tend to do it (Tomasevski 2003). Human Rights Watch, the largest US human rights NGO, has recently begun broadening its scope to include ESC rights, adopting by and large a violations approach that fits perfectly within its existing mandate and operational style:

> We focus particularly on situations in which our methodology of investigation and reporting is most effective, such as when arbitrary or discriminatory governmental conduct lies behind an economic, social and cultural right violation.
>
> We pay special attention to economic, social and cultural rights violations when they result from violations of civil and political rights. (HRW website)

As this statement suggests, the work is still basically limited to those cases where civil and *political* rights violations have economic, social, or cultural implications, and ESC rights as such still play only a marginal role in Human Rights Watch's work. Similarly, throughout the years it took me to write this book, Amnesty International has been going through a process of reflection with its worldwide membership on whether it should adopt a "full spectrum" approach—an approach that includes ESC rights— to human rights advocacy. While it seems likely that Amnesty International will eventually do so, it has still not happened. Note that for all these organizations, ESC rights are simply small add-ons to their "normal" mandates; they are not re-conceptualizing their aims in a more fundamental way or shifting paradigms as the development community does (Dorsey 2002, 6).

It is less clear what the development community ought to do with the violations approach. In theory, a violations approach has a number of advantages for aid agencies seeking to integrate human rights into their development work. It forces them to go beyond the usual feel-good development rhetoric and ideological blinders that ignore rights abuses. It could broaden the focus of attention away from states to include international agencies, firms, or NGOs—potentially including the development system itself. Finally, in exposing violations local partners would become aware of the impact of current economic and political practices, as well as of their rights to resist these, and they may well take more of the initiative for change into their own hands (Sano 2000, 747; see also Chapman 1996). A violations approach, then, could act as an empowerment device.

And yet, a violations approach may be less than appropriate for development actors. It is unclear how they would take on this mandate, for which they are hardly prepared. What methodology would they use? Should all development employees be trained in human rights violations data collection? And what should they do with the information collected? Should they engage in naming and shaming with all the attendant confrontational consequences? There seem to be many reasons to answer these questions negatively.

Development agencies live within a different political and social environment than human rights organizations. They stay longer on the ground, work more closely with much larger numbers of local partners, are more dependent on state collaboration, have many more local employees and partners who may not share such an antagonistic ideology and surely did not sign up to take the kind of risks human rights work entails, and are much more imbued (still not sufficiently in most cases, but surely more so than human rights NGOs) with a sense of the historical, political, and social constraints encountered in societies. A violations approach is bound to become rather antagonistic, and, unlike the case of supporting local human rights NGOs, the antagonism may be direct, without intermediaries between the development actor and the offending government. Development actors work in a world of trade-offs, of community and government ownership, of small, incremental changes—all of which a violations approach does not seem to fit into well.

Hence, both mandates are very different and fulfill important functions that are, a priori, of ethical importance. It is necessary to have watchdogs, organizations that expose violations, without fear, and—why not?—without compromise. There need to be some actors that do not make political compromises, that are not afraid to endanger their programs on the ground (partly because they hardly have any), and whose sole concern is to speak for those whose voices are silenced. The pressure they create remains indispensable for action; without it, it is too easy for everyone involved—the governments and the aid community—to look the other way, avoid rocking the boat, and lower their expectations. We need human rights organizations, social movements and interest groups, and possibly some highly politicized development NGOs to do this work consistently, untainted by the usual temptations of justification and accommodation. And at the same time, we need other organizations to do the long-term work, to be on the ground, to make some compromises, to strengthen a broad range of institutions, and so on. They should do this without being blind or complacent, but also without copying specialized human rights NGO mandates.

In the preceding paragraphs, I argued that while an explicit concern for human rights violations committed in the name of or in the process of development, is important, a strong violations approach based on investigating and documenting human rights abuses is not the best path forward for development actors. At the same time, there are situations where development (and, more so, humanitarian) agencies *have* played a role in documenting human rights violations. What can we learn from that? In addition, there are three approaches that development actors can adopt and that, while falling short of a full violations approach, may still bring them some of its benefits and strengths—the setting of standards, the pointing out of discrepancies between rhetoric and reality, the identifying of policies and actors that violate human rights, the creation of pressure for change. What these three approaches share is that they adopt a "lite" violations approach primarily to development agencies' *own* work.

To begin, then: In quite a few cases, development actors, and even more so humanitarian ones (for they often work in zones where massive violations take place and where few other formal organizations continue to exist) actually *are* prime sources of investigation and documentation of human rights abuses. As they are often the only foreign actors present in places where such abuses occur, and they seem relatively neutral, people come to them with tales and documents regarding human rights violations. The policy of most aid workers is to pass these on to the professional human rights organizations—national and international NGOs or UN human rights organizations. This is very risky for them when those responsible for the rights abuses get knowledge of this activity, and indeed, especially in the humanitarian case, it has repeatedly led to revenge killings. Courageous and noteworthy as this behavior is, it is not the same as the adoption of a human rights strategy by these same organizations. Passing such information happens "on the side," in an ad hoc manner, by necessity as silently as possible, and typically as fast as possible.

The main case I know where international development and humanitarian actors have tried to go beyond an ad hoc policy is Afghanistan, where, as part of the strategic framework, significant attempts *were* made by the international aid community to deal with human rights violations. The strategic framework has been evaluated negatively by many (for example, Duffield et al. 2001), but it did constitute a unique laboratory for the issues that concern us here. Norah Niland provides an excellent analysis and set of lessons from her three-year experience in Afghanistan during and after the Taliban. According to her, those adopting an RBA need to build coalitions that are as large as possible, so they do not stand alone; they need to feed their analyses into high-level UN and bilateral policymaking (ambassadors, special representatives, and the like are less vulnerable than specific aid agencies on the ground); and they need to be extremely careful, impartial, and context-sensitive, shining their lights equally on violations by all sides, and being willing to point out progress, achievements, and constraints as well as violations (behaviors that the specialized international human rights NGOs usually seem incapable of pulling off) (Niland 2003). Organizations could usefully begin such work on certain rather widely accepted economic and social rights, seeking to build coalitions of local and international actors that analyze issues that are not central to local high politics, providing a fine-tuned analysis of constraints, dynamics, progress made, steps to go, and so on—not to forget a self-critical look at donor practices in these fields. This way, they build on the strength of development organizations: their presence on the ground, their networks, their long-term vision, their sense of what is possible rather than what constitutes the moral high ground. None of this is easy, and even if well done, it may invite strong reactions, which is why coalitions of actors, high-level support, and the highest standards of impartiality and integrity are so important.

Let us continue now with a discussion of three methods for development actors to apply a "lite" violations approach to their work. One possible path is through work on human rights impact assessments, executed during the phase of project design, implementation, or evaluation (for example, NORAD 2001). Such methodologies can even be applied to development programs and policies (WTO policies, for example). As a consultant for CARE wrote:

> Benefit-harm analysis is intended to help us understand and, to the extent possible, anticipate and shape (i.e., maximize) the net positive impact our interventions are having. This type of analysis allows us to make sure that we are not ourselves violating or harming human rights attainment in the communities we serve in the course of our projects. (Neggaz 2001, 19)

These methods force practitioners and managers to do what we described above: name problems in different terms, before projects and programs start and while they are ongoing. It is a sign, however, of the weakness of the human rights agenda that, contrary to environmental impact assessments, the human rights agendas are still implemented rarely, and only voluntarily, and with methodologies that are ad hoc. No aid agency publishes annual reports on the human rights consequences of its development lending, for example (McGoldrick 1996, 806), even though calls for the use of such a methodology were already made by the UN secretary-general in 1979 (CESCR 1990, par. 8b).

A second solution resides in the application of the notion of non-retrogression. The non-retrogression rule essentially interprets the indivisibility of human rights as implying that no progress on one human right may be justified by reductions in the enjoyment of another one. In other words, development actors must ensure that in their attempts to promote the fulfillment of a particular right, they do not remove, violate, or decrease the preexisting attainment of another. It may be impossible to achieve all rights simultaneously (even though they are on a conceptual level all equally important, indivisible, and interdependent), but it is at least possible to avoid adopting strategies that endanger, undermine, or weaken existing levels of rights enjoyment (Sengupta 1999; Sengupta 2000b). The nonretrogression principle, then, provides a clear minimum standard for critical analysis of any development intervention and could constitute the basis on which to build a violations approach strategy. It does not judge every lack of full achievement of every human right as equally condemnable, but only regression from the prevailing situation. In other words, rather than focusing on all deviations from perfection (which is bound, for poor countries and the actors operating there, to produce a long list of failures and faults), it begins from the existing situation and judges trends and actions from there onward. Note that, although I qualified this as a minimal approach, it is still a tough criterion by which to judge actions and policies. To do it honestly requires a well-informed judgment about current rights (not just conditions that happen to prevail, but *rights,* that is, socially guaranteed equitable treatment of all people as citizens) and a critical analysis of how proposed and ongoing projects, programs, or policies affect current enjoyment of rights in all spheres of life and by all groups within society. Some of that work is being done by organizations that oppose structural adjustment policies, for example; they demonstrate how existing rights to water are endangered by proposed privatization policies. This is important work, where legal and development scholars and movements can find each other.

A third way ahead is for development organizations to subject themselves to occasional outside human rights scrutiny in order to ensure that their own processes and practices conform to human rights standards. One could envision development organizations extending formal invitations to human rights organizations critically to analyze aid agency portfolios and practices from a human rights perspective. True, this is risky: given the mode of functioning of human rights organizations, development actors may well come out of these assessments looking evil or ill-equipped for the job. Any agency working in countries where significant human rights violations take place, for example, may be simply condemned by the human rights purist as wrong-headed on the grounds that it should have withdrawn. This would be unfortunate, for it could lead to back-lashes against both the development agencies, if these results were widely known, and against the notion of human rights within development circles. The fear of exactly that happening makes it very unlikely that aid agencies will voluntarily consent to such assessments. It may be best to organize harm-benefit assessments initially as internal, confidential processes applied only to *past* projects, trying to tease out the human rights dimensions involved as learning exercises. Such a self-analysis could function as a training tool for employees to better understand the nature of the challenge of adopting a rights-based approach to development in a particular context.

Development actors who do consent to such a self-analysis could reap significant benefits from it. It could encourage them and their employees to confront the deeply social and political nature of the problems they seek to address. It could also force them to face up to their passive (if not active) complicity with the dynamics of exclusion, discrimination, and human rights violations that exist in many development programs. This may lay the groundwork for the adoption of a true rights-based approach to development.

The Inward Look

Many local employees and partners of development organizations are very aware of the human rights stakes in their own societies and in their own professional practice; they constantly deal with these matters in many ways. They may try to protect some people from potential or actual abuses by using their own networks and authority (or they may try to heap abuse on some people by using the same tools—there is, after all, no automatic reason why employees and partners of development agencies should be totally immune to the temptations of human rights abuse). They may try to avoid becoming targets of human rights abuses themselves by toning their own rhetoric and aligning themselves clearly with foreigners and/or with sufficiently powerful groups inside the country (including, possibly, groups that are guilty of human rights violations). They may try not to rock the boat by under-reporting human rights problems to their (foreign) superiors and by misrepresenting the situation on the ground, including closing an eye to how project funds, employees, and partners are part and parcel of ongoing patterns of discrimination and exclusion. Most of the foreigners who are in senior positions in the aid system typically understand little of these multiple strategies used by local employees to deal with the constraining human rights environment they live in. To the extent that the foreigners see human rights violations, they tend to see only the very visible instances—the famous dissidents who were unlawfully arrested, the dramatic disappearances of opposition figures—and fail to notice the equally important and pernicious daily forms of exclusion, discrimination, and lack of respect for human rights, and the way their own employees and funds are part and parcel of these daily dynamics. To the extent that they wish to act upon human rights outcomes, they too often invest solely in a few visible national human rights NGOs and legal mechanisms (important and positive as this may be).

All development agencies would benefit enormously if they managed to create an atmosphere of critical internal debate about human rights with their own staff and direct partners. Agencies would have to invest significant time in creating the required atmosphere of understanding and trust and security to make this happen; it will not happen overnight. But if agencies manage to do this, they can radically reinvent themselves: people may begin reporting the truth to their superiors (orally in cases where the written word is too scary), create explicit ethical bases for joint action, develop with senior foreign staff strategies of advocacy and protection of their employees, and learn to think in advance through the likely human rights impacts of various scenarios of action. All these would be breakthroughs—truly new ways of living a rights-based approach to development in a daily way. This may sound ideal and rather hard to achieve, and it probably is, but any progress along these lines is part of the implementation of an RBA.

Another internal process-related aspect of the rights-based approach to development is for development agencies explicitly to set out to comply *internally* with human rights standards. The quality of the workplace of aid agencies can be evaluated in human rights terms: Are minorities, lower castes, vulnerable groups, or women, for example, discriminated against in hiring and compensation? Do local employees participate significantly in organizational decision-making? Is there oversight and counter-power in internal management? One may argue that these issues are not strictly human rights matters (they are, after all, hardly matters of public guarantees for all citizens), but they seem to be a good place to begin when it comes to adopting an RBA—an instance of getting one's own house in order before spreading the gospel to others. These are complicated issues, of course, but also issues that are often important for many employees, local and foreign alike. Making progress on these matters, then, may convince them that the organization is serious when it talks about an RBA and that it is willing to look critically at itself. This can only help staff morale and internal ownership—apart from being the right thing to do.

Rule of Law

All organizations that seek to adopt a rights-based approach to development should focus their work on dramatically improving the rule of law at the level of daily life. It is worth nothing to have laws and policies—even if these laws and policies conform to human rights standards—if they are not implemented, if certain groups are excluded from them, if the relevant facts are not known to most people, if channels of redress do not function, if laws are systematically circumvented, or if money, guns, and political influence always tend to get the better of them. In many countries there are no or few instances of control of and redress for the many small and large abuses of power, instances of corruption, and the like that ordinary people suffer from.

Rule of law is crucial to a rights-based approach to development because it empowers ordinary people. Whatever the nature of the laws on the books—even if none of them explicitly refers to human rights standards or conforms to human rights—where rule of law exists, where there is an expectation that laws are applied, and rules are to be followed, where knowledge about the rules and the actions undertaken is widely spread, and where mechanisms of redress and counter-power exist, people can start organizing for social change (including changing the law to conform more to human rights standards). Without rule of law providing a basis for it, no human rights victories will ever be won by local people. Development actors interested in promoting human rights outcomes can do no better than using all their clout, imagination, networks, and resources to strengthen rule-of-law dynamics.

Rule of law is not the same as democracy, nor is it primarily a legal thing. Admittedly, in the longer run the mechanisms of accountability that are created by electoral democracies are propitious to the rule of law. They create incentives for elected people from the local to the national level, to ensure that laws not only represent the interests of a majority of people, but also are applied (for, if not, elected people would presumably lose their jobs). Note that this does not guarantee laws that conform to human rights, but simply that laws, even "bad" ones, are applied. But, for many developing countries this is far away. Elections are hardly more than contests between competing systems of clientelism; high-quality and critical information is not widely available; and many other historical, social, and economic conditions on which democracies rest are not present. Progress, however, can be made, slowly but surely, and it can constitute one of the bases on which, eventually, functioning democracies arise.

Progress on establishing rule of law is in part, of course, a matter of the legal and judicial sector; writing good laws, including civil and criminal procedures must be part of it, along with judicial reform that seeks to guarantee the competence and independence of the judiciary sector, and a panoply of legal-aid organizations, as well as ways that render the functioning of courts less expensive and time-consuming (World Bank 2000b, chap. 6). This sort of work requires not only technical competency but also an explicitly political yet hands-off approach by the international community. Examples of the latter include the long-term provision of significant salary complements; the creation of peer networks of discussion with and feedback by foreign judges; continued training; and a strong, clear, and consistently applied commitment by donors not to tolerate intimidation against judges and their families.

But the promotion of the rule of law—and this is a most important point—can also take many nonlegal forms: the multiplication of channels of information and (administrative and social) mechanisms for redress; the mobilization of grassroots and citizen power in favor of certain rules and procedures; the example given by senior politicians who demonstrate through their own behavior their respect for the rule of law and their expectation that others will do so as well.

It seems that there are three main ways to promote rule-of-law improvements—or any other, more direct human rights and governance improvement. First, there are legal and judicial changes, taking place at the level of the state, that craft the public-sector machinery to create the desired outcomes. Without the right laws and competent and independent judiciaries, rule of law will not come about. But improved laws are not enough; they risk being more theoretical or cosmetic if they are not implemented well or at all. This essentially requires counter-power. The second mechanism, then, is social control: any and all mechanisms that increase the capacity and willingness of citizens to know the laws, to be aware of when their rights are being violated or circumvented, and to seek redress. This is no longer a matter only of the public sector or of legal texts, but of the flow of information, of the capacity for analysis, of paths for seeking redress and response. The third mechanism lies at the level of the aid machinery itself: by its very presence and its resources, it can act as a mechanism for increasing rule of law—or fail to do so. As the World Bank admits: "Most investment projects and institutional reform projects, whether at the community level or at the national or global level, underestimate the need for information and underinvest in information disclosure and dissemination" (World Bank 2002, 15).

Improving flows of information for the poor is one of the most important things international aid actors can assist with. We know from basic political-science thinking that the dismantling of asymmetrical information is crucial for the establishment of civil society and eventually of democracy (see, for example, Diamond 1999). But the point can be made empirically also. I have repeatedly been told by practitioners that when small and poor farmers have access to at least two independent sources of information, their degree of empowerment rises dramatically. Suddenly they can compare information about prices, policies, rights, and rates without being dependent on middlemen and local leaders, and they can make up their own minds on these matters, availing themselves of opportunities that may have existed but were denied them for lack of information and knowledge (in other words, like markets, systems of governance need widespread information to function effectively). No wonder that in India the right-to-information movement that has come into existence in the last decade is considered by many an enormously powerful tool for any struggle for social change and human rights. And note that the information required is of an absolutely mundane nature. Harsh Mander and Abha Joshi argue that these campaigns are the corner stone of empowerment and human rights in India; the examples they give include the following (partial list):

- All estimates, bills, sanctions, vouchers, and muster rolls (statements indicating attendance and wages paid to all daily wage workers) for all public works.
- Criterion and procedure for selection of beneficiaries of any government programme. . . .
- Per capita food eligibility and allotments under nutrition supplementation programmes, in hospitals, welfare and custodial institutions.
- Rules related to award of permits, licenses, house allotments [and so forth]. . . .
- Rules related to imposition of taxes. . . .
- Copies of all land records.
- Statements of revenue, civil and criminal case work disposal. . . . (Mander and Joshi 2001, 3)

When the World Bank undertakes participatory anti-corruption surveys or Brazilian and Indian NGOs publish citizen report cards and scorecards on state government behavior (CRS 2003, 5–7; World Bank 2002, 232 ff.), they are at the very least laying the groundwork for a rights-based approach to development. I strongly believe that this—increasing the channels of information available to ordinary people about ordinary things—is absolutely a rights-based approach to development. It may not be about the famous professor imprisoned for teaching things the powers-that-be did not want to hear (although that is important too), but it is about human rights nonetheless.

Sometimes aid actions themselves have to take the lead, at least for those domains that fall within their control. Take a fascinating example: the Kecamatan Development Programme (KDP) managed by the World Bank in Indonesia. The program is basically a giant distributor of small grants to kecamatans, the lowest level of Indonesia's decentralization; people at that level can use the grants to invest in a jointly decided upon and managed project. They have a very large degree of freedom in the use of these block-grants. Interest in such block grant projects is growing everywhere, not because they will eradicate poverty but because they may contribute to achieving a set of higher-order aims, such as promoting decentralization and local-level community engagement therein, acting as a learning school for local democracy, strengthening local conflict resolution mechanisms. What interests us here in this project, however, are the manifold small mechanisms the World Bank created to ensure that corruption, clientelism, and local abuse could be counteracted. The following is a list of measures taken by the project (see World Bank 2003a, 11; World Bank 2003b):

Direct transfer of funds
- Funds pass through local government "in situ" only

Community control
- Villagers control budgets
- Financial formats are simplified so villagers can understand them.
- Public accountability meetings

Transparency
- Community notice-boards, village meetings
- Complaints database in newspapers

Monopolies—breaking
- Financial transactions require three signatures
- Procurement requires three quotations
- Breaking monopoly over information: facilitators

Monitoring and supervision
- By Alliance of Independent Journalists, NGOs—criticism and publicity encouraged
- Intensive ongoing supervision by network of hundreds of facilitators
- Sanctions and follow-up
- Handling Complaints Unit, World Bank has power to block disbursement

In essence, these mechanisms seek to ensure that people possess correct information, tools for control, and mechanisms of redress. I believe that this is rule-of-law work and an instance of a rights-based approach to development, even though it may not involve a single explicit reference to human rights law. Note that some of the most original mechanisms can be found at the bottom of the list. Further, they are all dependent on the World Bank's presence and its willingness to act as a counter-power—and this is where the originality but also the contestation come in. Indeed, the World Bank obliged the government of Indonesia to accept that the Independent Journalists Alliance (which was still formally banned at the time of the signing of the agreement) would write a number of independent investigative articles every year about the project's unfolding in particular locales; it similarly insisted on a key role for independent NGOs in a system of province-based monitoring, as well as independent impact evaluation studies to be conducted by the Demographic Institute at the University of Indonesia. Finally, the World Bank made a contract with a commercial company to act as an ombudsman to the project; villagers can file complaints about manipulation and interference through a special post office box or through the Complaints Handling Unit established at the central KDP secretariat (Sardjunani et al. no date; World Bank 2003b).

The World Bank is clearly throwing its weight around here. The government of Indonesia (or any other government I have ever worked with) would not have created these mechanisms by itself. Nor are these mechanisms as currently set up ultimately sustainable; they depend on the World Bank's money and its presence, and to some extent deliberately avoid and work around the official public mechanisms of accountability and control. This is what makes these mechanisms contested: they seem to depend a lot on pressure from outside, the sort of heavy-handedness for which the World Bank is infamous. And yet, there is something appealing about the setup of this project. I have just evaluated a project in Rwanda that is extremely similar in its aims and methods (it too consists of block grants to the lowest decentralized level in the country, with the aim of promoting local collective action and engagement in decentralization) but lacks the World Bank's mechanisms of independent control and counter-power. The difference is dramatic. The former is beset by a multitude of small irregularities that together may add up to disempowerment and risk negating the aims of the project, while the latter seems much closer to achieving its aims (admittedly, the history and level of state capacity of Rwanda and Indonesia are also not really comparable). In countries where the rule of law does not exist, where corruption and clientelism prevails, and where human rights are regularly violated both in high politics and low politics, it may be that only outside agencies can create, at least temporarily, the mechanisms required for rule of law to emerge. Without their engagement, it will not spontaneously occur. How much pressure to use and in favor of what types of mechanisms are clearly very difficult questions to answer, and the answers will probably vary from country to country, but these are not questions development actors can avoid by hiding behind nice rhetoric about ownership and local capacity.

This, then, is what an RBA can amount to, among others: a systematic and constant concern with the creation of mechanisms of accountability, information, control, and redress, available to all citizens, and especially those who are historically most subject to exclusion and discrimination; a willingness in development agencies explicitly to address these things and not act as if they are not problematic; a capacity to look critically at their own practice, from the top of the agency to the bottom, and the creation of a professional atmosphere that encourages this; a desire to learn and innovate in the creation of small mechanisms for daily adaptation to the human rights challenges faced by ordinary people.

But there is more.

Re-conceptualization of the Overall Aims of Development Agencies

One of the main advantages of a rights-based approach to development is that it can bring people to reframe the nature of the problems they seek to address and the levers for change they can employ. As I outlined earlier, human rights act here as a heuristic device, broadening the definition of the problems to be addressed as well as, consequently, the range of actions required to affect them.

Take the fight against hunger. In the usual approach to development, this was achieved primarily by technical projects to increase national food production through improved seeds and the use of more and better inputs. When these programs were criticized for not sufficiently targeting the poor, projects increasingly came to target smallholders or women (which does not mean they were always very successful at such targeting). Public-health practitioners added nutrition projects targeting children, pregnant women, or other "vulnerable groups." Environmentalists insisted on a higher priority for projects that fight erosion or soil impoverishment. Others, meanwhile, said the problem of hunger was not due to a lack of food but rather to a lack of income; they argued that the key to overcoming hunger is to increase the incomes of the poor, since higher incomes will create food demand in markets, which will be satisfied through the supply of imports, national trade, or increased local production. Still others have argued that what is really needed is the creation of off-farm employment, allowing families to diversify and increase income streams, possibly reinvesting parts of these in the intensification of agriculture. Still others would focus on small-scale, community-initiated initiatives, producer cooperatives, and community storage mechanisms.

The key point here is that all these debates, interesting as they are, employ an almost exclusively technical and expert-based perspective. They draw on insights from agronomy and economics, public health and environmental sciences, with some occasional anthropology thrown in for good measure. A human rights perspective, however, could dramatically change all that. It would begin by redefining the problem in terms of guaranteeing the right to food to all people in a country and then try to identify the factors that limit the promotion, protection, and provision of specific groups' right to food. The focus, then, would fall on a very different set of problems: the wide range of mechanisms that exclude some groups from services or resources the state makes available; the way discriminatory employment, land, credit, inheritance, or education policies exclude certain groups from the possibility of fending for themselves; how the practices of local and multinational corporations undermine or strengthen people's capacity to feed themselves; the impact of monopoly marketing boards or monopsony traders on the prices received by smallholders; the absence of social security programs intended to ensure that all people, regardless of gender, ethnicity, and income, have access to basic health care and nutrition. The list could continue. The point is that this approach to development has the potential to become broader—as well as rather radical, it must be said.

The distinction among *respect, protect,* and *provide* may act as a useful analytical device here. *Respect:* What do we as development practitioners need to do to avoid harming people, reducing their rights? What discriminatory practices shall we not accept inside our own organizations or in our relations with our clients and partners? To what standards of behavior do we hold our partners and other relevant organizations? *Protect:* How can we support people when they organize to end violations of their rights? What kind of pressure ought we exercise to make actors desist from human rights violations? What kind of oversight bodies, counter-powers, mechanisms of accountability and redress could ensure that violations will occur less frequently in the future? *Provide:* How can we strengthen actors' capacities to provide for satisfaction of their own rights? What influence can be exerted on states, international organizations, and the international community to assure the provision of rights? How can we help people directly? The resulting actions—even if all motivated by the simple and single right to food—will be in different fields of endeavor, from the very technical to the political, and at different levels, from the local to the international (for an interesting discussion, see Frankovits 2002). Oxfam International is an excellent example of an organization that has gone through such a process:

> The Oxfams focus on the realization of economic and social rights within the wider human rights continuum. Equity is key in the realization of these rights. Equity is about making the rules fair for poor people and ensuring that justice prevails. . . . Five rights-based aims provide the framework for Oxfam's work in the coming years. Their unifying theme is to make globalization work for poor and excluded people by establishing and implementing new "fair rules for the global economy." (Oxfam 2001, 7, 9)

For each of the five key rights Oxfam identified—the right to a sustainable livelihood, the right to basic social services, the right to life and security, the right to be heard, and the right to an identity—it sets out a series of strategic change objectives. These range from strengthening accountable local social change organizations to public campaigns for debt relief; from pressure on the World Bank's PRSPs to campaigns for fair trade; from improvements in preparedness for disaster response to research on the environmental needs of the poor in order to inform its campaigns for environmental regulation. Oxfam is quick to point out that it cannot meet these objectives all alone; it will need to cooperate with many other organizations, including primarily those representing the poor themselves and human rights NGOs.

Choice of New Partners

One of the major—and by now totally evident—consequences of a rights-based approach to development is that it encourages development actors to identify different partners. In an RBA, development actors are no longer limited solely to traditional development partners, namely, organizations that locally reproduce the discourse, aims, and strategies of the foreign agencies themselves. Indeed, throughout the world a large array of organizations exists that does what human rights are all about, as described in this chapter: promoting human dignity through the development of claims that seek to empower excluded groups and that seek to create socially guaranteed improvements in policy (including but not limited to legal frameworks). These groups, often without ever saying so, "do" human rights (see also Cornwall and Welbourn 2002, 1). They do it differently from the usual manner of international human rights NGOs—the "naming and shaming" approach. They do it through grassroots organization, collective mobilization and bargaining, changing values throughout society, pushing for change in laws and policies and institutions, confronting discrimination (not only by governments but also by non-state actors, whether for profit or not). They may be composed of professionals, or they may be social movements; they may be alone or part of large networks that cross regions, countries, and continents. They deal with HIV-AIDS; sex trafficking; homelessness; discrimination along ethnic, gender, regional, religious, or linguistic lines; and access to water and land. Improving their capacities for learning and networking, their degree of internal democracy and representativeness, and their impact on other actors is part of rights-based development work.

The choice of local partners can be made using human rights criteria as well, privileging organizations that live by—as opposed to talk about—human rights standards, organizations that are internally democratic (for example, non-exclusionary in their membership) and representative of excluded groups. They can be assisted to become more accountable, better organized, more effective, and the like—progressive donor organizations have quite some experience with this.

This may be the moment to reflect more on the risks of external (financial) support. Does an RBA tell us anything about the way funding relationships ought to be construed? This is, after all, a very complicated issue, where good intentions often end up producing less than optimal results. The problems typically identified with donor funding include its short-term, administratively heavy, externally driven nature, leading both to inefficiency and to a strong sense of distrust and reproach among recipients.

Another fundamental problem relates to the prime instrument of funding, namely, the project—a typically short-term, time-bound, and predetermined set of actions with a clear aim, time line, and budget. At the same time, the donor side of the relationship is worried about dependence. There is the nagging fear that financial support creates a dependency relation, in which the recipients, counting on continued outside support, ceases to invest in their own capacities (Ostrom et al. 2002). There is also the fear that large funding removes local leaders from their social bases, turning them into aid parrots, at home in the international aid circuit more than in the communities they claim to represent, capable of proposing fundable projects but short-circuiting their own bases.

Does a rights-based approach to development allow us to avoid such outcomes? A priori, it seems that the notions of transparency and participation that are so central to an RBA in general could be usefully applied to the particulars of the funding relationship as well. This would suggest vastly greater clarity in the way donors make their decisions about partners and funding as well as offer much more local control over sectors and modalities. Possible systems include:

- long-term program support for organizations with proven track records, allowing them to grow on their own rhythm and through their own learning;
- separating accompaniment and technical support to local organizations from the mechanisms that channel funding to local organizations' projects, with the former being available for a large number of local organizations in creating their own development plan, and the latter being available to those who submit successful proposals to foundation-like autonomous agencies (partly advocated by Hyden 1993; see also discussion by Ojo 1998);
- supporting networks of NGOs and CBOs for a long period of time, giving them significant decision-making power about the nature of the support, with simple rules seeking to guarantee equitable distribution among members and between members and the center (often the center of these networks receives a disproportionate share of the funding at the expense of the members);
- public knowledge, discussion, and audits of the management costs of the intermediaries (usually Northern NGOs who channel the funds from donor agencies to local NGOs, often at disproportionate cost);
- mechanisms, as discussed above, that strengthen and diversify the capacity of all people involved to know what money is flowing where,

why, and how, and that ensure that possibilities for correction and redress exist (major advances in transparency are bound to be part of any such mechanisms);

- clear rules and procedures allowing for negotiation of funding relationships rather than unilateral imposition by donors.

These are not impossible, and yet they are so rarely achieved.

It also seems that as the focus shifts from services to rights, the exclusive focus on money may weaken as well. Let me explain. In the traditional development approach, money is at the heart of the game. Whether development assistance is seen as filling the gap between insufficient local savings/foreign currency and required levels of investment, or whether it is simply a matter of providing more social and economic services to the poor—money is the core of what development cooperation is all about. There is no development relation without significant injections of money. In a rights-based approach to development, money is much less crucial, at least in a first run. What matters are organizational capacity, mutual influence, internal and external accountability, exchange of innovation and ideas, mechanisms of voice and control and redress, inclusive processes of decision-making, increased availability of information, improvements in policymaking and legal environments and the quality of justice, and the like. While none of these things comes for free (and none comes easily or rapidly), none of them depends solely or primarily on massive injections of external funding.

All the above clearly pleads for relationships between donors and recipients that are more long term and programmatic rather than of a short-term, project/service delivery nature—away from the subcontracting relationship that still prevails in much development aid and toward genuine partnerships. Admittedly, these things have been discussed for decades and little progress has been made, apart from European NGOs, who tend to be significantly ahead of the other players. An RBA can restate the importance, the urgency, of this sort of work, but it cannot really make it happen. Fundamentally, a lot of the institutional and procedural aspects of the daily business of development cooperation make the sort of different funding relationships described above difficult. The RBA, then, at the end of the day, poses a very uncomfortable question for donors: what is it in their own structures, attitudes, behaviors, and incentive systems that makes progress along these lines so excruciatingly slow? The RBA, then, moves upward from the field to the top levels of any development agency, requiring fundamental decisions about its systems and procedures.

Conclusion

A rights-based approach to development contains great potential to alter profoundly the way the development enterprise goes about its business. Truly implementing it constitutes a radical change, though, demanding changes in choices of partners, the range of activities undertaken and the rationale for them, internal management systems and funding procedures, and the types of relationships established with partners in the public and nongovernmental sectors. An RBA, in other words, deeply affects the sorts of relationships that development actors have with actors on the ground (and even the scope of "the ground," which moves from the local to the global) as well as the way they function as organizations. It requires both external and internal changes.

The RBA is not the solution to all problems, a magical key that will finally unlock the gates of development nirvana. It is a lens, a way of looking at the world, of defining struggles and partaking in them. History shows that social struggles are messy, long term, and complicated, and thus an RBA will by necessity display these features as well. It seems likely that not all development agencies will be able to adopt the full RBA described in this chapter, nor should they necessarily. Multilateral organizations, especially, with their global state membership, their size, and their bureaucratic weight, seem to be structurally unable to do so—or at most they can only slowly adopt a few of the less radical tenets of the RBA (for the case of UNICEF, see Jonsson forthcoming). Bilateral agencies possess more of a margin for maneuvering, and NGOs more so still, and hence I would expect and hope that change in the direction of an RBA will take place primarily here.

7

Final Synthesis and Questions

Human rights are seen not as inalienable property but as claims, stakes, and occasionally as trumps which people play out locally and globally, nationally and transnationally. These rights emerge, not from declarations, but from a culture of conflict over human dignity and self-preservation.

—MICHAEL GEYER, member of Human Rights Program
at the University of Chicago

In this conclusion I begin by synthesizing the main arguments of the book—a brief reminder of the key practical insights for those who struggled through the entire thing or a lengthy executive synthesis for those who came straight away to the conclusions. After this synthesis I step back and identify some broader, more conceptual insights about what it means to accord human rights a central place in the practice of development. This part should be of relevance to human rights specialists as well. Finally, I deal with two questions that came up repeatedly throughout this book but were never fully solved. The first one deals with the need to make choices among rights, which is often required in the real world, as development practitioners well know. In case of lack of resources, how do we set priorities? In case of a conflict between rights, how do we make trade-offs? The second question is the one of interventionism. Much of what I propose in this book seems to constitute a license for ever further interventionism by outside actors, often unmatched by knowledge, legitimacy, modesty, or accountability. Is it possible to temper, constrain, and counterbalance the evident risks this poses? How do we marry outside support with internal autonomy? I have no clear, single, or fixed answers that will solve these questions once and for all. The way we face up to them lies at the heart of our engagement in social change and solidarity; the values we have, the risks we are willing to take, and the types of relationships we build with those around us determine who we are and where we end up, although we may not know either in advance.

A Synthesis of the Arguments

This book discussed four ways in which human rights have been integrated into the practice of development. At the lowest level of integration, we found rhetorical repackaging, in which little changes with regard to development practice but the rhetoric. At the next level, we discussed political conditionality, where donors set criteria or conditions that ought to be met to continue the flow of aid. The practice of development itself does not change, but it is linked to human rights criteria: From whom should donors withhold aid? At what point should donors threaten to cut aid? When should they execute that threat? The third level of integration, called positive support, consists of development actors seeking to create the conditions and infrastructure to promote and provide human rights: better laws, functioning courts, stronger NGOs, the machinery of democracy, more competent and transparent states. At this level actual money is spent on human rights–related concerns, although human rights are still mainly defined as CP rights rather than ESC ones. At the highest level of integration, human rights and development concerns merge into a rights-based approach (RBA) to development. Here, the entire current development practice is fundamentally challenged; its goals, levels of intervention, tools, partners, and processes all become subject to rethinking in the light of human rights concerns, including ESC rights. In the next pages I briefly synthesize my key insights regarding these different levels.

Rhetorical Repackaging

As usual in the business of doing good, rhetorical repackaging is very popular. Multilateral organizations, which always need to walk a tightrope between their claims to the moral high ground and the realpolitik pressures of member-states and bureaucracies, are most subject to tendencies toward simple repackaging, but bilateral donors and NGOs are by no means immune. Repackaging consists of the pleasant discovery that our development practice is actually, and has always been, a way of realizing human rights for millions of poor people. Our development projects are allowing people to realize their rights to food, housing, work, and the like. As a result, there is no reason to change much in the actual practice of development; all that is required is to add a few new labels.

Many scholars and diplomats argue that such rhetorical redefinition constitutes a first step to real change; out of new discourses grow redefinitions of the realms of acceptable behavior, new ways of judging progress and holding actors accountable, new definitions of interest and preference. Like all processes of institutional change, this is a slow affair, and repackaging may merely be the first step on a long road. It is true that no major policy change can begin without being first conceived and formulated, and some organizations have slowly but surely made small strides in trying to adopt new practices after changing their rhetoric, so one can only hope that this will be the case for many more development actors. It is at present too early to tell.

Still, dangers lurk in repackaging. Instead of constituting the first step toward a fundamental re-conceptualization of the practice of development, rhetorical repackaging may merely provide a smoke screen for the continuation of the status quo. It is also usually based on a fundamental misconception about human rights, one that holds that any positive result in the field—say, more wells in a village or improved access to food for a group of people—constitutes the achievement of a right (to water or to food, as the case may be). Rights work, however, is about long-term guarantees, about structural claims and social guarantees, information, accountability and capacities for redress, and a particular attention to the most vulnerable and underprivileged or excluded. Dominant development practice, even if successful on its own terms of yielding aggregate growth in income, health care, or nutrition, is usually a far cry from that.

Conditionality

When one asks development or human rights experts to consider the relation between their two fields, most begin by talking about conditionality. They argue that donors should threaten to cut off development assistance—and execute that threat—to recipients who consistently violate human rights, with the aim of forcing them to change their behavior. The major international human rights NGOs—but also members of, say, the US Congress or the European Parliament—have often campaigned for a greater use of precisely such political aid conditionality.

Yet, four major arguments against conditionality can be made. The first is that conditionality is unethical and thus ought not to be employed. This may be so because (a) it hurts the poor and vulnerable, who are made to suffer for the sins of their rulers; (b) it is much less likely to be attempted,

and less likely to be effective, with larger, richer, or more strategically important countries than with smaller, poorer, and unimportant ones; and
(c) it constitutes a form of forceful interventionism, violating a country's
sovereignty or, worse, a people's right to self-determination (another human right, bringing us to the question of trade-offs we will discuss below).
Solving these issues poses some difficult questions, including: On what
basis do we make decisions about the appropriateness of conditionality,
and who should make these decisions? Does it make a difference if governments are democracies or if they are autocratic?

To be ethically acceptable, a nuanced practice of conditionality should
to the utmost extent possible,

- be designed not to impose costs on the most vulnerable groups;
- take into consideration internal debate in the country concerned; if
  significant portions of the population, or groups that can reasonably
  be held to represent them, are in favor of the use of conditionality (for
  example, South Africa, Burma), its legitimacy is greatly strengthened;
- be done in a graduated manner, with sufficient time and flexibility to
  allow for local responses to emerge;
- build on the existing laws of the country concerned, so as to ensure
  that the aim of conditionality is locally anchored;
- not be employed when the behavior to be changed enjoys major popular backing or when the government is democratically elected.

A second argument against conditionality is that it is never fully implemented; even if it were ethical, it is simply not doable. Whether because
donors assess the situation on the ground differently or because they have
different interests and face different domestic pressures, conditionality is
always applied only *to* some countries and not to others, or only *by* some
countries (or multilateral agencies) and not by others. Note also that traditional conditionality is useless in the face of human rights violations
committed by non-state actors, which may produce a deeply resented bias,
especially in situations of conflict. Such partial and ad hoc conditionality
is bound to suffer from very low legitimacy and effectiveness. Only closer
coordination and multilateralism, based exclusively on human rights criteria, would solve these criticisms, yet, although this has been on the agenda
for decades, it seems unlikely to happen anytime soon.

A third criticism against conditionality is that it does not produce the
results it aims for; even if were to be consistently employed, it would not
work. The rights-abusing governments possess too many tools for evasion.

They will, at most, engage in financially driven tactical compliance, but not in anything resembling real or lasting policy change. They will, for example, organize elections—pressure for elections has been a very popular form of conditionality—but stack the cards to ensure their victory. It is only in cases where strong domestic pro-democracy opposition movements already exist that such an outcome can be avoided. In other words, conditionality is most likely to work where it is needed least.

The fourth argument against conditionality goes further and argues that conditionality destroys that which it seeks to achieve. Heavy-handed external pressure often leads to a backlash, and domestic groups may become suspect if they are too cozy with foreign agencies. On a more structural level, while the aim of conditionality (especially in the structural adjustment variant) is to place limitations on the economic and political power of incumbent regimes, these same regimes are the ones who will need to implement the policies contained in the conditionality; as a result, incumbent power elites are strengthened rather than weakened by conditionality. Finally, conditionality, by its external nature, destroys the very domestic accountability and social transformation it seeks to achieve. The development of a local social contract between a government and its citizens is short-circuited, and sovereignty is transferred to outsiders (one could argue this is a problem of all aid, not only conditional aid).

If any of these points is considered correct, conditionality emphatically ought *not* to be employed. In short, conditionality is about shortcuts and absolute power, the alluring but empty idea that money can "buy" human rights—and, of course, that *we* know what's good for *them*. This is a dream, if not a nightmare. One cannot push buttons to make human rights happen, not even in societies where one invests a lot of money. This does not mean that donors ought to close their eyes when confronted with significant human rights violations in the countries they work in. Some form of action that goes beyond passive acceptance but is not traditional conditionality seems required.

The most promising tactic may be the inclusion of human rights criteria in the PRSP process of the World Bank. PRSPs consist of broad-based processes of national dialogue around economic and social policies—open discussions on the use of the national budget that could eventually lead to national policies that are truly locally owned. Once these PRSPs exist, the need for further conditionality of the arm-twisting type should disappear and aid actors ought to take a much more hands-off approach to their assistance. This approach has until now been implemented in an almost totally rights-devoid conceptual framework, focusing mainly on getting popular ownership of neoliberal economic policies. If infused by human rights, however, PRSPs could constitute a form of progress, based as they are on internal dialogue and international partnership.

Great progress could be made in two more alternatives to traditional conditionality. One is principled behavior, in which donors do not seek to reform governance systems but simply set a few basic criteria, lack of respect for which automatically leads to the suspension of aid. There seems to be a growing consensus that organizing genocide and overthrowing democratically elected governments are the most acceptable trigger points. Such principled behavior does not necessarily reform the offending situation but simply demonstrates principled unwillingness by donors to become complicit. Over time, this may become part of the international "rules of the game."

In addition, aid agencies need to break the habit of self-censorship when it comes to matters of human rights abuse. This holds especially for senior expatriates. It still remains standard operating procedure for the entire official aid rhetoric and all the written aid documents to tiptoe around the key human rights challenges in recipient countries, preferring silence, gentle insinuation, and massive doses of self-censorship to any frank mention of the stakes, the problems, and the unfulfilled challenges. The risk here is that over time these sanitized versions of reality become real; they become the intellectual framework in which aid practitioners conceptualize and judge their actions, leading to passivity or cynicism.

This means that donors—bilateral agencies as well as NGOs—must be more willing to face up to human rights violations, to discuss them with other agencies and arrive at joint positions, to check these positions with local partners to ensure the relevance and validity of their insights, to plan their interventions in explicit acknowledgment of these facts and positions, and to the extent possible, to convey these positions formally and informally to the offending parties—foremost, typically, the government, but possibly also non-state actors. In other words, an explicit concern for human rights violations ought to be standard operating procedure of development aid. This would make daily relations with recipient governments more difficult, but that may be the price to pay. As we will see below, this does not mean that development actors have to become mirrors of human rights NGOs.

Positive Support

Unlike conditionality, positive support is about collaboration and construction, not punishment and threat. Donors create projects that seek to encourage human rights outcomes, typically by creating or strengthening the institutions deemed necessary for human rights respect and promotion. Positive support projects seek to achieve a broad variety of goals, such as strengthening civil society or legislative bodies, writing constitutions and laws, supporting independent media or human rights watchdog organizations, creating electoral mechanisms, providing human rights training, promoting judicial reform programs, and so on. These projects engage a wide range of political entities including ministries, courts, local governments, people's organizations, journalists, policemen, political parties, NGOs of all kinds, and the population at large.

In practice, most positive support measures have focused on democracy, for this is the bundle of rights donors think they know best; in the early years democracy was basically interpreted as "elections." The World Bank has added its own, distinctly more technocratic notion of "good governance," consisting of the sorts of government attributes—transparency, absence of corruption, predictability, accountability—that favor stable and efficient markets. Whether promoting democracy or good governance, most donors have tried to break human rights down to a manageable subset of technical problems easily solved. Donors do so for reasons of convenience (it is easier to deal with recipient countries if we all pretend the work is not political), ideology (we know that liberal free-market policies are good for all, so no debate is required), and ignorance (development practitioners lack the in-depth historical and political knowledge required for a nuanced judgment about political trends and maneuvering).

This tendency toward technicality sits uncomfortably with the fact that all the objectives sought by positive support projects are fundamentally about power and counter-power, about overcoming the resistance of those who favor the status quo and strengthening those who seek positive change, about reshuffling political cards and changing deeply ingrained attitudes and practices. Thus, more often than not, positive support projects manage to create the form but not the process of democracy and human rights. Courts exist but no justice is done.

Let us be clear: Positive support to ensure human rights outcomes is not easy. Human rights promotion and democratization are nonlinear, unpredictable, messy, and reversible processes, in rich countries as much as in poor ones. Donors do not remotely possess the institutional flexibility, locally appropriate knowledge and foresight, or political persistence for such policies, and it is highly unlikely that they will develop them anytime soon.

In addition, almost the entire positive support approach is implemented using the oldest and by far weakest tool in the development toolbox: project aid. Projects are short-term, administratively top-heavy, and inflexible, and they foster bureaucratic conformity and a fixation on disbursements over processes. Projects are the most regressive and ill-suited conceptualization and management methods imaginable to promote human rights outcomes. This holds for projects with both governments and CSOs. In the case of civil society, the project system reward those who are well connected and master the project language rather than those who are engaged in grassroots-supported social change and fails to get at the crucial levers for promoting collective action and citizenship. Donor project support may actually undermine NGOs and CBOs as democratic actors in a similar way to conditionality: weakening their mechanisms of accountability and making them highly outward oriented.

Most of the positive support system, then, no matter how promising it looks on paper, collapses—or rather, systematically under-performs—under the weight of its internal contradictions. It is a highly interventionist machinery of social engineering that pretends to be simply technical and does not dare to discuss its political bases properly. It seeks to influence dynamics that are unpredictable and complicated with tools that are inflexible and short term. It fails to come to grips with the complicated ways in which it contributes to further undermining and weakening accountability and legitimacy of both state and non-state actors. Like an anti-Midas, it turns to lead all it touches. Some projects may work, of course, and produce excellent pro–human rights and pro-democracy results—maybe as a consequence of a particularly able set of people involved, some fortunate external constellation of propitious circumstances, or other idiosyncratic reasons—but these are the exceptions. The way they are currently implemented, external support projects for human rights are largely doomed to fail.

Short of a dramatic rethinking of the way the development enterprise functions—its procedures, its ideologies, is tools, its habits—there are no evident solutions to these problems. Some scholars and donors, DFID in particular, talk about rebuilding development assistance relations on a contractual basis, which in the field of human rights could lead to what has been called political pacts for governance reform. These would be negotiated conventions, detailing mutual obligations, likely in terms of medium-term goals rather than short-term projects, including in the field of governance. International support would be programmatic and long term, and annual reviews would explicitly discuss trends, progress made, constraints encountered, and so on. Violations by either side of the terms of this accord would lead to renewed discussion and possibly suspension. All this, then, would contain stronger elements of partnership, dialogue, contractuality, stability, and predictability. The potential explicitness, mutuality, and security of commitments, foremost in the political realm, make this approach seem promising. Current practice, however, is a far cry from these ideals; all sides to the contract have a hard time living by it or accepting its vision. This is a structural problem, for the underlying power differences as well as the political pressures on both parties have not suddenly disappeared when such contracts are signed.

More radically, some small NGO donors have displayed a strong commitment to a radical vision of capacity building, which almost obsessively assures that aid will be complementary to local knowledge and initiative but never a substitute for them. Aid will not act without or in lieu of local actors. Outside support will be long term, guaranteed, enacted only upon local request and after local investment, and based on clear and transparent procedures of negotiation and mutual control. Deep trust is necessary for this approach to work, and as a result it seems likely to be undertaken only by a limited number of NGOs. Its impact has thus been small until now, although interest is large, and it could be applied much more widely than has been the case until now.

The Rights-Based Approach to Development

At this highest level, development and human rights become inseparable aspects of the same process, like two strands of the same fabric. The boundaries between human rights and development disappear, and both become conceptually and operationally inseparable parts of the same processes of social change. Recently, there have been some major intellectual statements of such a vision, most notably Amartya Sen's *Development as Freedom*. Donors and NGOs, however, by signing up to Sen's vision, remain uncommitted to anything more than improved discourse. In this book I sought to go further, specifying what would concretely change in a rights-based approach to development, as well as suggesting some practical steps to help agencies get there.

At the most general level, there are two basic ways in which the rights-based approach to development differs from its predecessors: one relates to the fact that it is based on claims and not charity (in other words, the *goal* of development work changes), and the other relates to the way development actions are implemented (the *process* changes).

As to the first point, a human rights focus means that the nature of development work is about helping people realize claims to rights, not providing them with charity. As a result, development practitioners will begin thinking more in terms of policy, inequality, exclusion, social structures, and discrimination—and not just poverty as a fact of nature or some original state everyone departs from. Human rights act as heuristic devices, then, broadening the definition of the problems to be addressed and, consequently, profoundly changing the range of actions (and partners) that can be undertaken by development actors to promote social change. Typically, with a rights-based approach to development, the vantage point changes simultaneously from the individual to the structural and from the aggregated to the disaggregated, as well as from the technical to the political.

When arguing that human rights are claims, one immediately encounters the fact that justiciability—the capacity to adjudicate a claim before a court of law—seems impossible for many human rights (although it *is* possible for some rights and for aspects of other rights). Hence, a rights-based strategy must extend beyond a legal approach and also work on the many nonlegal, social, and political paths for ensuring enforcement of rights claims. These include the dissemination and internalization of new social norms, the mobilization of grassroots and citizen power in favor of certain rights, and the creation of ombudsmen, whistle-blowers, and other administrative complaint mechanisms.

At the end of the day, then, notwithstanding the seemingly clear and formal legal basis upon which human rights claims rest, the nature of the duties that are created by human rights claims is a deeply political and constantly shifting matter, for what is socially and legally feasible and warranted is never fixed. A rights-based approach to development is not about asserting the existence of legal claims, therefore, but about political struggles, in which human rights are tools that crystalize the moral imagination and provide power in the political struggle, but do not substitute for either. This may put development agencies in a more confrontational position toward developing country governments and social power structures (and toward other aid agencies such as the World Bank and the IMF, as well as foreign policy establishments of donor countries), but there is no way to adopt an RBA without engaging in political dynamics.

The second main aspect an RBA brings to development work is the realization that the *process* by which development aims are pursued should itself respect and fulfill human rights. Frankovits argues for the need "to apply the human rights practices to the aid program itself and not simply to attempt to assess the human rights implications of aid's outcomes" (Frankovits 1996, 125). Human rights impact assessments that focus on both the external and internal practices of development actors can be useful here. Occasional studies by human rights NGOs, confidential if necessary, could provide occasions for critical discussion and learning. An important conceptual tool is the non-retrogression rule, which states that no

progress on one human right may be justified by reductions in the enjoyment of another one. Development actors must ensure that in their attempts to promote the fulfillment of a particular right, they do not remove, violate, or decrease the preexisting attainment of another right. It
may be impossible to achieve all rights simultaneously (even though they
are on a conceptual level all equally important, indivisible, and interdependent), but it is at least possible to avoid adopting strategies that endanger, undermine, or weaken existing levels of rights enjoyment.

In the concrete practice of development work, an RBA could lead to a
wealth of activities and approaches, such as:

- Investing in the human rights law machinery. This is the most evident
  type of activity, and, while useful, may be the least crucial one.
- Supporting and building the capacity of local human rights NGOs.
  This has already been happening for a few years, especially in
  (post)conflict societies.
- Advocacy by international development actors themselves—possibly
  the first major policy change many people think of when they reflect
  on the RBA. More and more NGOs are engaging in this field, confronting major and not easily solved ethical problems related to who
  decides on the substance of the advocacy campaigns and who deter-
  mines their success.
- Adoption of a violations approach, in which development actors monitor actual violations of human rights. While fruitful for human rights
  actors, this may be too difficult and incompatible for development
  actors. Still, the latter can engage in human rights impact assessments,
  executed during the phase of project design, implementation, or evaluation. Some progressive NGOs could also subject themselves to occasional outside human rights scrutiny as learning tools for understanding the nature of an RBA. And, as said earlier, the non-retrogression
  principle could act as an important critical lens here.
- *The inward look.* For any RBA to succeed, employees need to begin
  reporting the truth about human rights matters to their superiors, to
  create explicit ethical bases for joint action, to develop explicit strategies of advocacy and protection with senior foreign staff, and to learn
  to think in advance through the likely human rights impacts of various scenarios of action. Another internal process-related aspect of the
  rights-based approach to development is for development agencies to
  set out explicitly to comply *internally* with human rights standards
  (simple matters like nondiscrimination in hiring and pay inside development agencies, for example).

- *Rule of law.* Organizations that seek to adopt a rights-based approach to development should focus their work on improving the rule of law at the level of daily life. It is worth nothing to have laws and policies—even if these laws and policies conform to human rights standards—if they are not implemented; if they are systematically circumvented; if power, money, and influence get the better of them; if there are no instances of control of and redress for the many small and large abuses of power, instances of corruption, and the like that ordinary people suffer from. Achieving rule of law is not foremost a legal matter but rather involves working on social, political, administrative, ideological, and economic dynamics, which are precisely the fields where development actors are typically active.

- *Choice of new partners.* An RBA opens the door for development actors to broaden the realm of potential partners to new organizations. They can and should work with the large array of organizations that do what human rights are all about: assuring the existence of effective claims in favor of excluded groups, developing social guarantees, and creating improvements in policy. Many local groups, often without ever saying so, "do" human rights, albeit not in the "naming and shaming" of international human rights NGOs so well known to most of us. They do it instead through grassroots organization, collective mobilization and bargaining, changing values throughout society, pushing for change in laws and policies and institutions, confronting discrimination (by governments, but also by non-state actors, whether for-profit groups or not). The sorts of relationships development actors ought to create with these groups should be long term and programmatic rather than short term and project/service delivery—away from the subcontracting relationship that still prevails in much development aid and toward genuine partnerships and with different financial modalities. The RBA, then, at the end of the day, forces donors to modify their own structures, attitudes, behaviors, and incentive systems.

A Step Back: Big Trends and Questions

There are a few basic insights about human rights in the practice of development that have resurfaced throughout this book. Admittedly, they are primarily taken from the chapter on the RBA, which, I am sure the reader will have deduced, is the only approach I believe contains the potential to provide the necessary changes in current development practice. I provide them here briefly; they do not need much explanation, as I have come back to them over and over, albeit without always naming them this way.

Human rights act as lenses, framing social problems in different ways. Human rights push the border of the moral imagination and re-conceptualize the nature of change, away from technical problems and toward policies, matters of discrimination and redress, and the responsibilities of different actors—foremost but not exclusively the state—to protect and promote certain outcomes. Rights approach matters in terms of people's dignity and the claims they have on others, which is a very different lens from the lens of overpopulation, under-productivity, over-grazing, or under-investment. To be sure, development agencies still need economists, public health specialists, agronomists, and the like, but they will work within a different and broader overall framework.

Human rights place the bar higher. With an RBA, development work is no longer just a service, a gift, an aid; it is a duty and a contribution to the creation of claims. This entails much higher obligations for those who engage in development work: their aims and their processes ought to conform to human rights standards. They must pay more attention to structures, accountability, agency, participation, nondiscrimination, transparency, and redress—applying all these to themselves as much as to local actors.

Human rights are political not legal matters. A rights-based approach to development means listening to and respectfully working with marginalized groups, not hiring more lawyers—and the same holds for positive support. Providing human rights training to employees, partners, and/or target groups may be useful, but it is not remotely what the introduction of human rights in development is about. The same holds for legal initiatives, such as support for human rights commissions, ratification of human rights treaties, rewriting of laws, or support for justice systems. While all these are necessary and important, the key issues in an RBA lie both upstream and downstream from these legal initiatives, in the social, political, ideological, cultural, and economic dynamics of societies—and in agenda setting, organization, information, and the like.[1]

Human rights are but a subset of broader social struggles, many of which can properly be said to be about rights as well. Throughout the world people engage in social struggles, making claims on not only states but also communities, enterprises, and indeed other members of the household (Cornwall and Welbourn 2002, 5). What we call human rights is a subset thereof, which has at some point in time been codified in international law and is still in the process of developing. This codification has provided these rights claims with certain strengths (a clear language, a strong claim to universality, and supposed backing by government commitment) and certain weaknesses (overly legalistic language, weak links with social movements, and, like so much international law, the absence of strong procedures for enforcement). When international domestic actors or development agencies use human rights language, they can benefit from exactly these strengths and suffer from these weaknesses.

Two important insights follow from the above: (1) these internationally codified human rights are not the only possible rights struggles, and (2) all rights struggles are local struggles. Indeed, making rights happen, as said before, is eminently a matter of local politics. Not all human rights are being struggled for in all places at all times; what is concretely fought for, and resisted, depends on local political factors—balances of power; definitions of interest and preference; opportunities for change; redefinitions in values, cultures, and attitudes; and deep economic and social trends. In addition, the rights struggles people engage in go beyond the ones defined in major human rights instruments; struggles for respect for indigenous cultures and modes of living, for the environment, for reproductive control, and for freedom of sexual orientation have all been fought without being part of the original human rights edifice. Some of these struggles (rights of indigenous peoples and reproductive rights and women's rights) have become more or less codified in international law, albeit typically in a weak manner, that is, through soft law only. Others (for example, sexual orientation and the environment) remain off the books.

Human rights allow, if not oblige, development agencies to create new alliances and partnerships with a much broader range of actors. Adopting a rights-based approach to development not only means that development practitioners should work with human rights organizations, but also that they position themselves in ongoing local rights struggles by financially, intellectually, and politically supporting all people and organizations that are engaged in such struggles; by themselves behaving in ways that conform to human rights standards; and especially, in many countries, by helping to promote conditions that allow other rights-based struggles to take shape and advance. Campaigns that combine advocacy, capacity building, and service on the ground to stop the spread of blood diamonds (involving Amnesty International, Global Witness, and development NGOs), or on treatment for HIV/AIDS (involving Physicians for Human Rights, Amnesty International, but also Oxfam, Doctors without Borders, and others)—these are all examples of the new sort of human rights–inspired coalitions that can emerge.

And yet, development actors should not become more like human rights NGOs (and international organizations). Human rights and development

NGOs (and international organizations) do not fulfill the same function, nor do they have the same position in the broader social and political scene. There are opportunities for interaction: training and critical discussion can be provided by human rights NGOs to development organizations, for example, or the latter can reasonably teach human rights NGOs something about community participation and capacity building. Especially useful for development agencies is the possibility for a human rights analysis of their work and a subsequent mainstreaming of such concerns and debates in the organization. But, by and large, I do not think that doing traditional "naming and shaming" or protection work should be the centerpiece of a human rights approach to development.

Human rights NGOs have typically remained close to the basic legal texts, for this closeness provides them with some of their strength: the solid, almost immutable legal basis, the claim to universality, the political power of the law and governments' consent with it. From this appearance of universality and objectivity they derive their strength as lobbyists, as voices of criticism, as accusers—and this has provided them with considerable power to speak out, to end certain abuses, to put pressure and speak in the name of some of the oppressed. This is important work. Development actors, however, engage in different struggles, assisting long-term dynamics of social change on the ground. I believe that they can and should do so with a human rights approach, but this does not mean that they ought to do the same things as human rights NGOs.

At the same time, there are ways to ensure principled, human rights-grounded behavior in development cooperation. At the very least, development agencies should jointly agree to minimum standards for the recipient government to follow below which they refuse to be engaged. This is not so much a matter of believing they can change the situation on the ground as of refusing to condone or become complicit. In addition, the development world should dare to be much more explicit in its analyses, reports, and interactions with local actors about the human rights violations that do take place. This is not the same as playing the naming and shaming role of major human rights NGOs. Rather, it is ending the systematic and deliberate obfuscation and self-censorship that still prevail in most development cooperation.

There is no neutrality. Clearly, a human rights approach to development has to drop the pretense of neutrality and technicality so dear to development practice. It means a focus on structural issues of inequality and power, on dynamics of exclusion and discrimination, and on institutions and processes of accountability and redress. Human rights provide the development practitioner with an intellectual language for conceptualizing these changes and a well-developed lens for approaching matters of institutional change, accountability, and politics.

Social enforcement mechanisms are crucial. An RBA is about promoting the establishment and strengthening of formal and informal, legal and nonlegal mechanisms of creating and enforcing claims. This can be done through improvements in the law and the functioning of the courts, certainly, but also through the systematic mobilization of coalitions of advocacy; the strengthening of institutions that exert grassroots and citizen power; changes in attitude and knowledge; the creation of ombudsmen, whistle-blowers, and other complaint and information exchange mechanisms; and the development of networks of social change organizations.

Human rights, like a gas, will permeate the entire development enterprise. Introducing human rights in the practice of development cannot be limited to creating a few new human rights projects, no matter how well designed they are. If agencies, whether governments, NGOs, or international organizations, profess attachment to human rights in their development aims, they must be willing to apply the rights agenda to *all of their own actions* (the inward focus) and to the global political, social, and economic dynamics within which rights problems are nested (the outward focus). In the absence of these moves, the human rights agenda is little more than a projection of power, and the world has had enough of that already.

In other words, the promotion of human rights begins at home. As with most ethically desirable aims, organizations seeking to promote human rights outcomes through the use of aid have a very easy place to start: themselves. Ensuring that their internal personnel management and decision-making procedures are nondiscriminatory, non-exclusionary, transparent, and accountable, for example, especially for field offices, may well be a minor revolution. Creating workplaces where all people—foreigners and local staff of all backgrounds—can speak freely and equally; where doubts and criticisms, including about the human rights aspects of the work, can be voiced before or during project implementation; where "doublespeak" does not reign—all of that is a necessary part of the introduction of human rights in development work. Rethinking financial and administrative procedures and systems, finally, in order to be able to work with partners in more long-term, flexible, and appropriate manners remains a priority.

The human rights approach to development demands an absolute requirement of participation and transparency, whose suspension, abrogation, or limitation is only allowable in the most extreme of circumstances. In practice, this means that aid agencies shall ensure that they provide all relevant information to those concerned, in local languages if necessary; that they strictly monitor and ensure the security of those whom they encourage to participate; that they do all that is possible to ensure that under-represented groups are brought into the process as well; that they meet all the costs (and build in the time) participation may cause, both to themselves and to the potential participants; that they ensure that their aims, assessments, resources, and constraints are known (or could be known) by all those concerned; that they multiply the mechanisms by which all this can happen; and the like. This is a deep form of participation, precisely because it is based on claims and rights and not on self-determined claims of effectiveness and sustainability (although it will also do the latter, most of the time).

The strict participation approach is not limited to the narrow confines of project implementation or even project design and selection; it is also more broadly a commitment by aid agencies to give much more priority to promoting local dialogues, to stimulating local knowledge generation and research, to finding ways of making people's voices heard by those in power—both out of respect for the dignity of people and because they are the ones who have to live with the consequences of being wrong. As a matter of fact, this may well be one of the things in which external aid agencies have a comparative advantage: to create spaces for discussion, for innovative knowledge, for thinking—and listening. Their external nature allows them to be less implicated than locals and thus to take a leadership role in the emergence of new knowledge.

Human rights are indivisible. For many observers the relation between development and human rights is all about ESC rights, which are considered the natural terrain of overlap. For others within the traditional human rights movement, it is all about development actors finally speaking out about CP rights violations. Both these approaches are incorrect. While most of what the development enterprise traditionally does indeed falls within the realm of what ESC rights are all about (food, shelter, income, and so on), development work does not automatically constitute or even lead to the provision or protection of ESC rights. In addition, in both the positive support approach and the RBAs, CP rights are crucial as well. At the end of the day, rule of law, multiple and transparent flows of information, strong social movements, the existence of administrative and social mechanisms of control and counter-power, deeply participatory processes that include the dispossessed—all these things are good for CP rights as much as for ESC rights, and vice versa, all these consist of and would not be possible without ESC and CP rights. In daily life they cannot be separated.

Finally, donors need to face up to the need to make choices, set priorities, and accept trade-offs. While most traditional human rights organizations can live with the pretension that no such choices are necessary and can simply repeat the mantra that all rights are indivisible and equally important at all times (which is true, but there is more to social change than saying that), the practice of social change very often demands that choices be made. This issue is important enough to deserve more attention.

Choices Among Rights

The human rights edifice provides no tools for making choices or setting priorities. Every specialist on some right and every committee devoted to some right—to food, to education, to water, to a clean environment, and the like—essentially "proves" that the right exists and finishes the job by arguing that this right needs to be respected, protected, and provided— period. However, as development specialists know from practical experience, there is no way that most countries in the world can achieve all of these in an "indivisible" and "simultaneous" manner, even if they sincerely wished to do so. Craig Scott lays the problem out best:

> The 1993 Vienna Declaration on Human Rights states: "All human rights are universal, indivisible and interdependent and interrelated." This trend is, on the whole, to be welcomed for its potential to promote less legalistic and category-dominated interdependence analysis. There are dangers, however, to keep in mind. One such danger is that the Vienna Declaration expresses the interconnection of human rights in so many abstract ways that it risks conveying the impression of meaningless sloganeering and thereby undermines attempts at more serious invocations of the ideas of interdependence and indivisibility. Another danger is of a flattening effect created by undifferentiated references to "all" human rights. While it is true that the interdependence of overarching, grand categories of human rights speaks to the equal importance of those broad categories for human dignity, all legally recognized human rights cannot be of equal importance. This is especially true in concrete contexts where (hopefully principled) trade-offs among human rights are sometimes necessary. Rights advocates and defenders must encourage the idea of interdependence but not to the point that it helps to promote a discourse where all human rights, and thus all human rights violations,

are treated as legally indistinguishable. (Scott 1999, 643–44; see also 648)

This debate is of great importance to the development community, which constantly faces the need to make tough choices about priorities and trade-offs (UNDP 2001, 23). The need for explicitly addressing issues of trade-off and prioritization is even more acute in post-conflict situations, where it is more likely than elsewhere that not all rights can be respected at once (including CP ones), and that tough choices need to be made (Uvin 2001; Jonathan Moore 1998).

There can be many reasons to make choices. One involves the necessity to determine priorities, as resources and administrative capacity—for both developing country governments and development aid agencies—are insufficient to make significant progress on all human rights simultaneously. In a country like Rwanda, for example, many say that "everything is a priority"—and they are right. Justice, rural development, education (up to tertiary), health, labor-intensive public works, demobilization, reconstruction of housing and infrastructure, all compete for resources, and all seem equally urgent. But the funds as well as the administrative capacity to do it all are not remotely available. How do we determine priorities in such cases, going beyond the current practice, which is that de facto priorities eventually emerge as a result of accident, personal whim, and inertia? At other times, choices need to be made between human rights as they conflict in particular instances, or between the short term and the long term, or between the rights claims of some *vs.* those of others. In this book we saw that conditionality can constitute an instance of such a conflict between rights; in Chapter 6 on the RBA, we mentioned potential trade-offs between advocacy and work on the ground as well as choices of partners—between government and civil society organizations, for example, or between NGOs who take different positions in contentious debates about religion, justice, or cost recovery.

The human rights edifice seems to provide little in the way of answers. As Karl Klare writes:

Many of the most important rights are formulated at an exceedingly high level of abstraction. . . . Thus rights concepts are sufficiently elastic so that they can mean different things to different people. But there is an even deeper problem. Even those who would consistently invoke rights in the service of self-determination, autonomy and equality find that rights concepts are internally contradictory. This is because, like all of legal discourse, rights theory is an arena of conflicting conceptions of justice and human freedom. . . . Thus choices must be made in elaborating any structure of human rights guarantees. . . . The problem is that rights discourse itself does not provide neutral decision procedures with which to make choices. (Klare 1991, 98ff.)

On what grounds should choices about these matters be made? And, just as important, by whom should such choices be made? These are questions the human rights community has hardly addressed. They are almost heretical questions, for they cast into doubt the entire basis of self-evidence and solidity upon which the entire rights edifice is built. Fundamentally, the human rights community does not like to address the issue of choice and priority, for it takes the dogma out of the religion. Human rights advocates like to behave like Moses, having come down the mountain of wisdom bearing the stone plates of progress, safe in the knowledge that they occupy the moral high ground, relaying revealed wisdom that is beyond human doubt. Yet, development practitioners who adopt an RBA need tools for making choices, for they encounter them all the time in their work.

Looking at both the literature and practice, we can distinguish five possible solutions to the trade-off/priority problem: the first is denial, the second is to allow for temporary exceptions, the third and the fourth use empirical and theoretical methods respectively for arriving at choices, and the fifth uses a participatory method to elicit the opinions of those concerned.[2]

Denial

Denial is not really a solution, but, as said before, it is the most popular way of addressing the issue of prioritization and trade-offs in the human rights literature. Like their development colleagues, human rights practitioners prefer to pretend there is no problem here. Like most people in the business of doing good, they enjoy the feeling of not being questioned too much, of relaying evident knowledge, of feeling secure that they represent the right path. This essentially consists of minimizing or trivializing the relevance or even the existence of the problem. Arjun Sengupta, the special rapporteur for the right to development, argues:

The problem [of prioritization] should not be blown out of proportion or used as a pretext for avoiding action. Many of the activities needed to fulfil these rights do not need many financial resources. They may require more input of administrative or organizational

resources whose supplies are relatively elastic, depending on political will rather than on finance or physical infrastructure. Similarly,
the resources requested may not be limited to national availability
but also can be complemented by international supply. (Sengupta
1999, par. 29)

A good deal of work by the Committee on Economic, Social and Cultural
Rights displays the same categorical optimism.

While it is true that developing countries possess significant resources
and could spend more of these resources on guaranteeing basic human
rights, it is equally true that merely asserting this fact does nothing to alter
the existence of the problem. No state in the world, including in the North,
has ever spent *all* of its resources on guaranteeing the basic rights of the
poor. None of them has ever been willing to forego military spending, or,
for that matter, any other goal. None of them will make major progress in
the direction of more equitable resource allocation overnight. Hence, in
the real world, the problems of scarcity and the need for prioritization
constantly exist, and simply defining them away is no solution. Doing so
is the typical "castle in the air" approach that has made so much human
rights writing (especially regarding ESC rights) irrelevant and easy to dis-
miss. Resources are indeed no problem in a world where every government is suddenly and exclusively committed to the realization of basic
human rights for all to the exclusion of all other concerns, knows how to
achieve this goal efficiently, and is fully supported by the international
community and international organizations. Unfortunately, this world does
not exist, and no amount of legal proselytizing will bring it into being.
Resource and priority questions, therefore, are bound to be crucial for all
people seeking social change, whether within their own communities or
across borders.

Some Legal Exceptions

It must be admitted that the legal community actually *has* developed some
answers to the question of choice, though they are rather limited in scope.
Some jurists, for example, distinguish a certain hierarchy of rights based
on their significance and solidity in international law. The criteria jurists
use to make that determination include the number of states that are parties to the instruments that provide for the right in question; whether states
that are parties to the conventions are allowed to derogate from the protection of the right; whether the right is construed as a peremptory norm;
whether the violation of the right is characterized as an international crime;

and whether the right is considered *jus cogens* (Yasuaki 1999, 117; Meron 1986). In addition, article 4 of both the 1966 covenants allows for temporary derogations of certain rights due to a state of emergency. The suspensions ought to be limited in time and subject to some process of control, and they ought to be proportionate to the challenge faced. Some rights, however, are explicitly prohibited from suspension, even in times of emergency. One can thus suppose that these rights are more inviolable, more sacred, than the others.

In addition, legal scholarship tells us that any suspension or trade-off, to the extent that it can be justified, is bound to be *temporary*; it "cannot represent an inherently desirable form of government. Such sacrifices ought to be a matter of profound regret and discomfort" (Donnelly 1999b, 72). They cannot constitute the basis for a long-term vision. They are no ideals for a healthy society; indeed, they are literally trade-offs, in which something desirable is lost, and this loss is recognized, regretted, and, to the extent possible, compensated.

It would serve the development community well to feel the same sense of regret and discomfort when it condones human rights violations in its own work, even in the name of economic growth and development. Yet, more generally, article 4 of the International Covenant on Civil and Political Rights does not serve the development practitioner very well. It deals only with one possible instance, namely, public emergencies, and it focuses on only one actor, namely, the state. All of this may be of some relevance to development practitioners as they decide whether they can ethically or legally work with a certain state that is violating human rights, or what to do during wars and natural catastrophes. It does not help them make concrete choices in the many routine and much more ordinary cases where conflicts or priorities among human rights (or development aims) exist. Article 4 of the Covenant on Economic, Social and Cultural Rights is more closely related to the kinds of issues the development practitioner typically deals with, allowing for limitations on the enjoyment of rights "for the purpose of promoting welfare in a democratic society." However, apart from telling us that such matters can at least be considered, this article, too, tells us nothing about how to implement any of this. Thus, the question remains: how should human rights and development practitioners approach the matter of choices and trade-offs among human rights?

Empirical Reasoning: The Priority of Economic Growth

The second solution is to engage in empirically based reasoning, seeking to assess on the basis of case-specific evidence to what extent claims for

---
Box 2

The International Covenant on Civil and Political Rights

Article 4.1

In time of public emergency which threatens the life of the nation and the existence of which is officially proclaimed, the States Parties to the present Covenant may take measures derogating from their obligations under the present Covenant to the extent strictly required by the exigencies of the situation, provided that such measures are not inconsistent with their other obligations under international law and do not involve discrimination solely on the grounds of race, colour, sex, language, religion or social origin.

Article 4.2

No derogation from articles 6, 7, 8 (paragraphs 1 and 2), 11, 15, 16 and 18 may be made under this provision.

Other rights specifically mentioned include:
- the right to life; also, no derogation is possible from the obligations expressed in the Genocide Convention; right to seek amnesty, pardon, or commutation of a death sentence; no death penalty for people under eighteen or for pregnant women. (Article 6)
- no torture, or cruel, inhuman or degrading punishments. (Article 7)
- no slavery or keeping of people in servitude, except in prisons. (Article 8)
- no imprisonment for inability to fulfill contractual obligations. (Article 11)
- no one can be held for something not a crime when the act occurred; punishment cannot be harsher than the punishment when the act occurred. (Article 15)
- the right to appear as a person before the law. (Article 16)
- the right to freedom of conscience, thought, and religion; states must have respect for parents to raise children in conformity with their own beliefs. (Article 18)

The International Covenant on Economic, Social and Cultural Rights

Article 4

The States Parties to the present Covenant recognize that, in the enjoyment of those rights provided by the State in conformity with the present Covenant, the State may subject such right only to such limitations as are determined by law only in so far as this may be compatible with the nature of these rights and solely for the purpose of promoting welfare in a democratic society.

trade-offs or priorities are justified and what kind of choices and temporary derogations are allowable. As it stands, such empirical analysis is entirely missing from the human rights literature (Bauer and Bell 1999, 22), and, indeed, fundamentally contrary to its mode of functioning. One possible method for such an empirical approach could be anthropological, with decisions about priorities being made on the basis of specialists' deep understanding of specific local cultural and religious norms and practices (see the discussion in Chapter 2 on the "empirical" and "incremental change" solutions to the Eurocentrism charge).

In practice in the development community, by far the most common empirical approach to make choices has been of an economic nature. The yardstick here is efficiency: experts seek to determine, based on economic data and models, which activities—or possibly rights—have the highest pay-off or which ones will bring about the highest rate of economic growth, on the basis of the argument that this, in turn, will facilitate the achievement of other rights.[3] The advantages of this empirical approach are many. It is scientific, building on the foundations of the most quantitatively rigorous of all social sciences. It employs the language of economics, a politically powerful language that has dominated development thinking for decades. In addition, economics provides us with a set of tools to think analytically through the trade-offs and policy choices we are discussing here. It is exceedingly good at working through the short-term and long-term effects of a given action, for example, or at apprehending the often unintended consequences of an action taken for one specific purpose on another area of human life. Finally, economic criteria hold the promise of constant improvement: choose this option and not only can you make scientifically based choices about priorities right now, but in addition your need to make such choices will automatically decrease as economic growth increases the size of the resource pie (assuming the gains from growth are distributed progressively). The resource optimism of economists—given the right incentives, every pie can grow forever, and when it grows, everyone's piece will be bigger and tastier—is very appealing. There are, however, a number of problems with this strategy.

The first is most evident: economic growth does not automatically lead to improvements in human rights or well-being for all, and significant progress can be made at very different levels of national income. The extent to which economic growth produces benefits for all, instead of for a small minority, depends partly on the degree of popular participation, democracy, accountability, and lack of repression that exist within the polity—in other words, the realization of at least some human rights precedes any such empirical economic calculation. If all economic pies were equally or justly distributed, there would be no struggles about economic and social rights! So, clearly, while economic reasoning may be of importance, it cannot act as the sole criterion for addressing rights choices.

Still, it seems likely that with economic growth the possibility of countries being able to protect and promote a larger range of rights for a larger number of people increases. In addition, the opposite is certainly true: there is overwhelming evidence that, in the *absence* of economic growth, poverty and inequality always increase, and with them the enjoyment of rights declines for many, if not most, poor people. Hence, at the very least one could make the strong point that, all things being equal, if trade-offs or setting priorities among human rights are required, those choices that do not (or least) retard economic growth should be privileged.

But even this does not solve the matter, for three very fundamental reasons. One is that usually all things are *not* equal, and determining priorities and trade-offs by their likely economic impact may amount to a less than optimal rights strategy. As Arjun Sengupta observes: "Those rights that require least expenditures of the resources which are most binding or in short supply will tend to be realized first. There is a risk that this may, as a result, fail to bring about the social change that is the ultimate objective of following the rights approach to development" (Sengupta 1999, par. 31). In addition, once we get to these choices, we enter squarely into the domain of uncertainty, for opinions clearly differ dramatically, even among economists, on the best way to achieve growth, the best ways to deal with the efficiency-equity trade-off—or even the exact nature of that trade-off. Once one leaves the domain of mainstream US economics, one finds fundamental disagreements on almost all trade-offs and policy issues. And finally, the resource constraints that underlie the need to set priorities and/or make trade-offs are themselves political in nature, the result of past choices—choices in which, very often, human rights were trampled. For example, the poverty prevalent in so many countries, or among specific groups, is not a natural fact only; it may result from past practices of colonization, exploitation, or marginalization. Economics is totally unequipped to face up to history, whereas a human rights approach could and should. In short, a human rights approach demands that we question the status quo, render explicit the concerns of the oppressed and the poor when thinking through policies, and not take resource constraints as natural givens but to treat them as the results of past choices. In practical terms, then, a strong human rights approach seems to lend strong credence to a significant national and international redistribution of incomes and assets (Schacter 1983, 4020), whereas a strong economist approach does the opposite, almost always disfavoring any form of redistribution.

Purely economic discussions, then, typically provide no answer to the "choices among rights" questions, for they take place in a parallel universe in which rights questions simply do not exist—and the opposite seems to be the case as well, with much human rights work taking place in a world in which economic limitations or dynamics seem mysteriously not to exist (for exceptions, see Steiner 1998; Tomasevski 2003). Clearly, there are dramatic differences in treating certain things as good (as economists do) *vs.* treating them as rights. Three decades ago, in a time more inclined to radical scholarship than now, Susan George wrote *How the Other Half Dies* (1974), a book about world hunger that deeply influenced me and countless other people (she is still around, playing a significant role in the ineptly named anti-globalization movement). One of the key insights of that book was that in our current world food is a good and not a right. Imagine how different our agricultural and food systems would be if food were a right and not a good! In 2003 Katarina Tomasevski, the current rapporteur for the right to education, made a similar analysis, juxtaposing approaches that treat education as a good and those that treat it as a right. Treating such things as rights rather than goods should not automatically mean one is anti-market or ignorant of opportunity costs and economic constraints; it should mean, however, that one applies a different lens, a different starting point and end point, when thinking about matters like education and food. Most development work these days implicitly or explicitly works within a goods framework, adding social concerns preferably in "marketized" terms such as *human resource investment*. A rights perspective, whether applied to development work or to social change in the rich countries, would constitute a dramatic change, especially if it managed to take matters of opportunity cost and incentives seriously.

One of the most important challenges facing scholars and activists is to develop a language, a framework, a methodology for conversations between economic thinking and rights thinking. Such an integration could be based on the recognition by human rights specialists that choices and policies that most favor economic growth are superior (and that, hence, they ought to try to understand these choices), and the acceptance by economists that choices that least violate human rights (and protect and promote them as well) are also superior. Development practitioners could be at the forefront of this search for a better integration between the economics and the human rights lenses.

Theoretical Reasoning: Basic Rights

The third solution has been developed by Henry Shue in his seminal 1980 book, *Basic Rights,* in which he attempts to reason through the issue of priorities rather than to solve it empirically. He sets out to define a subset of rights that can be seen as taking priority over others. Shue then defines basic rights as *those required for the enjoyment of all other rights,* that is, those without which no other right could be meaningfully said to exist. He identifies three such categories of basic rights: subsistence or minimal economic security; physical security (that is, "not to be subjected to murder, torture, mayhem, rape, or assault"); and liberty. Together these constitute "everyone's minimum reasonable demands upon the rest of humanity" (Shue 1980, 19). Shue explicitly allows for the fact that "if a right is basic, other, non-basic rights may be sacrificed, if necessary, in order to secure the basic right" (Shue 1980, 19). He thus offers us a compelling criterion for setting priorities and making trade-offs. Note that Shue takes great care to argue that these basic rights are not more valuable or more satisfying or somehow morally superior than the other human rights. They are merely functional and operational—a matter of sequencing, not of assigning value.

Such a basic rights approach allows nonspecialist practitioner organizations to define a minimum of core rights about which there can be no doubt—rights that cannot be traded off or made secondary to other concerns. This is an appealing idea. However, the devil lies in the details. Shue does not attempt to tackle the extraordinarily difficult task of specifying the concrete and complete list of basic rights, even using his own criteria. As Jack Donnelly demonstrates, once one actually attempts to do so in a logically and ethically consistent manner, it is not clear if it can be done without more or less reconstructing the entire human rights system, save dropping a few evident ones such as the right to paid holidays (Donnelly 1989, 38ff.).

As we discussed earlier, Oxfam recently developed a list of five key rights as a basis for its operations (Oxfam International 2001, 7, 9). The choices—the right to a sustainable livelihood, the right to basic social services, the right to life and security, the right to be heard, and the right to an identity—suffer from the same problem as Shue's basic rights choices: once one starts spelling out what is required to achieve these rights, it seems one basically ends up reaffirming the entire human rights edifice—a testament to the truthfulness of the claims to indivisibility, certainly, but not of much use in a world where choices must be made.

Still, one could argue that while the definition of a minimum set of basic rights can never be 100 percent foolproof, it is still relevant and useful for development actors, for whom *any* set of basic rights, no matter how short, no matter how intellectually shaky, is better than the current agnosticism toward rights. Such a set can be relatively limited, for agencies can justify being specialized in certain domains—economics tells us there are major gains from specialization. In other words, more specialized agencies can very usefully redefine their existing mandate—health, HIV/AIDS, education, children, whatever—in human rights terms, and, from there, develop a limited set of rights to focus on (not because these rights are somehow more important, but because these agencies are specialized and thus possibly more efficient).

Participatory Methods

Both the previous solutions—the economist's one of selecting the right with the greatest pay-off in terms of growth or Shue's method of defining a subset of basic rights that need to be satisfied before all others—are expert-based solutions in which outsiders develop the tools allowing them to make tough choices (see also Sano 2000, 748). The following solution differs from these two in this respect.

The last solution is participatory, consisting of the development of mechanisms that allow those most concerned to play an active role in setting priorities or making trade-off of rights. This strategy follows from the human rights approach itself, which, as we saw, strongly stresses deep participation, transparency, and empowerment (Sengupta 1999, par. 32; Donnelly 1999a). Both ethically and legally, when aid agencies need to make tough choices on how to spend their resources in a given community, the key criterion ought to be the opinion of the people concerned themselves (even if they do not express these choices in rights terms). This is also the solution I have repeatedly advocated throughout this book.

A human rights approach dictates that utmost care be taken to associate those concerned with the tough choices that affect them—a requirement significantly more stringent than current development practice. For people to participate, they need information and knowledge, and consequently any human rights approach to development cares very much about donor clarity and transparency. As DFID's "Principles for a New Humanitarianism" states: "We recognize that humanitarian intervention in conflict situations often poses genuine moral dilemmas. We will base our decision on explicit analyses of the choices open to us and the ethical considerations involved, and communicate our conclusions openly to our partners" (as cited in Smillie 1998, 67). The resulting clarity may benefit frank discussion and mutual understanding among donors, send clearer signals to recipients, and increase donor credibility.

A Fear: Is This Agenda Too Interventionist?

In this book, I have lauded and encouraged the willingness of donors to become more politically explicit, to engage in human rights struggles, to define their mandate more broadly. At the same time, I have repeatedly voiced my fears and misgivings about the questions of power, of interventionism, and of who decides.

Indeed, I worry that much of the agenda I have described in this book produces a broad license to intervene and thus a dramatic extension of the power of outsiders. It is us, the outsiders, who are redefining our mandate to include more facets of poor societies, ranging from the overtly political to the deeply personal. So, while I applaud the move away from the dominant reductionist and technical approaches of the past, I shudder at the thought of the limitless intervention seemingly condoned if not morally justified by the emerging agenda.

This critique pertains especially to the extension of the development mandate to include all that relates to both human rights and conflict prevention. Historically, pressure for human rights (defined as CP rights only) has been selectively applied by wealthy citizens in rich countries to poor countries and often consisted of the use of Western military might in poor parts of the world. Michael Ignatieff writes: "As the West intervenes ever more frequently but ever more inconsistently in the affairs of non-western societies, the legitimacy of its rights standard is put into question. Human rights is increasingly the language of moral imperialism just as ruthless and just as self-deceived as the imperialism of yesteryear" (Ignatieff 1999, 13). As a result, while "a right of humanitarian intervention has prevailed," it occurred "not by virtue of international consensus, but as an unwilling concession to Western power" (Ignatieff 2000, 6). And he adds: "All unlimited forms of power are open to abuse, and there is no reason why power that legitimizes itself in the name of human rights does not end up as tyrannous as any other. Those who will end up with more power may only be those who have power already; the coalitions of the willing, the Western nations with the military might necessary for any successful human rights intervention" (Ignatieff 2000, 10). These wise words did not stop Ignatieff from enthusiastically endorsing the Iraqi war less than three years later (Ignatieff 2003; for similar positions by prestigious moral authorities see Wiesel 2003; Ramos Horta 2003).

The same fear holds, for that matter, for the extension of the development aid mandate into conflict resolution, which is also currently taking place (and which obviously interacts with the human rights debates we had in this book, as the relation among human rights violations, conflict, and development are obvious). This agenda also constitutes a major extension of the development mandate, and another justification for more intervention in the name of the good. As donors, working in pre- or post-conflict societies engage in matters that are deeply political, domestic, complicated, and uncertain, while at the same time being totally unaffected by the effects of their choices (if things go wrong, they're on the next plane out) or unconstrained by domestic control over these choices (they owe accountability only to their sources of funding), I believe the whole venture of extending the mandate of the development enterprise faces major—David Rieff would argue insurmountable—ethical problems. As I wrote elsewhere:

> Taken to its extreme, the new post-conflict agenda . . . amounts to a license for interventionism so deep and unchecked it resembles neo-colonialism: in the name of a totalizing, missionary-style ideology (based on a deeply romanticized vision of the situation "at home"), foreigners are encouraged to make deeply interventionist life or death decisions for other societies, unbound by outside control, unconstrained by procedure, unaffected by outcomes. (Uvin 2001; see also Rieff 2002a; Chandler 2001; for an excellent case study of East Timor, see Chopra 2002).

Things become even worse in those cases where the development enterprise has become intertwined with the military and foreign-policy establishment, as has often been the case in recent years: Kosovo, Afghanistan, Iraq (these are precisely the sort of cases Rieff focuses on). At such a point the development enterprise is part and parcel of a violently coercive and interventionist machinery, which often couches itself in the rhetoric of human rights and development. I do not believe (or hope) that these cases are the norm or even the harbingers of things to come; they are exceptions, which have always existed and always will, but they do not constitute the rule. As a result, I do not want to generalize from them. It seems that the number of these exceptions has increased compared with historical trends during the last decade, but I surmise it will fall again over the next, as US missionary zeal is bound to decline (Lieven 2003). This book has focused less on the highly political cases and more on the ordinary ones, where the largest (but not the most visible) share of development aid takes place. That said, I share with Rieff the fear that current trends in the aid enterprise provide too much license for intervention by foreigners (which they will often do heavy-handedly if not militarily) and are too often un-matched by knowledge, legitimacy, modesty, or accountability.

I do not believe that the answer is to cease all development aid; that is the easy solution that is popular among academics in need for a quick fix. As Mary Anderson states: "It is a moral and logical fallacy to conclude that because aid can do harm, a decision *not* to give aid would do no harm" (Anderson 1999, 2). This moral responsibility to act in solidarity and in favor of social change—and at the same time intelligently, self-critically, consciously—is stronger because often those who favor human rights and peace are not the powerful but the weak, and all of us who can ought to take their side (Anderson 1999, 68). Nor is the answer to main-tain aid but return to the previous narrower, "cleaner" practice (this is what Rieff advocates for humanitarian aid). I can understand the tempta-tion, and I myself, in my professional practice, have sometimes nostalgi-cally recalled the "good old days" when things were so much simpler, more straightforward, and I felt less that I was constantly fighting to stay afoot on a slippery slope. But the past practice is what allowed the devel-opment community to become horrendously caught up in, and even to feed into or magnify, the dynamics of exclusion and violence. It is not a practice to return to; it deserves to be jettisoned.

It seems to me, then, that *the development community must find ways to counter the necessary expansion of its mandate with an equally neces-sary reduction in its power, its capacity for conceptualization and initia-tive, its control over finances, and its lack of accountability.* This with-out doubt very hard to achieve, for almost everything—vast gaps in knowledge and wealth; institutionalized systems of inequality; dominant attitudes and paradigms; bureaucratic constraints—creates incentives for outsiders to be in the driver's seat, to control the flows of information and money and decisions. As Alex de Waal states with typical eloquence and bluntness, writing about humanitarian assistance:

> Within the specialist institutions there are sharp differences of opin-ion and interest, which give the appearance of lively debate. But none of this debate questions whether famine relief, or any other form of emergency response, should be controlled by international 'experts,' any more than warring barons ever contemplated the abolition of feudalism. (De Waal 1997, 70)

How, then, to deal with this conundrum?

There is no magical solution to this problem, which lies at the heart of all social struggles that bring together people from different backgrounds, classes, cultures, opportunities, and resources. In the case of international development aid, I can see a few imperfect paths for change that, if added to what I have suggested in this book, may limit the worst excesses of unchecked interventionism and the pretenses of moral high ground.

One path is the radical capacity building approach we already discussed, which entails a transfer of the power of initiative and conceptualization to local actors. When combined with a deep commitment to participation (Chopra 2002) and a strong contractual approach—with clear procedures for negotiation and criteria for suspension—this way of working can overcome many of the fears I discussed in the previous paragraphs. Admittedly, a solution like this, which is based on a voluntary abandonment of power by donors, is not likely to be adopted rapidly or widely, although cognitive and attitudinal change *is* possible. Maybe, as time goes by, recipients of aid will demand such a radical capacity building approach—the transfer of power, then, will not be voluntary only, but forced, demanded—and thus more likely to work.

A second path forward lies, I believe, in social movements using human rights as a tool to focus on reform in the international political economy. This trend redirects the human rights spotlight back onto the rich countries and their citizens (including those who are development professionals) and the global international political economy in which rich country corporations and citizens occupy such a privileged position. From a legal perspective, two processes are at play here, and both are very new and highly contested. One is a merger of international economic law (the law that deals with economic transactions, such as contracts, disputes, investments, trade flows) and human rights law. The other is the extension of the parties concerned by human rights obligations to include private corporations, individuals, and third states (if not the famous but vague "international community" as well). The overall aim of this process is to rethink and reorient the dynamics of international economic governance toward its impact on development—to add "development" as part of a "quality assurance" mechanism for the global governance system (Slinn 1999, 317). From a development perspective, the main novelty here is that development is not considered to be something that is missing, something to be solved "out there" in hot and poor countries, but an issue that binds us all as global citizens. As Oxfam states:

Global citizenship . . . concerns many aspects of our daily lives:
- How we inform ourselves about other peoples and their cultures;

- The daily choices we make as shoppers, holiday-makers and investors;
- How we welcome strangers and refugees and question stereotypes;
- How we respond to humanitarian crises in countries far away from our own;
- The attitudes we communicate to our children, colleagues, neighbors and friends;
- The political choices we make as citizens. (Oxfam International 2001)

All this does not necessarily immediately undo the dangers of interventionism as described in previous pages. Rather, it weakens the temptation of claiming the moral high ground, it redirects the spotlight of human rights and development inquiry and criticism back to the rich countries and their citizens, it allows for mutual claims to be created, and it permits for new coalitions of change to emerge.

The third path is for the development enterprise to do far less, but to do it far better—and within a rights framework. For some time now I have been suggesting to colleagues—totally devoid of success, by the way—that they need to reduce dramatically their areas of operation. This is so for two main reasons: first, to provide much more space for local social forces to define the future and engage in social struggle for it; and second, in order to do at least something well, rather than everything halfway (if that). I have argued that the development community seriously consider a policy of engaging in each country in only three or four sectors, areas, or goals, while staying entirely out of all the rest. These sectors could be chosen according to the specific and urgent needs of each country, or they could be set in a fixed manner for the whole world—there are advantages and disadvantages to each system.

Such an approach could be implemented through country-specific compacts, in which the international community negotiates with the government and society a limited set of areas the international community will massively invest in for the long run, and the modalities for this investment, as well as minimal human rights–based suspension clauses. A strong a priori would exist in favor of investing in education, nutrition, and health, as well as in doing so in rights terms. In other words, this approach would then amount to a basic rights approach, in which the international community seeks to guarantee every single person in the world access to the key elements of the right to life.

Financially, this is possible. In *Human Development Report 1997*, the UNDP calculated the annual cost over a period of ten years of providing every single person in the world with basic social services. The estimated cost for basic education is $6 billion; for basic health and nutrition $13 billion; for reproductive health and family planning $12 billion; and for water and sanitation $9 billion. Even if these are underestimated and if one should add other sectors—the fight against HIV/AIDS would surely increase the cost—these are still affordable figures.

There are multiple advantages to this radical approach. It avoids the current difficulties with sovereignty and especially people's empowerment: it does not seek to run people's lives but leaves that up to the people themselves. It does not seek to mold political dynamics, not because it considers them unimportant, but because it treats them as people's own business (and also because it has a healthy sense of limitation as to its own intelligence and foresight in making political decisions for others). It does guarantee absolute key elements in both equitable economic growth and political empowerment: the right to life (nutrition and health) and the right to education. Another advantage to such an approach is that it provides an original way to deal with the fungibility issue; because much of the funding for these few sectors would replace domestic investments, the governments concerned would receive budget support. This fungibility is encouraged here. Those governments that are already spending a significant amount of funds on programs to guarantee these rights would receive much more de facto budget support than those that are not—a situation that rewards those governments with better social sector track records over those with worse ones.

One of the most vocal proponents of such a redefinition has been Arjun Sengupta, the independent expert on the right to development. Since 1999 he has argued for a "development compact," a long-term understanding between rich and poor countries focusing on a few well-defined minimum rights, namely, the rights to food, to primary health care, and to primary education (Sengupta 2000a, 573; Sengupta 1999, par. 65ff.; Sano 2000, 744–45), while not lowering the level of enjoyment of any other right, including the CP ones (non-retrogression). If this is done, he argues—if significant progress is made by governments, supported by the international community, in realizing these basic indicators of the right to development without simultaneously lowering the enjoyment of any other right—there will be definite progress toward realizing the right to development.

A development compact along these lines could be constructed as an entitlement to all people throughout the world, conferring a duty on all members of the international community, and especially on those who are most in a position to afford the cost, that is, its richest members. Like the French "Revenu Minimal d'Insertion," all persons in the world would automatically be entitled to enjoy these rights, not in return for any action or behavior or ideology but as a simple result of being human, of being a citizen of this world; similarly, it would be incumbent on those who are in a position to do so to engage actively in seeking to make these rights realities. Such a compact would reaffirm our joint citizenness and humanity, that we all live on the same planet and are similar human beings, and that for all of us there are certain unquestionable rights—so fundamental and inherent that nothing can abrogate them—rights that the entire world community guarantees. Investment in these rights, then, is not an act of charity or a quid pro quo for certain desirable behaviors; neither is it a duty that simply follows from international law. Rather, then, it must be a citizens' affirmation of the fact that we all truly have become global citizens. In this deeply interconnected and globalized world where we wear on any single day sneakers made in Indonesia and garments sewn in El Salvador, Bangladesh, and Romania; drink Kenyan coffee; get our computers repaired by Indian software consultants; talk to Barbados-based travel agents before taking off for our Nepalese hiking holiday; play with baseballs sewn in the Dominican Republic, and so on—in this world, it makes sense to conceive of a certain social minimum we all guarantee nobody should be without. This is not because of charity but because of our joint humanity and daily interconnectedness; that is, tomorrow, any of them may make our next favorite shoes, study at our universities, guide us on exciting holidays, watch over or marry our children, mow our lawns, buy our computers. We are in this together.

Notes

Introduction
1. The right to food is probably the most well developed of all ESC rights; hence, the situation is even worse in all other fields of development.
2. See the Center for Human Rights and Conflict Resolution website.
3. Note that my professional experience is almost exclusively in sub-Saharan Africa, which is bound to color my insights. Most important, I am likely to over-estimate the impact of aid and foreigners in my writing, as the footprint of the development community is much bigger in African countries than elsewhere.

Chapter 1
1. The General Assembly was then a body of forty-eight states, of which fourteen were Western countries (all in favor), thirty-five third-world countries (thirty-three in favor, including India, Pakistan, Cuba, Egypt, Iran, Iraq; the two that abstained were Saudi Arabia and South Africa), and seven communist countries (all abstained, with the exception of China); two countries were not present to vote.
2. The United States still took twenty-six years to ratify even this covenant and did so with so many reservations and understandings that it substantially nullified its effect. It took until 1998 for China to ratify.

Chapter 2
1. For some excellent discussions, see An-Na'im 1992; Steiner and Alston 2000, part B.
2. Some of the major developing countries such as India, China, Cuba, Lebanon, Panama, Egypt, and the Philippines also played a role in its drafting and voted in favor; see Glendon 2002.
3. Donnelly 1999b, 68; Tatsuo 1999, 31 ff.; Ignatieff 1999. Arjun Sengupta argues that human rights are deeply imbued with the values of free-market systems, but Donnelly adds the important corrective that this is more the European, welfare-state, market system than the one that is prevalent in the United States or Hong Kong.
4. Perhaps the most important author taking such a position is Martha Nussbaum.
5. Nussbaum 1997, 275. For a nice overview of various critiques, see Kennedy 2002.
6. Nussbaum argues that this is so because of the phenomenon of "adaptive preferences": people at the bottom of society often lower their expectations of life, to the extent of considering their fate normal and deserved, while those who are used to great luxury may deeply resent not having more (Nussbaum 1997).

7. I must admit that I am giving short shrift here to an extremely rich and rewarding literature. Authors such as Rawls, Nussbaum, and many other political philosophers surely have thought of these criticisms as well and tried to deal with them, including in the few works I cite here, but following their arguments would take us very far indeed.

8. Bauer and Bell 1999, 17; for a very important case-specific discussion, see Kingsbury 1999, 367.

9. See the example by Steiner and Alston at the end of their female genital mutilation discussion (2000, 412ff.).

10. For excellent discussions of what has been called post-developmentalism, see Rahnema 1997; Nederveen Pieterse 2001; Peet 1999; Schuurman 1993.

11. Craven 1995, 109; de Feyter 2001, 262; Windfuhr 2000. Asbjorn Eide, a specialist on the right to food who is generally seen as the father of this division, actually distinguishes an additional level between the second and the third, namely, the obligation to *facilitate* or *promote* (states must promote activities intended to strengthen people's access to and utilization of resources and means to ensure their livelihood, including food security) (Eide 1995, 32–33). This level, while a very interesting one, seems not to be used by others, however, so we will stick to the usual triple categorization.

12. E-mail, André Frankovits, June 18, 2001; see also the tables in Frankovits 2000.

13. See Paul 1995; Bunn 2000, 1431; Marks 1999, 340; Sengupta 2000b, par. 29; Perry 1996, 227.

14. Primarily in the General Assembly and in the UN Conference on Trade and Development (UNCTAD), a newly created organization designed to counter the General Agreement on Tariffs and Trade's (GATT's) hegemony and to promote international commodity agreements, control over multinational corporations, and greater concessional resource flows between rich and poor countries. The organization's heydays ended in 1983, when the Reagan administration, followed by its Thatcher counterpart in the UK, unceremoniously ended its funding.

15. Quoted in Slinn 1995, 270; see also Craig Scott 1999, 643-44.

16. The declaration contains ten articles; the full text is available online at the UNHCHR website.

17. Any right to development aid was deliberately not mentioned (Slinn 1995, 275; see also Rosas 1995, 249-50); de Feyter goes on to discuss at some length the fact that there are no legal commitments of developed states to contribute to the development of populations in poor countries (de Feyter 2001, 23).

18. The text is available online at the UNHCHR website. Very similar wording also can be found in article 3 of the Cairo Programme of Action.

Chapter 3

1. The few exceptions I know of include FIAN (Food First Information and Action Network) and Equality Now. FIAN, an organization devoted to the right to food, was created in the late 1980s in Germany; during the 1990s it became more international, with offices and memberships in more than ten countries. Equality Now was founded in 1992 "to work for the promotion and protection of the human rights of women around the world" (Equality Now website). Colleagues often tell me that in the Third World there are human rights organizations devoted to "development" types of rights, but they typically offer no references, and I have not personally encountered many during my years in Africa.

Chapter 4

1. UNDP 1992; see also Tomasevski, quoted in Sano 2000, n. 39. This is undoubtedly related to the dictates of the Cold War.

2. Tomasevski 1993; Donnelly argues that "electoral democracy . . . falls far short of the demands of internationally recognized human rights" (Donnelly 1999a, 618), and, on the next page, "because rights of democratic participation are but a small set of internationally recognized human rights, the struggle for human rights is not only much more than the struggle for democracy, but also fundamentally different in character." Elizabeth Spiro Clark offers an argument that elections *are* the key, for they will eventually bring about the other conditions for a full-blown democracy (Spiro Clark 2000).

3. The African, Caribbean, and Pacific countries, consisting of mostly but not exclusively former colonies with whom the European Union creates five-year treaties governing all economic relations.

4. Of course, the ethical dilemma of aid conditionality and poverty can also run the other way around: if disbursements of foreign aid are at least partly guided by the needs of the poor, recipients, anticipating this, have little incentive to improve the welfare of the poor (Ostrom 2002). This is the oft-discussed disincentive effect of all aid.

5. This can go either way. During the 1980s, Central American allies of the United States received World Bank funding even though both their economic and political track records were bad, because of US pressure to stabilize their regimes. In the 1990s, on the other hand, the World Bank, notwithstanding its opposition to explicit human rights criteria, again under pressure from the United States, delayed or suspended loans to recipient countries for human rights reasons—China for a few months after Tiananmen, Burma, and Serbia are a few cases (see Forsythe 1997, 346, among others).

6. With the support of human rights luminaries as Elie Wiesel (2003) and Jose Ramos Horta (2003). I find myself much closer to the position of David Rieff (2002b) here.

7. "Conditionality is largely impotent as a driver of change" (DFID 2002, 13); "Conditionality as an instrument to promote reform has been a failure" (Deverajan et al. 2001); "Punitive political conditionality is an inadequate strategy to respond to crises of governance" (Santiso, 2002, 4); "What is surprising to see is that donors continue to cling to conditionalities against the prevailing understanding that conditionalities do not work and that they have humanitarian consequences" (Atmar 2001, 6). Atmar is current minister of Rural Development in the government of Afghanistan.

8. As Göran Holmqvist perceptively observes, the argument that conditionality does not work because recipients are always capable of resisting and subverting it seems implicitly to contradict the argument that conditionality cannot work because it is highly destructive of internal mechanisms for learning, accountability, and political change (Holmqvist 2000, 1-2).

9. For an interesting piece of contestation in favor of a more comprehensively conditional approach, see Neiss 2001.

10. The fungibility issue refers to the fact that even if aid is allocated to a specific project, it basically amounts to little more than savings for the government if the latter would have undertaken that project anyway. As a result, to the extent that fungibility exists, aid underwrites the entire government program and not the specific project it manifestly funds. There exists a long tradition of trying to determine empirically to what extent aid has been fungible; more recently, however,

following World Bank research, it has suddenly become agreed upon that *all* aid is basically fungible. While this may be a handy stylized fact for the development of economic models, it seems strangely at odds with the real facts; that is, if all aid were fungible, then the government would have funded with its own resources all of the expenditures aid finances—a logical impossibility, for the government's own budget without aid is by definition much smaller.

11. The rational of this name is that in traditional conditionality, the desired policy is negotiated first, and aid is then provided in conjunction with—and as a reward for—its implementation. With selectivity, the aid arrives *after* the policy. Governments have shown, through their actual behavior, that they implement good policies, and on the basis of that donors afterward allocate funds.

12. This is a complicated matter, which should be solvable through analytical means, but, of course, has not. Proponents of selectivity answer the ethical question by arguing that *not* giving aid to countries with good government policies is unethical, for it means that people who could have been lifted out of poverty through the judicial use of aid are not. Paul Collier and David Dollar argue that a redistribution of aid only to countries with good government policies would lift twenty million more people out of poverty than the current distribution (Collier and Dollar 1998). Other scholars dispute these data and develop econometric models suggesting that aid given purely according to poverty criteria lifts more people out of poverty than the same amount of aid disbursed on the basis of government effectiveness criteria (selectivity) (see, e.g., Beynon 2001; Hansen and Tarp 1999; Mosley and Hudson 2001).

13. According to Stephen Fidler, the breadth and vagueness of this project are deeply disliked within the World Bank itself (Fidler 2001).

14. Our colleagues in the military could possibly change the offending behavior through military means, but that is of course a totally different (and potentially highly worrisome) matter. David Rieff has this to say on the matter: "In theory, of course, those agencies that believed it was appropriate for them to withdraw when the regimes they had to deal with 'descended' below a certain human rights standard were not necessarily endorsing the doctrine of humanitarian military intervention. But in practice, they were increasingly unable to resist such calls, whether these were voiced by the powerful governments that funded them, private donors who had been persuaded by the idea of the right of intervention, or field-workers from within their own organizations" (Rieff 2002a, 321; see also Chandler 2001). It is not my aim to endorse such a slide. As should be clear from this book, forceful intervention, especially bilaterally, deeply worries me; too easily, the powerful manage to cloak their ambitions and pretensions in the garb of humanitarianism.

Chapter 5

1. There could still be a value to such action by NGOs, but it would reside not in their capacity to force change through their sheer weight, but rather in their capacity to put things on the agenda by taking visible actions that upset the status quo. This is what Médecins Sans Frontières (MSF)-France attempted, for example, when it withdrew from the refugee camps in Zaire in 1995 (see Terry 2002 for a good analysis). Note that MSF's action failed to produce the desired results.

2. "Even activities that appear highly apolitical or technical have the potential for unanticipated political consequence" (Wozniak Shimpp 1992). However, USAID admits that "the Agency's operating environment and institutional culture are

neither conducive to nor supportive of DG [democracy and governance] linkages with other sectors" (USAID 2001).

3. In August 1997 the executive board of the IMF adopted new guidelines regarding governance issues, allowing the IMF to deal with political matters insofar as it has "a significant impact on macroeconomic performance and the ability of the government to pursue policies aimed at sustainable growth" (IMF 1997). This constitutes an update of the same position.

4. For good overviews of the literature, see Rueschemeyer 1991; Tilly 1995; Bratton and van de Walle 1997, chap. 1; Mahoney 2003.

5. See this interesting quote from Thede: "Thus, the major characteristic of the shift towards democracy-building in the 1990s is that, although it has become a legitimate area for bilateral and multilateral involvement, democracy itself is depoliticized in the approaches of major funders. This depoliticization is manifested, for example, in the reluctance to recognize democracy as a system of contained conflict, rather than consensus" (Thede 2002, 2-3).

6. As Mark Duffield and his co-authors correctly observe about international aid to Afghanistan during the Taliban regime: "Promoting community forms of governance in a totalitarian environment means, in effect, that the UN is encouraging a political opposition" (Duffield et al. 2001, 9).

7. See also Lijphardt 1999; Beetham 1995; Held 1997; Diamond 1999; Bratton and van de Walle 1997; as well as practitioners such as Carothers 2002, 15; Thede 2002, 3.

8. As Nancy Thede, looking back at ten years of work by Rights and Democracy, Canada's main democracy promotion NGO (created by Parliament) says: "These lessons actually complicate rather than simplify our vision of democratic development. What we have learned takes us farther away from a simple formula for democratization. We cannot produce a manual on good democratic development, or even a booklet of 'best practices.' And by all means, *we should not*" (Thede 2002, 21).

9. Hearn 1999, 22. The organizations are human rights NGOs, women's organizations, and, in Ghana, organizations promoting economic liberalization (see Robinson 1996; Mendelson 2001).

10. "Citizenship must be an active condition of struggling to make rights real" (Phillips 1991, 76).

11. For these ideas I am deeply indebted to the work of Sue Unsworth, a senior DFID employee who has over the last years published some of the best work on positive support I have seen. The text in this paragraph closely mirrors an unpublished text we co-authored on donor policy to civil society in Rwanda (Unsworth and Uvin 2002; see also Unsworth 2001). She is influenced greatly by Mick Moore and his colleagues (see Joshi and Moore 2000; Moore and Punzel 2001).

12. "For political leaders, political survival is an overwhelming interest, and in general, they will promote actions that increase their chances for survival even if they are detrimental to development" (Brautigam 2000, 3).

13. This holds especially for humanitarian work, where a capacity building approach seems like an evident slow-down compared to a delivery one (for excellent discussions, see Minear 2002; Smillie 2002; Lautze and Hammock 1996). However, for the typical development approach, which is rather long term in any case, and which is often suboptimal in producing widespread benefits, the problem may well be much smaller than it seems. Adopting a capacity building approach is not such a trade-off after all.

14. One quotation from this report illustrates the evident logic of coherence: "Conflicts between EC development policy and EC trade policy or the Common Agricultural Policy have received a lot of attention in the recent years. A significant case was the dumping of beef meat in West Africa. Due to surpluses within the EC, and due to high costs of storage, the EC used a 2 ECU/kilo subsidy to sell, (i.e., dump) beef in the West African market. This angered livestock producers in Burkina Faso, Mali and Niger. At the same time, the EC was using its development cooperation funds to promote the livestock industry in these countries. The matter was resolved after a public campaign, initiated by public interest groups in Europe through a 15 percent reduction of the export subsidy on beef to West Africa" (Box et al. 1997).

15. Stephen J. Stedman made this argument for the development community's growing role in conflict prevention: what is new, he argues, is not that conflict prevention is being considered at all, for it has always been on the agenda of international relations, but that development actors—many of them nongovernmental, which constitutes another contrast with the previous government monopoly on conflict prevention—claim they and their resources have a major role to play here. It is the aid folks who are the new kids on the block here, not the foreign policy and the military ones (Stedman 1995).

16. For critical discussions of this matter in the case of the conflict prevention role of development assistance, see Duffield 2001; Macrae and Leader 2000; Wood 2001.

Chapter 6

1. Sengupta describes the same idea more succinctly: "A prosperous community of slaves who do not have civil and political rights will not be regarded as a society with well-being" (Sengupta 1999, par. 54).

2. "Methodologically and theoretically sound" describes his major theoretical contributions preceding his development work, made during the 1960s and 1970s, on matters of public choice and preference aggregation. "Empirically rich" characterizes, for example, his work on intra-household distribution, famine, and hunger, made in the 1970s and 1980s. Finally, note that in the community of his economist peers the latter qualifiers—all the ones that follow the words "methodologically and theoretically," in fact—are much less appreciated. As a colleague of mine recently remarked, Sen couldn't get tenure in any good American economics department on the basis of his most famous work.

3. Other authors arrive at the same place as the UNDP. Hamm (2001, 1011) argues that a rights-based practice of development contains four factors: (1) reference to and starting from human rights treaties; (2) nondiscrimination, special focus on disadvantaged groups, explicitly women and children; (3) participation and empowerment; and (4) good governance (Hamm 2001, 1011). As Hamm herself admits, there is little that is new here; apart from the first point, development practitioners have already been trying to do all the other elements for at least a decade, and, as we saw in the first section, the first one isn't exactly a guarantor of a major breakthrough. Paul Nelson and Ellen Dorsey, analyzing the same question, provide a slightly different list but also observe repeatedly that there is little new here (Nelson and Dorsey 2003).

4. See also Tomasevski 1989, 155; Donnelly 1999b, 61; Windfuhr 2000, 35. André Frankovits argues that the rights-based approach "transforms beggars into claimants" (Frankovits 1996, 125)—a nice sound bite, but one that should not be

taken too literally, for many of the world's poor never begged aid agencies for anything really, nor did they ever receive much.

5. Or are they second best? Some critics have argued that they are best, for they are based on deep social mechanisms rather than individualistic and antagonizing legal procedures (Kennedy 2002; Sunstein 1995; Glendon 1991).

6. That, precisely, was the main lesson drawn from my previous book (see Uvin 1998). See also Benedict Kingsbury, who documents the same for indigenous peoples in Asia (Kingsbury 1999); and Arundati Roy's touching and well-written piece on the Narmada dam in India (Roy 1999).

7. This argument was first described in a famous article by Audrey Chapman (1996).

8. See Roy 1999; Uvin 1998; CESCR 1990, par. 7; Kingsbury 1999, 369ff.; Tomasevski 2003.

Chapter 7

1. Ben Cousins makes these points in a fine case study of South Africa (Cousins 1997).

2. The reader may recall that these five paths mirror five of the solutions in our earlier debate on Eurocentrism: the legalistic solution, and the soft relativist, empiricist, philosophical, and incrementalist ones.

3. Haddad 1999, 13; see also Bauer and Bell 1999, 21. Arjun Sengupta clearly and repeatedly argues that no right to development can be sustainable without economic growth, and thus adds economic growth to equity and participation as key elements of the right to development. As a matter of fact, Sengupta goes so far as to argue that growth should be a human right as well (Sengupta 2001).

Bibliography

Abbott, Kenneth W., and Duncan Snidal. 2000. "Hard and Soft Law in International Governance." *International Organization* 54.

Alexander, Nancy, and Charles Abugre. 1997. *NGOs and the International Monetary and Financial System*. Paper prepared for the Technical Group of the Inter-Governmental Group of Twenty-Four in International Monetary Affairs. Washington D.C.

Anders, Mary. 1999. *Do No Harm*. Boulder, Colo.: Lynee Rienner.

An-Na'im, Abdullahi Ahmed. 1990. *Toward an Islamic Reformation: Civil Liberties, Human Rights and International Law*. Syracuse: Syracuse University Press.

———. 1992. *Human Rights in Cross-Cultural Perspectives: A Quest for Consensus*. Philadelphia: University of Pennsylvania Press.

———. 1999. "The Cultural Mediation of Human Rights: The Al-Arqam Case in Malaysia." In *The East Asian Challenge for Human Rights*, edited by Joanne Bauer and Daniel Bell. Cambridge: Cambridge University Press.

Atmar, Mohammed Haneef. 2001. *Politicisation of Humanitarian Aid and Its Consequences for Afghans*. ODI Conference Politics and Humanitarian Aid: Debates, Dilemmas, and Dissension. London, February 1. Available online.

Baehr, Peter R. 2000. "Controversies in the Current International Human Rights Debate." *Human Rights Review* 2/1 (October-December): 7–32.

Bauer, Joanne R., and Daniel A. Bell. 1999. "Introduction." In *The East Asian Challenge for Human Rights*, edited by Joanne Bauer and Daniel Bell, 3–25. Cambridge: Cambridge University Press.

Bauer, Peter T. 1983. *Equality, the Third World and Economic Delusion*. Cambridge, Mass.: Harvard University Press.

Bayart, Jean-François. 1989. *L'Etat en Afrique. La politique du ventre*. Paris: Fayard.

Beetham, David. 1995. *Defining and Measuring Democracy*. London: Sage.

Bell, Daniel A. 1996. "Minority Rights: On the Importance of Local Knowledge." *Dissent* 45/1 (Summer): 36–41.

Benoit, André, Johan Cottenie, Koen De Feyter, Han Verleyen. 2000. *Filling the Gap: Development and Economic, Social, and Cultural Rights: An NGO Challenge*. NCOS/11.11.11. Brussels: May. Available online.

Beynon, Jonathan. 2001. *Policy Implications for Aid Allocation of Recent Research on Aid Effectiveness and Selectivity: A Summary*. Paper presented at DAC/DC seminar "Aid Effectiveness, Selectivity, and Poor Performers," Paris, January 17.

Booth, David. 2001. "Overview of PRSP Processes and Monitoring." In *PRSP Institutionalisation Study: Final Report*. London: ODI, October.

Booth, David, Melissa Leach, and Alison Tierney. 1999. *Experiencing Poverty in Africa: Perspectives from Anthropology*. Background paper no. 1(b) for the World Bank Poverty Status Report 1999, final draft. London: World Bank, April.

Bourque, André. 2002. *Le programme d'appui de 11.11.11 aux Droits Humains au Rwanda: perspectives 2003–2008*. Kigali: 11.11.11., December.

Box, Louk, and Andrea Koulaïmah-Gabriel. 1997. *Towards Coherence? Development Cooperation Policy and the Development of Policy Cooperation*. ECDPM Working Paper no. 21. Maastricht: ECDPM. Available online.

Bratton, Michael, and Nicolas van de Walle. 1997. *Democratic Experiments in Africa: Regime Transitions in Comparative Perspective*. Cambridge: Cambridge University Press.

Brautigam, Deborah. 2000. *Aid Dependence and Governance*. Stockholm: Almqvist & Wiksell International.

Brown, Susan. 2002. *Why Conflict Prevention?* Paper presented at a conference "Development, Conflict and Peacebuilding: Responding to the Challenge," Centre for the Study of Global Issues, University of British Columbia, Vancouver, February 14–15. Available online.

Bunn, Isabella D. 2000. "The Right to Development: Implications for International Economic Law." *American University International Law Review* 15/6: 1425–68.

Burnell, Peter. 1999. "Good Government and Democratization: A Sideways Look at Aid and Political Conditionality." *Democratization* 1/3: 485–503.

Burnside, Craig, and David Dollar. 1997. *Aid, Policies and Growth*. World Bank Policy Research Working Paper 1777. Washington D.C.: World Bank.

Burton, John W. 1997. *Violence Explained: The Sources of Conflict, Violence and Crime and Their Prevention*. Manchester: Manchester University Press.

CARE. 2001. *Defining Characteristics of the Rights-Based Approach* (by Andrew Jones). Atlanta: CARE.

Carothers, Thomas. 1999. *Aiding Democracy Abroad: The Learning Curve*. Washington D.C.: Carnegie Endowment for International Peace.

———. 2002. "The End of the Transition Paradigm." *Journal of Democracy* 13/1 (January): 5–21.

Carothers, Thomas, and Marina Ottaway, eds. 2000. *Funding Virtue: Civil Society Aid and Democracy Promotion*. Washington D.C.: Carnegie Endowment for International Peace.

Cassen, Robert. 1986. *Does Aid Work?* Oxford: Oxford University Press.

CESCR (Committee on Economic, Social and Cultural Rights). 1990. *International Technical Assistance Measures (art. 22): CESCR General Comment No. 2*. Geneva: CESCR. Available online.

———. 1994. *The Nature of State Parties Obligations Under Article 2(1) of the ICESR: General Comment No. 3*. UN Doc HRI/GEN/1/Rev. 1. Geneva: United Nations.

———. 1997. *The Relationship Between Economic Sanctions and Respect for Economic, Social, and Cultural Rights: CESCR General Comment No. 8*. Geneva: CESCR. Available online.

———. 1998. *The Domestic Application of the Covenant: CESCR General Comment No. 9*. Geneva. Available online.

Chabal, Patrick, and Jean-Pascal Daloz. 1999. *Africa Works: Political Disorder as Policy Instrument*. London: Currey.

Chambers, Robert. 1986. *Rural Development: Putting the Last First*. London: Longman.

———. 1995. *Poverty and Livelihoods: Whose Reality Counts?* Institute for Development Studies Discussion Paper no. 347. Sussex: IDS.

Chandler, David. 2001. "The Road to Military Humanitarianism: How the Human Rights NGOs Shaped a New Humanitarian Agenda." *Human Rights Quarterly* 23/3: 678–700.

Chapman, Audrey R. 1996. "A 'Violations Approach' for Monitoring the International Covenant on Economic, Social and Cultural Rights." *Human Rights Quarterly* 18/1: 23–66.

Chatterjee, Partha. 1993. *The Nation and Its Fragments: Colonial and Post-colonial Histories*. Princeton, N.J.: Princeton University Press.

Cheru, Fanta. 2001. *The Highly Indebted Poor Countries (HIPC) Initiative: A Human Rights Assessment of the PRSPs*. Geneva: Commission on Human Rights, E/CN.4/2001/56, January. Available online at the UNHCHR website.

Chomsky, Noam. 1973. *For Reasons of State*. New York: New Press. Reprinted 2003.

Chopra, Jarat. 2002. "Building State Failure in East Timor." *Development and Change* 33/5: 979–1000.

Christie, Daniel J. 1997. "Reducing Direct and Structural Violence: The Human Needs Theory." *Peace and Conflict: Journal of Peace Psychology* 3/4: 315–32.

Clapham, Christopher. 1996. *Africa and the International System: The Politics of State Survival*. New York: Cambridge University Press.

Claude, Inis L. 1966. "Collective Legitimization as a Political Function of the United Nations." *International Organization* 20/3 (Summer): 367–79.

Clayton, Andrew, Peter Oakley, and Jon Taylor. 2000. *Civil Society Organizations and Service Provision*. UNRISD Program on Civil Society and Social Movements Paper no. 2. Geneva: UNRISD, October.

Cohn, Elizabeth. 1999. "U.S. Democratization Assistance." *Foreign Policy in Focus* 4/20 (July): 1–4.

Collier, Paul. 1997. "The Failure of Conditionality." In *Perspectives on Aid and Development*, edited by Catherine Gwin and Joan Nelson. Washington D.C.: Overseas Development Council.

———. 1999. "Learning from Failure: The International Financial Institutions as Agencies of Restraint in Africa." In The Self-Restraining State: Power and Accountability in New Democracies, edited by Andrea Schedler, Larry Diamond, and Marc Plattner, 313–30. Boulder, Colo.: Lynne Rienner.

Collier, Paul, and David Dollar. 1998. *Assessing Aid—What Works, What Doesn't, and Why*. Washington D.C.: World Bank Policy Research Report no. 7.

Cornwall, Andrea, and Alice Welbourn. 2002. "Introduction: Realizing Rights: Transforming Approaches to Sexual and Reproductive Well-being." In *Realizing Rights: Transforming Approaches to Sexual and Reproductive Well-being*, edited by Andrea Cornwall and Alice Welbourn, 1–20. London: Zed Books.

Cortright, David, ed. 1997. *The Price of Peace: Incentives and International Conflict Prevention*. New York: Rowman & Littlefield Publishers/Carnegie Commission on Preventing Deadly Conflict.

Cousins, Ben. 1997. "How Do Rights Become Real? Formal and Informal Institutions in South Africa's Land Reform." *IDS Bulletin* 29/2 (October).

Craven, Matthew. 1995. *The International Covenant on Economic, Social and Cultural Rights: A Perspective on Its Development.* Oxford: Clarendon Press.

Crawford, Gordon. 1997. "Foreign Aid and Political Conditionality: Issues of Effectiveness and Consistency." *Democratization* 4/3 (Autumn): 69–108.

CRS (Catholic Relief Services). 2003. *Social Accountability Mechanisms: Citizen engagement for Pro-Poor Policies and Reduced Corruption.* Baltimore, Md.: CRS, January.

Dalai Lama. 1999. "Buddhism, Asian Values, and Democracy." *Journal of Democracy* 10/1: 3–7.

De Feyter, Koen. 2001. *World Development Law.* Antwerp: Intersentia.

De Waal, Alex. 1997. *Famine Crimes: Politics and the Disaster Relief Industry in Africa.* Bloomington, Ind.: University of Indiana Press.

———. 2000. "Democratic Political Process and the Fight Against Famine." Institute for Development Studies Working Paper 107. Sussex: IDS.

Dembele, Demba Moussa. 2003. *The Myths and Dangers of PRSPs.* Dakar: Forum des alternatives africaines. Available online.

Deng, Francis M., Sadikiel Kimaro, Terrence Lyons, Donald Rothchild, and William Zartman. 1996. *Sovereignty as Responsibility: Conflict Management in Africa.* Washington D.C.: Brookings.

Devarajan, Shantayanan, David Dollar, and Torgny Holmgren. 2001. *Aid and Reform in Africa: Lessons from Ten Case Studies.* Washington D.C.: World Bank.

DFID (Department for International Development). 2000. *Realizing Human Rights for Poor People.* DFID Strategy Paper. London: DFID.

———. 2002. *How Should DFID Respond to PRSPs?* London: DFID Africa Policy Department, February. Available online at the DFID website.

Diamond, Larry. 1999. *Developing Democracy: Toward Consolidation.* Baltimore, Md.: Johns Hopkins University Press.

Donnelly, Jack. 1989. *Universal Human Rights: In Theory and Practice.* Ithaca, N.Y.: Cornell University.

———. 1999a. "Human Rights, Democracy, and Development." *Human Rights Quarterly* 21/3: 608–32.

———. 1999b. "Human Rights and Asian Values: A Defense of 'Western' Universalism." In *The East Asian Challenge for Human Rights*, edited by Joanne Bauer and Daniel Bell, 60–87. Cambridge: Cambridge University Press.

Dorsey, Ellen. 2002. *Economic, Social and Cultural Rights Initiative, Amnesty International, USA.* Paper delivered at Oxfam/CARE Workshop, Boston, September 16.

Duffield, Mark. 2001. *Global Governance and the New Wars: The Merging of Development and Security.* London: Zed books.

Duffield, Mark, Patricia Gossman, and Nicholas Leader. 2001. *Review of the Strategic Framework for Afghanistan.* London: AREU. Available online.

Easterly, William. 2001. *The Elusive Quest for Growth.* Cambridge, Mass.: MIT Press.

———. 2002. "The Cartel of Good Intentions." *Foreign Policy* 131 (July-August): 40–44.

Eide, Asbjørn. 1989. "Realization of Social and Economic Rights and the Minimum Threshold Approach." *Human Law Journal* 10/1–2: 36, 38.

———. 1995. "Human Rights Requirements for Social and Economic Development." *Food Policy* 21/1: 23–39.

Ellerman, David. 2000. *The Indirect Approach*. World Bank Staff Working Paper 2417. Washington D.C.: World Bank.

Ellerman, David. 2001. *Helping People Help Themselves: Toward a Theory of Autonomy-Compatible Help*. World Bank Staff Working Paper 2693. Washington D.C.: World Bank. Available online.

Escobar, Arturo. 1994. *Encountering Development: The Making and Unmaking of the Third World*. Princeton, N.J.: Princeton University Press.

Esteva, Gustavo 1997. "Basta! Mexican Indians Say 'Enough!'" In *The Post-Development Reader*, edited by Majid Rahnema with Victoria Bawtree, 302–5. London: Zed Books.

EU (European Union). 2001. *The European Union's Role in Promoting Human Rights and Democratisation in Third Countries*. Brussels: Communication from the Commission to the Council and the European Parliament, COM (2001) 252 final, May 8.

Farer, Tom J., and Felice Gaer. 1993. "The UN and Human Rights: At the End of the Beginning." In *United Nations, Divided World*, edited by Adam Roberts and Benedict Kingsbury. Oxford: Clarendon Press.

Farmer, Paul. 1999. "Pathologies of Power: Rethinking Health and Human Rights." *American Journal of Public Health* 89/10: 1486–96.

Farmer, Paul. 2003. *Pathologies of Power: Health, Human Rights, and the New War on the Poor*. Berkeley and Los Angeles: University of California Press.

Ferguson, James. 1990. *The Anti-Politics Machine: "Development," Depoliticization, and Bureaucratic Power in Lesotho*. Cambridge: Cambridge University Press.

Ferguson, Niall. 2003. *Empire: The Rise and Demise of the British World Order and the Lessons for Global Power*. New York: Basic Books.

Fidler, Stephen. 2001. "Who's Minding the Bank?" *Foreign Policy* 126 (September-October).

Filali-Ansary, Abdou. 1999. "Muslims and Democracy." *Journal of Democracy* 10/3: 18–32.

Fino, Daniel. 1996. *De l'aide internationale au renforcement des capacités nationales*. Geneva: Nouveaux Cahiers de l'Institut Universitaire d'Etudes du Développement, 13–26.

———. 2001. "Le programme hydraulique Niger-Suisse (PHNS): quelques leçons à retenir." *Cahiers africains d'administration publique* 57: 51–65.

Foot, Philippa. 1981. "Moral Relativism." In *Relativism: Moral and Cognitive*, edited by Jack W. Meiland and Michael Krausz. Notre Dame, Ind.: University of Notre Dame Press.

Forsythe, David P. 1997. "The United Nations, Human Rights, and Development." *Human Rights Quarterly* 19/2: 334–49.

Frankovits, André. 1996. "Rejoinder: The Rights Way to Development." *Food Policy* 21/1: 123–28.

———. 2000. "Background Paper." In *Asia-Pacific Inter-Sessional Workshop on the Right to Development and Economic, Social and Cultural Rights*, organized by the Office of the High Commissioner for Human Rights, Sana'a, Yemen, February 5–7. Available online at the UNHCHR website.

———. 2002. "Rules to Live By: The Human Rights Approach to Development. *Praxis* 17: 1–14. Available online.

Frankovits, André, and Patrick Earle. 2000. *Working Together: The Human Rights Based Approach to Development Cooperation*. Human Rights Council of Australia Stockholm Workshop, Stockholm, October 16–19.

George, Susan. 1974. *How the Other Half Dies*. London: Penguin Books.

Ghai, Yash. 2001. *Human Rights and Social Development: Toward Democratization and Social Justice*. UNRISD Democracy, Governance and Human Rights Programme Paper 5. Geneva: UNRISD, October.

Gil, David G. 1986. "Sociocultural Aspects of Domestic Violence." In *Violence in the Home*, edited by M. Lystad. New York: Brunner/Mazel.

———. 1996. "Preventing Violence in a Structurally Violent Society: Mission Impossible." *American Journal of Orthopsychiatry* 66/1 (January): 77–84.

Glendon, Mary Ann. 1991. *Rights Talk: The Impoverishment of Political Discourse*. New York: Free Press.

———. 2002. *A World Made New: Eleanor Roosevelt and the Universal Declaration of Human Rights*. New York: Random House.

Gopin, Mark. 2000. *Between Eden and Armageddon*. Oxford: Oxford University Press.

Guttal, Shalmali, Alejandro Bendaña, and Helen Wanguza. 2001. *The World Bank and the PRSP: Flawed Thinking and Failing Experiences*. Bangkok: Focus on the Global South, November. Available online.

Gwin, Catherine, and Joan Nelson, eds. 1997. *Perspectives on Aid and Development*. Policy Essay no. 22. Washington D.C.: Overseas Development Council.

Haddad, Lawrence. 1999. "Symposium Synthesis and Overview." *SCN News* 18 (July), special issue on Adequate Food: A Human Right: 14–17.

Hamm, Brigitte L. 2001. "A Human Rights Approach to Development." *Human Rights Quarterly* 23/4: 1005–31.

Hansen, Henrik, and Finn Tarp. 1999. *Aid Effectiveness Disputed*. Copenhagen: Development Economic Research Group, Denmark. Available online.

Harrison, Graham. 1999. "Clean-ups, Conditionality and Adjustment: Why Institutions Matter in Mozambique." *Review of African Political Economy* 81 (September): 323–33.

Hearn, Julie. 1999. *Foreign Aid, Democratization and Civil Society in Africa: A Study of South Africa, Ghana, and Uganda*. Institute for Development Studies Discussion Paper 368. Sussex: IDS.

Heinz, Walter, Hildegard Lingnau, and Peter Waller. 1995. *Evaluation of EC Positive Measures in Favour of Human Rights and Democracy*. Berlin: German Development Institute.

Held, David. 1997. *Models of Democracy*. Stanford, Calif.: Stanford University Press.

Hibou, Béatrice. 2002. "The World Bank: Missionary Deeds (and Misdeeds)." In *Exporting Democracy. Rhetoric vs. Reality*, edited by Peter Schraeder, 173–91. Boulder, Colo.: Lynne Rienner.

Hirschman, Albert O. 1991. *The Rhetoric of Reaction: Perversity, Futility, Jeopardy*. Cambridge, Mass.: Harvard University Press.

Holland, Martin. 2003. "20/20 Vision? The EU's Cotonou Partnership Agreement." *The Brown Journal of World Affairs* 9/2 (Winter/Spring): 161–75.

Holmqvist, Göran. 2000. *Conditionality and Sustainability of Policy Reforms.* Stockholm: Swedish International Development Cooperation Agency. Available online.

Howell, Jude, and Jenny Pearce. 2001. *Civil Society and Development: A Critical Exploration.* Boulder, Colo.: Lynne Rienner.

HRCA (Human Rights Council of Australia). 2001. *Submission to the Joint Standing Committee on Foreign Affairs, Defense and Trade Inquiry into the Link Between Aid and Human Rights.* Canberra: February. Available online at the HRCA website.

Hyden, Goran. 1993. *From Bargaining to Marketing: How to Reform Foreign Aid in the 1990s.* Department of Political Science Working Paper no. 6. East Lansing, Mich.: Michigan State University.

Hyman, Gerald. 2002. "Tilting at Straw Men." *Journal of Democracy* 13/3 (July): 26–32.

Ibhawoh, Bonny. 2000. "Between Culture and Constitution: Evaluating the Cultural Legitimacy of Human Rights in the African State." *Human Rights Quarterly* 22/3: 838–60.

ICISS (International Commission of Intervention and State Sovereignty). 2002. *The Responsibility to Protect.* Ottawa: Department of Foreign Affairs and International Trade and Ralph Bunche Institute. Available online.

Ignatieff, Michael. 1999. *Whose Universal Values? The Crisis in Human Rights.* Amsterdam: Praemium Erasmianum Essay.

———. 2000. *Human Rights Culture: The Political and Spiritual Crisis.* The Andrei Sakharov Lecture on Human Rights. Boston: Brandeis University, January 25.

———. 2003. "The Way We Live Now: I Am Iraq." *The New York Times,* March 23: 6–13.

IMF (International Monetary Fund). 1997. "Guidelines Regarding Governance Issues." *IMF Survey 1997* 26/15: 234–38.

———. 2001. "Conditionality in Fund-Supported Programs—Overview Prepared by the Policy Development and Review Department." Washington D.C.: IMF, February 20. Available online at the IMF website.

Johnson, Juliet. 2002. "In Pursuit of a Prosperous International System." In *Exporting Democracy: Rhetoric vs. Reality,* edited by Peter Schraeder, 31–51. Boulder, Colo.: Lynne Rienner.

Jonsson, Urban. 1999. "Historical Summary on the SCN Working Group on Nutrition, Ethics, and Human Rights." *SCN News* 18 (July), special issue on Adequate Food: A Human Right: 49–51.

Jonsson, Urban. Forthcoming. *A Human Rights Approach to Development Programming.* New York: UNICEF.

Jordan, Lisa, and Peter van Tuijl. 1998. *Political Responsibility in NGO Advocacy: Exploring Emerging Shapes of Global Democracy.* Amsterdam: NOVIB.

Joshi, Anuradha, and Mick Moore. 2000. "The Mobilising Potential of Anti-Poverty Programmes." Institute for Development Studies Discussion Paper no. 374. Sussex: IDS.

Kabou, Axelle. 1991. *Et si l'Afrique refusait le développement?* Paris: L'Harmattan.

Kanbur, Ravi. 2000. "Aid, Conditionality and Debt in Africa." In *Foreign Aid and Development: Lessons Learnt and Directions for the Future,* edited by Finn Tarp. London: Routledge.

Kanbur, Ravi, Todd Sandler, and Kevin Morrison. 1999. *The Future of Development Assistance: Common Pools and International Public Goods*. Policy Essay no. 25. Washington D.C.: Overseas Development Council.

Kapur, Devesh, and Richard Webb. 2000. *Governance-related Conditionalities of the International Financial Institution*. UNCTAD G-24 Discussion Paper Series no. 6. Geneva: UNCTAD.

Keck, Margaret, and Katherine Sikkink. 1998. *Activists Beyond Borders*. Ithaca, N.Y.: Cornell University Press.

Kennedy, David. 2002. "The International Human Rights Movement: Part of the Problem?" *Harvard Human Rights Journal* 15 (Spring): 101–26.

Killick, Tony. 1997. *Donors as Paper Tigers: Why Aid with Strings Attached Won't Work*. London: id21.

———. 1998. *Aid and the Political Economy of Policy Change*. London: Routledge.

Kingsbury, Benedict. 1999. "The Applicability of the International Legal Concept of 'Indigenous People' in Asia." In *The East Asian Challenge for Human Rights*, edited by Joanne Bauer and Daniel Bell, 336–77. Cambridge: Cambridge University Press.

Klare, Karl. 1991. "Legal Theory and Democratic Reconstruction." *University of British Columbia Law Review* 69: 97–122.

Kyi, Aung San Suu. 1995. *Opening Keynote Address at the NGO Forum on Women, Beijing '95*. Available online.

Klingebiel, Stephen. 1999. *Impact of Development Cooperation in Conflict Situations: Cross-section Report on Evaluations of German Development Cooperation in Six Countries*. German Development Institute Reports and Working Papers 6. Berlin.

Knack, Stephen. 2001. "Aid Dependence and the Quality of Governance: A Cross-Country Empirical Analysis." *Southern Economic Journal* 68/2 (October): 310–29.

Koh, Harold H. 1997. "Why Do Nations Obey International Law?" *Yale Law Journal* 106, 2599ff.

———. 1999. "How Is International Human Rights Law Enforced?" *Indiana Law Journal* 74 (Fall): 1397–1417.

Kothari, Rajni. 1989. *Rethinking Development: In Search of Humane Alternatives*. New York: Apex Press.

———. 1993. *Poverty: Human Consciousness and the Amnesia of Development*. London: Zed Books.

Krasner, Stephen D. 1999. *Sovereignty: Organized Hypocrisy*. Princeton, N.J.: Princeton University Press.

Küng, Hans. 1998. *A Global Ethic for Global Politics and Economics*. New York: Oxford University Press.

Küng, Hans, ed. 1996. *Yes to a Global Ethic*. New York: Continuum.

Küng, Hans, and Jurgen Moltmann, eds. 1990. *The Ethics of World Religions and Human Rights*. Philadelphia: Trinity Press International.

Laakso, Liisa. 2002. "Promoting a Special Brand of Democracy: Denmark, Finland, Norway and Sweden." In *Exporting Democracy: Rhetoric vs. Reality*, edited by Peter Schraeder, 55–71. Boulder, Colo.: Lynne Rienner.

Lautze, Sue, and John Hammock. 1996. *Coping with Crisis, Coping with Aid: Capacity Building, Coping Mechanisms, and Dependency, Linking Relief and Development*. New York: UN Department of Humanitarian Affairs.

Lecomte. Bernard. 1986. *L'aide par projet: Limites et alternatives*. Paris: OECD.

Lieven, Anatol. 2003. "The Empire Strikes Back." *The Nation*, July 7: 25–30.

Lijphardt, Arend. 1999. *Patterns of Democracy: Government Forms and Performance in Thirty-Six Countries*. New Haven, Conn.: Yale University Press.

Lovelace, James Christopher. 1999. "Will Rights Cure Malnutrition? Reflections on Human Rights, Nutrition, and Developments." *SCN News* 18 (July). Special issue on Adequate Food: A Human Right: 27–30.

Macrae, Johanna, and Nicholas Leader. 2000. *The Politics of Coherence: Humanitarianism and Foreign Policy in the Cold War Era*. London: ODI.

Mahoney, James. 2003. "Knowledge Accumulation in Comparative-Historical Research: The Case of Democracy and Authoritarianism." In *Comparative Historical Analysis in the Social Sciences*, edited by James Mahoney and Dietrich Rueschemeyer. Cambridge: Cambridge University Press.

Mander, Harsh, and Abha Singhal Joshi. 2001. *The Movement for Right to Information in India: People's Power for the Control of Corruption*. Paper delivered at a conference on Freedom of Information and Civil Society in Asia, Tokyo. Available online.

Marglin, F. A., and S. Marglin. 1990. *Dominating Knowledge: Development, Culture, and Resistance*. Oxford: Clarendon Press.

Marks, Stephen P. 1999. "The United Nations and Human Rights: The Promise of Multilateral Diplomacy and Action." In *The Future of International Human Rights*, edited by Burns H. Weston and Stephen P. Marks. New York: Transnational Publishers.

McGoldrick, Dominic. 1996. "Sustainable Development and Human Rights: An Integrated Conception." *International and Comparative Law Quarterly* 45 (October): 796–818.

Mendelson, Sarah E. 2001. "Democracy Assistance and Political Transition in Russia." *International Security* 25/4 (Spring): 68–106.

Meron, Thomas. 1986. "On a Hierarchy of International Human Rights." *American Journal of International Law* 80: 1–23.

———. 1998. *Human Rights and Humanitarian Norms as Customary Law*. New York: Oxford University Press.

Minear, Larry. 2002. *The Humanitarian Enterprise: Dilemmas and Discoveries*. Bloomfield, Conn.: Kumarian Press.

Moore, Jonathan, ed. 1998. *Hard Choices: Moral Dilemmas in Humanitarian Intervention*. Lanham, Md.: Rowman and Littlefield.

Moore, Mick. 1998. "Death Without Taxes: Democracy, State Capacity, and Aid Dependence in the Fourth World." In *The Democratic Developmental State*, edited by Mark Robinson and Gordon White. Oxford: Oxford University Press.

Moore, Mick, Madhilka Choudhary, and Neelam Singh. 1999. *How Can We Know What They Want? Understanding Local Perceptions of Poverty and Ill-Being in Asia*. IDS Working Paper 80. Sussex: IDS.

Morrissey, Oliver. 1998. *Promises, Promises: Can Aid with Policy Reform Strings Attached Ever Work?* London: id21, August.

Morss, Elliott R. 1984. "Institutional Destruction Resulting from Donor and Project Proliferation in Sub-Saharan African Countries." *World Development* 12/4: 465–70.

Mosley, Paul, Jane Harrigan, and John Toye. 1991. *Aid and Power: The World Bank and Policy-Based Lending*. London: Routledge.

Mosley, Paul, and John Hudson. 2001. *Aid, Poverty Reduction and the "New Conditionality."* Sheffield: University of Sheffield, Department of Economics Working Paper, October. Available online.

Mukasa, Stella, and Florence Butegwa. 2001. *An Overview of Approaches to Economic and Social Rights in Development in Uganda*. Draft report for Danida. Kampala: Nordic Consulting Group, June.

Ndegwa, Stephen N. 1996. *The Two Faces of Civil Society: NGOs and Politics in Africa*. Bloomfield, Conn.: Kumarian Press.

Nederveen Pieterse, Jan. 2001. *Development Theory. Deconstructions/Reconstructions*. London: Sage.

Neggaz, Ana Meira. 2001. *The Rights-Based Approach*. Salvador: CARE El Salvador, August.

Neier, Aryeh. 2003. *Taking Liberties: Four Decades in the Struggle for Rights*. New York: PublicAffairs.

Neiss, Hubert. 2001. "Conditionality and Program Ownership." Remarks by the chairman, Asia, Deutsche Bank IMF Seminar on Conditionality, Tokyo, July 10. Available online at the IMF website.

Nelson, Joan, and Stephanie Eglington. 1993. *Global Goals, Contentious Means: Issues of Multiple Conditionality*. Policy Essay 10. Washington, D.C.: Overseas Development Council.

Nelson, Paul. 1995. *The World Bank and Non-Governmental Organizations*. New York: St. Martin's Press.

Nelson, Paul J., and Ellen Dorsey. 2003. "At the Nexus of Human Rights and Development: New Methods and Strategies of Global NGOs." *World Development* 31/12: 2013–26.

Niland, Norah. 2003. *Humanitarian Action: Protecting Civilians. Feedback from Afghanistan*. Paper prepared for OCHA. New York: OCHA, June.

NORAD. 2001. *Handbook in Human Rights Assessment: State Obligations, Awareness, and Empowerment*. Oslo: Norwegian Agency for Development Cooperation, February. Available online.

Nussbaum, Martha C. 1997. "Capabilities and Human Rights." *Fordham Law Review* 66 (November): 273–300.

————. 2000. *Women and Human Development: The Capabilities Approach*. Cambridge: Cambridge University Press.

Nyamu-Musembi, Celestine. 2002. *Towards an Actor-Oriented Perspective on Human Rights*. Institute for Development Studies Discussion Paper 169. Sussex: IDS, October.

Obiora, L. Amede. 1996. "Beyond the Rhetoric of a Right to Development." *Law and Policy* 18/3&4 (July–October): 355–418.

OECD (Organisation for Economic Co-operation and Development). 1997. *Guidelines on Peace, Conflict, and Development Cooperation*. Paris: OECD.

Ojo, Olatunde J. B. 1998. "Rethinking Hyden's Development Fund Model: A Critique and Suggestions for Modification." *African Studies Quarterly* 2/2. Available online.

Olsen, Gorm R. 2002. "The European Union: An Ad Hoc Policy with a Low Priority." In *Exporting Democracy: Rhetoric vs. Reality*, edited by Peter Schraeder, 131–45. Boulder, Colo.: Lynne Rienner.

Osberg, Lars. 2001. "Needs and Wants: What Is Social Progress and How Should It Be Measured?" In *The Review of Economic Performance and Social Progress. The Longest Decade: Canada in the 1990s,* edited by Keith Banting, Andrew Sharpe, and France St-Hilaire, 23–41. Montreal: McGill University Press.

Ostrom, Eleanor, et al. 2002. *Aid, Incentives, and Sustainability: An Institutional Analysis of Development Cooperation.* Stockholm: Sida Studies in Evaluation (02/01). Available online.

Oxfam International. 2001. *Towards Global Equity: Strategic Plan 2001–2004.* Oxford: Oxfam. Available online.

———. 2002. *Five Aims.* Oxford: Oxfam. Available online. ·

Panday, Devendra Raj. No date. *Can Aid Conditionality Help Governance Reform in Needy Countries?* Katmandu: Transparency International Nepal. Available online.

Paul, James. 1995. "The United Nations and the Creation of an International Law of Development." *Harvard International Law Journal* 36 (Fall).

Peet, Richard. 1999. *Theories of Development.* New York: Guilford Press.

Perry, Richard W. 1996. "Rethinking the Right to Development: After the Critique of Development, after the Critique of Rights." *Law and Policy* 18/3&4 (July-October): 225–49.

Perry, Michael J. 1998. *The Idea of Human Rights. Four Inquiries.* Oxford: Oxford University Press.

Phillips, Anne. 1991. "Citizenship and Feminist Theory." In *Citizenship,* edited by G. Andrews. London: Lawrence and Wishardt.

Plank, David N. 1993. "Aid, Debt, and the End of Sovereignty: Mozambique and Its Donors." *Journal of Modern African Studies* 31/3 (September): 407–30.

Poate, Derek, Roger Riddell, Nick Chapman, Tony Curran. 2000. *The Evaluability of Democracy and Human Rights Projects: A Logframe Assessment.* Swedish International Development Authority Evaluation Studies 00/03. Stockholm. Available online.

Rahnema, Majid, with Victoria Bawtree, eds. 1997. *The Post-Development Reader.* London: Zed Books.

Ramos Horta, Jose. 2003. "War for Peace? It Worked in My Country." *New York Times,* February 25: A-29.

Rawls, John. 1971. *A Theory of Justice.* Cambridge: Harvard University Press.

———. 1996. *Political Liberalism.* New York: Columbia University Press.

Rieff, David. 2002a. *A Bed for the Night: Humanitarianism in Crisis.* New York: Simon and Schuster.

———. 2002b. *Genocide and Humanitarian Response.* Washington D.C., Holocaust Memorial Museum Committee on Conscience Talk, December 12. Available online.

Rist, Gilbert. 2002. *The History of Development: From Western Origins to Global Faith.* London: Zed books.

Robinson, Mark. 1996. "Strengthening Civil Society Through Foreign Political Aid. Institute for Development Studies Report to ESCOR no. 6234. Sussex: IDS.

Rosas, Allan. 1995. "The Right to Development." In *Economic, Social and Cultural Rights: A Textbook,* edited by Asbjorn Eide, Catarina Krause, and Allan Rosas, 247–56. Dordrecht: Martinus Nijhoff.

Rose, Gideon. 2000. "Democracy Promotion and American Foreign Policy: A Review Essay." *International Security* 25/3 (Winter): 186–200.

Roy, Arundhati. 1999. "The Greater Common Good." In Arundhati Roy, *The Cost of Living*. New York: Modern Library. Also available online at the narmada.org website.

Rueschemeyer, Dietrich. 1991. "Different Methods—Contradictory Results? Research on Development and Democracy." *International Journal on Comparative Sociology* 32/1&2: 9–38.

Sachs, Wolfgang, ed. 1992. *The Development Dictionary: A Guide to Knowledge as Power*. London: Zed Books.

Sahn, David E. 1997. *Structural Adjustment Reconsidered: Economic Policy and Poverty in Africa*. Cambridge: Cambridge University Press.

Sano, Hans-Otto. 2000. "Development and Human Rights: The Necessary, but Partial Integration of Human Rights and Development." *Human Rights Quarterly* 22/3: 734–52.

Santiso, Carlos. 2001a. *Good Governance and Aid Effectiveness: The World Bank and Conditionality*. Washington D.C.: Paul Nitze School of Advanced International Studies, Johns Hopkins University.

———. 2001b. "International Cooperation for Democracy and Good Governance: Moving Towards a Second Generation?" *European Journal of Development Research* 13/1: 154–80.

———. 2002. *The Reform of EU Development Policy: Improving Strategies for Conflict Prevention, Democracy Promotion, and Governance Conditionality*. Centre for European Policy Studies Working Document no. 182. Brussels: March.

Sardjunani, Nina, Haryo Raharjo, and Rosniaty Syamsidar. No date. "Kecamatan Development Programme: How to Make the National Poverty Alleviation Program Relevant to the Decentralization Process." In *ASEAN—Australia Social Safety Net Project, Workshop Papers and Proceedings, Final Synthesis Report*, chap. 9. Available online.

Schachter, Oscar. 1983. "Human Dignity as a Normative Concept." *American Journal of International Law* 77. Reprinted in *International Human Rights in Context: Law, Politics, Morals*. 2d ed., edited by Henry J. Steiner and Philip Alston. Oxford: Oxford University Press, 2000.

———. 1985. *International Law in Theory and Practice*. Dordrecht: Nijhoff.

Schacter, Mark. 2000. *Monitoring and Evaluation Capacity Development in Sub-Saharan Africa: Lessons from Experience in Supporting Sound Governance*. World Bank Operations Evaluation Department Working Paper Series no. 7. Washington D.C.: World Bank, February.

Schmitter, Philippe, and Imco Brouwer. 1999. *Conceptualizing, Researching and Evaluating Democracy Promotion and Protection*. European University Institute Working Paper SPS 99/9. Florence.

Schuurman, Frans J. 1993. *Beyond the Impasse: New Directions in Development Theory*. London: Zed Books.

Scott, Craig. 1999. "Reaching Beyond (Without Abandoning) the Category of 'Economic, Social and Cultural Rights.'" *Human Rights Quarterly* 21/3: 633–60.

Scott, James C. 1999. *Seeing Like a State: How Certain Schemes to Improve the Human Condition Have Failed*. New Haven, Conn.: Yale University Press.

Seligman, Adam B. 2000. "The Idea of Human Rights." *Human Rights Review* 1/3 (April-June): 140–44.

Sen, Amartya 1993. "Capability and Well-Being." In *The Quality of Life*, edited by Martha Nussbaum and Amartya Sen. Oxford: Oxford University Press.

———. 1999. *Development as Freedom*. New York: Alfred A. Knopf.

Sengupta, Arjun. 1999. *Study on the Current State of Progress in the Implementation of the Rights to Development*. Commission on Human Rights, 56th session, E/CN.4/1999/WG.18/2. Geneva: United Nations, July 27.

———. 2000a. "Realizing the Right to Development." *Development and Change* 31: 553–78.

———. 2000b. *Right to Development*. Note by the Secretary-General for the 55th session, A/55/306. New York: United Nations, August.

SGTS. 2002. *Civil Society Participation in Poverty Reduction Strategy Papers (PRSPs)*, vol. 1, *Overview and Recommendations*. Report to the DFID. London: SGTS & Associates. Available online at the DFID website.

Shestack, Jerome J. 2000. "The Philosophical Foundations of Human Rights." In *Human Rights: Concepts and Standards*, edited by Janusz Symonides, 31–60. Aldershot: Ashgate with UNESCO.

Shihata, Ibrahim F. 1991. *The World Bank in a Changing World: Selected Essays*. Dordrecht: Martinus Nijhoff.

Shiva, Vandana. 1988. *Staying Alive*. London: Zed Books.

Shue, Henry. 1980. *Basic Rights: Subsistence, Affluence and U.S. Foreign Policy*. New York: Basic Books.

Simma, Bruno, J. B. Aschenbrenner, and C. Schulte. 1999. "Human Rights Consideration in the Development Cooperation Activities of the EC." In *The EU and Human Rights*, edited by Philip Alston. Oxford: Oxford University Press.

Slim, Hugo. 2002. "A Response to Peter Uvin—Making Moral Low Ground: Rights as the Struggle for Justice and the Abolition of Development." *Praxis* 17. Also available online.

Slinn, Peter. 1995. "The Contribution of the United Nations to the Evolution of International Development Law." *African Society of International and Comparative Law Proceedings* 7: 263–78.

———. 1999. "The International Law of Development: A Millennium Subject or a Relic of the Twentieth Century?" In *Development and Developing International and European Law*, edited by Wolfgang Benedek, Hubert Isak, and Renate Kicker, 299–318. Frankfurt: Peter Lang.

Smillie, Ian. 1998. *Relief and Development: The Struggle for Synergy*. Humanitarianism and War Project Occasional Paper no. 33. Providence: Brown University, Watson Institute. Available online.

Smillie, Ian, ed. 2002. *Patronage or Partnership: Local Capacity Building in Humanitarian Crises*. Bloomfield, Conn.: Kumarian Press.

Smith, Karen E. 1998. "The Use of Political Conditionality in the EU's Relations with Third Countries: How Effective?" *European Foreign Affairs Review* 3/2 (Summer): 253–74.

Sorensen, Georg. 1998. *Democracy and Democratization*. Boulder, Colo.: Westview.

Spiro Clark, Elizabeth. 2000. "Why Elections Matter." *The Washington Quarterly* 23/3 (Summer): 27–40.

Stedman, Stephen J. 1995. "Alchemy for a New World Order: Overselling 'preventive diplomacy.'" *Foreign Affairs* 74/3 (May-June).

Steiner, Henry J. 1998. "Rights and Economic Development: Converging Discourses?" *Human Rights Law Review* 4: 25–42.

Steiner, Henry J., and Philip Alston. 2000. *International Human Rights in Context: Law, Politics, Morals.* 2d ed. Oxford: Oxford University Press.

Stiglitz Joseph. 1998. *Distribution, Efficiency and Voice: Designing the Second Generation of Reforms Conference on Asset Distribution, Poverty, and Economic Growth Sponsored by the Ministry of Land Reform, Brazil and the World Bank.* Brazilia, Brazil, July 14. Available online at the World Bank website.

Stokke, Olav. 1995. *Aid and Political Conditionality.* London: Frank Cass.

Sugisaki, Shigemitsu. 2001. *Ownership and Conditionality.* Speech by the deputy managing director of the IMF at the International Policy Dialogue, Berlin, June 11. Available online at the IMF website.

Sunstein, Cass. 1995. "Rights and Their Critics." *Notre Dame Law Review* 70: 727–48.

Tatsuo, Inoue. 1999. "Liberal Democracy and Asian Orientalism." In *The East Asian Challenge for Human Rights,* edited by Joanne Bauer and Daniel Bell, 27–59. Cambridge: Cambridge University Press.

Taylor, Charles. 1996. "A World Consensus on Human Rights?" *Dissent* 45/1 (Summer): 15–21.

———. 1999. "Conditions of an Unforced Consensus on Human Rights." In *The East Asian Challenge for Human Rights,* edited by Joanne Bauer and Daniel Bell, 124–45. Cambridge: Cambridge University Press.

Terry, Fiona. 2002. *Condemned to Repeat? The Paradox of Humanitarian Action.* Ithaca, N.Y.: Cornell University Press.

Tharoor, Shashi. 1999. "Are Human Rights Universal?" *World Policy Journal* 16/4 (Winter): 1–6.

Thede, Nancy. 2002. *Democratic Development 1990–2000, An Overview.* Montreal: Rights and Democracy.

Therkildsen, Ole. 2002. "Keeping the State Accountable: Is Aid No Better than Oil?" *IDS Bulletin* 33/3 (July).

Thin, Neil. 2002. *Social Progress and Sustainable Development.* Bloomfield, Conn.: Kumarian Press.

Tilly, Charles. 1995. "Democracy Is a Lake." In *The Social Construction of Democracy, 1870–1990,* edited by George Reid Andrews and Herrick Chapman, 365–87. London: Macmillan.

Tomasevski, Katarina. 1989. "The World Bank and Human Rights." In *Yearbook on Human Rights in Developing Countries 1989,* edited by Manfred Nowak and Theresa Swinehart. Kehl am Rein: Engel.

———. 1993. *Development Aid and Human Rights Revisited.* New York: Pinter.

———. 1995. "International Development Finance Agencies." In *Economic, Social, and Cultural Rights: A Textbook,* edited by Asbjorn Eide, Catarina Krause, and Allan Rosas, 403–14. Dordrecht: Martinus Nijhoff.

———. 2003. *Education Denied: Costs and Remedies.* London: Zed books.

Tsikata, Tsidi. 1998. *Aid Effectiveness—A Survey of the Recent Empirical Literature.* Washington D.C: IMF.

UN (United Nations). 1994. *An Agenda for Development: Report of the Secretary-General.* A/48/935. New York: United Nations.

UNDP (United Nations Development Programme). 1992. *Human Development Report 1992.* New York: Oxford University Press.

———. 1998. *Integrating Human Rights with Sustainable Development.* UNDP Policy Document 2. New York: UNDP.

————. 2001. *Human Development Report 2001*. New York: Oxford University Press.

Unsworth, Sue. 2001. *Understanding Pro-Poor Change*. London: DFID.

Unsworth, Sue, and Peter Uvin. 2002. *A New Look at Civil Society Support in Rwanda*. Kigali: DFID, October 7. Available online.

USAID. 2001. *Linking Democracy and Development: An Idea for the Times*. US Agency for International Development Evaluation Highlights no. 75. Washington D.C.: USAID, December.

Uvin, Peter. 1998. *Aiding Violence: The Development Enterprise in Rwanda*. Bloomfield, Conn.: Kumarian Press.

————. 1999a. *The Influence of Aid in Situations of Violent Conflict*. Paris: OECD. Available online.

————. 1999b. "NGOs and Global Governance." In *Global Institutions and Local Empowerment*, edited by Kendal Stiles. Basingtoke: MacMillan Press.

————. 2001. "Ethics and the New Post-Conflict Agenda: The International Community in Rwanda after the Genocide." *Third World Quarterly* 22/3 (April): 177–89.

————. 2002a. "On High Moral Ground: The Incorporation of Human Rights by the Development Enterprise." *Praxis* 17. Also available online.

————. 2002b. "The Development/Peacebuilding Nexus: A Typology and History of Changing Paradigms." *Journal of Peacebuilding and Development* 1/1.

————. 2003a. *Rwanda's Draft Constitution: Some Personal Reflections on Democracy and Conflict and the Role of the International Community*. Paper commissioned by the embassies of the Netherlands, UK, and United States. Kigali, February 14 (draft). Available online at http://129.194.252.80/catfiles/2601.pdf.

————. 2003b. "Wake Up! Some Personal Reflections and Policy Proposals." Providence: mimeo, June.

Uvin, Peter, and Isabelle Biagiotti. 1996. "Global Governance and the "New" Political Conditionality." *Global Governance* 2/3 (Fall).

Van de Walle, Nicolas. 2001. *African Economies and the Politics of Permanent Crisis 1979–1999*. Cambridge: Cambridge University Press.

Welch, Claude E. 1995. *Protecting Human Rights in Africa: Roles and Strategies of Non-Governmental Organizations*. Philadelphia: University of Pennsylvania Press.

Wiesel, Elie. 2003. "Peace Isn't Possible in Evil's Face." *Los Angeles Times*, March 11.

Windfuhr, Michael. 2000. "Economic, Social and Cultural Rights and Development Cooperation." In *Working Together: The Human Rights Based Approach to Development Cooperation*, compiled by André Frankovits and Patrick Earle, 24–35. Human Rights Council of Australia NGO Workshop, Stockholm, October 16–19. Available online at the HRCA website.

Wood, Bernard. 2001. *Development Dimensions of Conflict Prevention and Peace-Building*, 2d draft. An independent study prepared for the Emergency Response Division. New York: UNDP.

Wood, Angela, and Matthew Lockwood. 1999. *The "Perestroika of Aid"? New Perspectives on Conditionality*. Washington D.C.: Bretton Woods Project/Christian Aid. Available online.

World Bank. 1992. *Governance and Development*. Washington D.C.: World Bank.

————. 1999. *Development and Human Rights: The Role of the World Bank*. Washington D.C.: World Bank.

————. 2000a. *Voices of the Poor—Can Anyone Hear Us?* Washington D.C.: World Bank.

————. 2000b. *World Development Report 2000/2001: Attacking Poverty*. New York: Oxford University Press/World Bank. Also available online at the World Bank website.

————. 2002. *Empowerment and Poverty Reduction: A Sourcebook*. Washington D.C.: World Bank. Available online.

————. 2003a. *Anti-Corruption Guide: Developing an Anti-Corruption Program for Reducing Fiduciary Risks in New Projects. Lessons from Indonesia*. Jakarta: World Bank Office Jakarta. Available online.

————. 2003b. *Third Kecamatan Development Project: Project Appraisal Document*. Washington D.C.: World Bank, June 2.

Wozniak Schimpp, Michelle. 1992. *Aid and Democratic Development: A Synthesis of Literature and Experience*. Washington D.C.: USAID, May.

Yasuaki, Onuma. 1999. "Toward an Intercivilizational Approach to Human Rights." In *The East Asian Challenge for Human Rights*, edited by Joanne Bauer and Daniel Bell, 103–23. Cambridge: Cambridge University Press.

Index

absolutism, 9, 30
accountability, 68, 197; colonialism and, 131–32; conditionality and, 65, 68, 73, 77, 171; contractual mechanisms for, 117; democracy and, 48, 49, 103; dependence and, 111; donor, 65, 104, 107, 110, 112–13; interventionism and, 167; positive support and, 118, 173; RBA and, 131–34, 139, 179, 182; redress and, 162, 165, 169, 181–82; rhetorical repackaging and, 169; rule of law and, 155, 159–60; transparency and, 92, 139; World bank on, 87, 88
ACP (African, Caribbean, and Pacific) countries, 58
acquiescence, 147
activists: on charity, 53; on ESC rights, 14; on Eurocentrism, 16; on non-state actors, 15, 16
adaptation, 36
adaptive preferences, 203n6
adjustment loans: IMF, 74; World Bank and, 87
advocacy, 19, 109, 180; RBA and, 141, 143–46, 148, 154, 177, 182, 185
affirmative approach, 24–25, 32, 34, 35t
Afghanistan, 121, 150, 196, 207n6
Africa, 12. *See also* South Africa; impact of aid and foreigners in, 203n3; PRSPs in, 73; sub-Saharan, 65, 112
Africa Works (Chabal/Daloz), 117
Agenda for Development (UN secretary-general), 125
agricultural projects, 50–51
agricultural techniques, 1
agronomy, 161, 179
aid. *See also* humanitarian aid: budgets, 83; reforms, 41; as rights-based development, 55

aid agencies, 36, 37. *See also specific agencies*; poor countries' relationship with, 103; risks for, 80–81, 137
Aiding Violence: The Development Enterprise in Rwanda (Uvin), 2–3
Algeria, 78
Alliance of Independent Journalists, 159
Alston, Philip, 132
ambassadors, 96, 97, 150
American Revolution, 9
Amnesty International, 22, 180; on conditionality, 57; on ESC rights, 148
ANC (African National Congress), 62
Anderson, Mary, 197
An-Na'im, Abdullahi Ahmed, 25
anthropologists, applied, 34
anthropology, 161
anti-globalization movement, 15, 192
arms: dumping in third-world countries, 88; embargoes, 143
Asian countries, 38. *See also specific countries*
Asian values, 17–18
assembly, right to, 58, 85
Assessing Aid (Collier/Dollar), 70
assessments: conditionality and, 170; motives and, 142; and programming, participatory, 19; RBA and, 151–53, 176–77
association, freedom of speech and, 62
attitudes, 28, 31
Aung San Suu Kyi, 128
authoritarianism, 95; democracy v., 48–49, 58
autonomy, 114, 138; support v., 167

Baaré, Anton, 146
Baehr, Peter R., 22
Bangladesh, 201
bank accounts, freezing, 60

About the Author

Nancy Soukup

Peter Uvin is the Henry J. Leir Professor of International Humanitarian Studies at the Fletcher School, Tufts University. He received his doctorate in international relations from the Institut Universitaire de Hautes Etudes Internationales, University of Geneva. He has been a research associate professor at the Watson Institute of International Affairs, Brown University, and has taught at New Hampshire College and the Graduate School of Development Studies, Geneva. For the last twenty years, he has worked periodically in Africa as a development practitioner and consultant, recently collaborating with UNDP, the OECD, and Belgian, Dutch, Danish, and British bilateral agencies. His earlier book for Kumarian Press, *Aiding Violence: The Development Enterprise in Rwanda*, won the 1999 African Studies Association Herskovits Award for the most outstanding book on Africa.

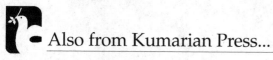 Also from Kumarian Press...

Humanitarianism

Aiding Violence: The Development Enterprise in Rwanda
Peter Uvin

The Humanitarian Enterprise: Dilemmas and Discoveries
Larry Minear

Nation-Building Unraveled? Aid, Peace and Justice in Afghanistan
Edited by Antonio Donini, Norah Niland and Karin Wermester

Patronage or Partnership: Local Capacity Building in Humanitarian Crises
Edited by Ian Smillie for the Humanitarianism and War Project

Protecting the Future: HIV Prevention, Care and Support Among Displaced and War-Affected Populations
Wendy Holmes for the International Rescue Committee

War's Offensive on Women
The Humanitarian Challenge in Bosnia, Kosovo and Afghanistan
Julie A. Mertus for the Humanitarianism and War Project

War and Intervention: Issues for Contemporary Peace Operations
Michael V. Bhatia

International Development, Global Issues

Going Global: Transforming Relief and Development NGOs
Mark Lindenberg and Coralie Bryant

Governance, Administration and Development: Making the State Work
Mark Turner and David Hulme

Managing Policy Reform: Concepts and Tools for Decision-Makers in Developing and Transitioning Countries
Derick W. Brinkerhoff and Benjamin L. Crosby

New Roles and Relevance: Development NGOs and the Challenge of Change
Edited by David Lewis and Tina Wallace

Reinventing Government for the Twenty-First Century
State Capacity in a Globalizing Society
Edited by Dennis A. Rondinelli and G. Shabbir Cheema

Southern Exposure
International Development and the Global South in the Twenty-First Century
Barbara P. Thomas-Slayter

Visit Kumarian Press at **www.kpbooks.com** or
call **toll-free 800.289.2664** for a complete catalog.

Kumarian Press, located in Bloomfield, Connecticut, is a forward-looking, scholarly press that promotes active international engagement and an awareness of global connectedness.